INDIA'S STATIC POWER STRUCTURE

BY THE SAME AUTHOR

Problems of Monetary Policy in Underdeveloped Countries
Central Banking in Theory and Practice

INDIA'S STATIC POWER STRUCTURE

J.D. SETHI

VIKAS PUBLICATIONS

© J. D. Sethi, 1969

Jai Dev **Sethi** (1924)

Printed in India
at the Oxford Printcraft India Pvt. Ltd., 68 Scindia House, New Delhi-1, and published by Sharda Chawla, Vikas Publications, 5 Daryaganj, Ansari Road, Delhi-6

To the Memory of

C. WRIGHT MILLS

PREFACE

All the fifteen essays and short articles on Indian politics included in this volume were written over a period of three and a half years, beginning with Mrs. Indira Gandhi's rule in early 1966. Some of them were published, while others were prepared for discussions, seminars or symposia and remained unpublished for one reason or another. During this period several eassys on other subjects also, particularly economics, my main field of study, were published. But in order to focus attention directly on only one subject, namely, contemporary Indian politics, these have been omitted.

The book was in the press when the crisis in the Congress Party exploded in mid-July and continued unabated till the end of August. A new chapter has been added to bring the analysis to date. As the typewriter rattled, the political weather-vane over New Delhi kept veering waywardly backward and forward until it settled down in a breezeless lull that was brought about by the so-called unity resolution of the Congress Working Committee. This new chapter appears at the beginning and not at the end of the book so that the readers can prospectively evaluate the problems of Indian political development discussed in other chapters, as well as retrospectively judge the predictive quality of the major conclusions drawn therefrom.

Except for some editorial changes, the essays appear as they were written originally. Although no general apology or excuse is offered for the collection, apology is given without reservation for a few repetitions which are bound to creep into such a collection. These essays have been divided into two parts. In Part One are included those which deal with the static structure of power in which the Congress Party, its leaders, and the Prime Minister carry on their struggle either for power or for survival. Despite repeated shocks administered to it, the structure of the Congress Party remains static. The structure also remains unstable because it cannot manage change within itself and without a crisis. The political strategy of Prime Minister Mrs. Indira Gandhi is the focal point of the analysis of Part One. Part Two covers some of the basic motivations, forces, power, groups, etc., which have a more dynamic and durable impact on politics and power structure. The crisis in Indian politics is the crisis of a static power structure resisting the pulls and pressures of dynamic, macro political and economic forces in the country. Readers can apply two criteria in their judgment of this collection. Looking back from a vantage point one should be able to say how relevant, correct, and comprehensive the analyses were when made some time in the past. Second, how far the basic, durable factors are correctly identified and their significance determined.

No writer can fully acknowledge the debt he owes to others who directly or indirectly may have helped him in his work. However, I cannot refrain from mentioning two names: Romesh Thapar and Raj Thapar of the *Seminar*, who initiated me into political writing and who now, though, almostly totally disagree with, if not disapprove of, my analysis. Thanks are also due to those journals and newspapers who originally published some of these essays and articles.

September 1969   J. D. SETHI

CONTENTS

Introduction xi

PART ONE

1. The New Prime Minister *3*
2. Congress Left and Indira Gandhi *19*
3. Struggle for Leadership *29*
4. Consensus and All That *40*
5. The Structure and Division of Power in the Congress Party *46*
6. Mrs. Gandhi's Strategy of Static Balance *67*

PART TWO

7. Cracks in the Indian Party Structure *85*
8. Centre-State Relations *98*
9. Parties, Power, and Pelf *113*
10. Anatomy of Political Defections *126*
11. Democracy to Populism *131*
12. Back to Nationalism: Consensus and Democracy *141*
13. Back to Nationalism: Quasi-Indian Power Elite *163*
14. Political Change and Democratic Alternative *175*
15. Qualitative Content of Political Life in India *200*

Glossary of Events *213*

INTRODUCTION

IN RECENT WEEKS the static political super-structure of India was given uncharacteristic jolts one after another. Factional politics took over command everywhere, followed by an unending series of crises in which all conceivable weapons were used by the contenstants, more effectively by the Prime Minister's faction than by her opponents. Never before had the succession of events been so swift and hallucinatory and yet so consequential as to have shaken the ramshackle empire of the Congress Party.

For nearly two months the real business of the nation came to a standstill at the governmental level. The anticlimax came as the brinkmanship was dissolved into a compromise resolution, presented by that cryptic peace-maker, Y. B. Chavan, and passed by the Congress Working Committee, calling for unity and discipline, both of which were flouted and would meet all the more the same fate from now on. The resolution, that comic parable, did paper over the cracks temporarily, leaving the structure of power as static as it was before the crisis began, but with Mrs. Gandhi emerging relatively stronger than other components of power.

How does all that has happened change the role, functioning, and drift of the power structure of the Congress Party, as described in the following chapters? Has the unity resolution of the Congress Working Committee really closed the chapter that began at Bangalore? Was it all a bad joke, a soap opera, or an irreversible and momentous political change? Will the Congress Party split before 1972 and if it does how will it split? Will Mrs. Gandhi's Government continue till 1972, or will she herself go to the polls sometimes next year? Will a coalition rule at the Centre before or after the next elections? What will be the magnitude of the Congress defeat or victory in the next elections? Will the very first coalition be a Left or Right coalition? These are important and relevant questions, but by their very nature also highly speculative and thus not significantly illuminating. Yet the answers must come, even though indirectly. The best way to approach these questions is to identify the nature of the crises inside the Congress as well as outside it, and in its relations with other competitive forces in the polity.

The struggle for power goes on unabated. But, however important the factional and leadership struggle may be, to rely on it for an analysis of the emerging crises in the Congress Party or the country can only yield distorted and unreliable predictions. One must make the analysis at several levels not only to get an integrated picture of the structure of power and the functioning of those who wield it, but also to judge in perspective and in full measure the impact of any new crisis, such as the one created recently by Mrs. Gandhi's jolting the Congress system of power, that the party may have to face in future.

The analysis given here is made at three levels: (*i*) at the level of leadership struggle, and the choice and effectiveness of techniques used by the leaders; (*ii*) the structure of the Congress Party and its relations with those parties and groups which exist primarily in cooperation or friction with it; and (*iii*) the emergence and role of new elemental forces, classes, mass movements, etc., which sustain or corrode the existing structure. The same classificatory approach has been followed in other chapters as well.

Let us first take the question of leadership struggle. Saying the obvious, namely, that the Congress Party will never be the same again or that the most serious crisis is generated by the fierce, fight-to-finish leadership struggle amounts to practically saying nothing, unless leaders' respective strategies, formal and informal tactics, and motivations are sharply brought out. Since it is to Mrs. Gandhi's strategies that other leaders react, it is enough to focus attention on how she conducts herself in power. In Chapter 6, I have discussed by now her well-known strategy at some length. To describe this strategy in the abstract and then to illustrate it by examples from the past will be of only academic interest. What I propose to do is to reveal, one by one, the major thrusts of that strategy in direct relations to the current crises and thereby not only properly identify the crises themselves but also their possible outcome. Analysis of various strategies will also be related to various dilemmas, old and new, that Mrs. Gandhi faces today.

Introduction

On 12 July 1969, the Syndicate, the top political caucus of the Congress Party (about which more will be said later), decided to nominate Sanjiva Reddy as the party's candidate for the Presidency of the Indian Republic. This choice was made by the Congress Parliamentary Board, consisting of nine top leaders of unequal strength, against the clear opposition of Prime Minister Mrs. Indira Gandhi. Although it was argued, on the basis of precedents, that Mrs. Gandhi should have bowed to the decision of the Board, as her father did twice before, the choice before her was not so simple and the threat not ordinary. It was the logical result of the functioning of the static political structure, on which her power rested, that such a challenge should be thrown to her long before 1972 by those who had been the victims of her strategy.

What was the crucial aspect of her strategy which determined her extremely violent outrage and reaction against the choice of Sanjiva Reddy? It was the threat to the very core of her strategy of getting power through maintaining a series of balances in the system. Mrs. Gandhi survived all these years by keeping correct power balances between the party and the Government, between the Centre and the States, between Right and Left, between her friends and foes in the Council of Ministers, and by a whole set of other balances at lower levels. It did not matter to her whether one or more of these balances were functionally defunct or active, or without party or national purpose. So long as each balance served her purpose, no matter how much it depreciated the national power, she fully made use of it. These balances were not automatic or self-regulating but were maintained by such manipulations as were considered necessary by the Prime Minister. If now she were to face a President, who himself became a balancing factor with her as the Prime Minister, all other balances in the system would become highly unstable and a fundamental shift in the relative positions of the various components of the power structure would have taken place, to the definite detriment of her power and position. At least, the existing balance between Mrs. Gandhi and the Syndicate would have decisively and finally moved against her. Then it would have been only a matter of time before she was either forced to share power or removed from power altogether.

She acted the only way she could have, making use of every strategy and every instrument of governmental power at her disposal.

On 16 July 1969, Mrs. Indira Gandhi gave the first jolt to the static structure of the Congress Party, by summarily relieving Morarji Desai of the Finance portfolio and then, two days later, by nationalizing fourteen major banks. Without her taking the second climateric step, Morarji's dismissal would have doubtlessly appeared a brazen act of political vendetta against an ageing man who always chose to act, though unwittingly, as a catalyst or a shock-absorber between Mrs. Gandhi and her real rivals in the Congress Party. Morarji, of course, had made himself vulnerable by his having adopted for long this catalyst position, by his refusal to play the game of power politics according to its rules, and by adopting, apparently, a *status quo* economic ideology. The price for insisting on a code of conduct, such as Morarji did—party loyalty and discipline without purpose or policy—was no doubt to make onself a sitting duck for anyone who cared to shoot. Had the men of the Syndicate been able to defeat Mrs. Gandhi in the recent crisis, they would have, one and all, outdone Mrs. Gandhi in their treatment of Morarji. For him to be consistent, he should have realized that his vote with the Syndicate in Bangalore was completely out of place and a political blunder.

For the fact that the nationalization of banks was a desperate political act on the part of the Prime Minister to safeguard herself against the equally desperate men of the Syndicate, one does not have to go far to seek explanation. Nationalization has been demanded many a time before on various Congress forums, but at no occasion did Mrs. Gandhi give her support to that demand, despite the general opinion among the economists and politicians of the Left Centre that the measure was overdue for adoption. Ashok Mehta has revealed that for quite some time it was Mrs. Gandhi who opposed nationalization of banks at the Cabinet level. Nationalization of banks seemed, therefore, quite out of proportion to, if not inconsistent with, her past economic strategy, if ever there was one. For example, over the last three years, her Ministers of Commerce and Industry, who happened to be closest to her politically, have been resorting to an almost total liquidation of

Introduction

control and licensing system, so elaborately structured over two decades, though for good operational reasons but not quite so. The era of *neo-laissez faire* unleashed by Mrs. Gandhi, ever since the old draft of Fourth Plan was given up and a Plan Holiday declared for three years, was least expected to find its climax in the nationalization of banks. Gradual liquidation, since Mrs. Gandhi came to power, of the control and licensing system had left with the Planning Commission very little to suggest by way of instruments to support the strategy of the new Fourth Five Year Plan. Nationalization of banks, therefore, was implicit in the strategy of the Plan, but without the Chairman of the Commission, Mrs. Gandhi, ever having cared to note it or spell it out. The claptrap about defence of the small man will not stand even a minute's scrutiny because only a few months before, if our memory is not short, Morarji's budget proposal of taxing agricultural wealth of big farmers, a measure of far-reaching importance, was shot down by Mrs. Gandhi herself.

Mrs. Gandhi was right in stressing, since there was not much else to stress, that banks had to be nationalized without notice to avoid financial manipulations by interested parties, but to have done so in a huff and without adequate preparations behind the scene made an eloquent commentary on Mrs. Gandhi's motives as well as economic strategy. The number of amendments moved by the Government to its own bill on nationalization was so large that no one took the Government seriously on its promises and intentions and Mrs. Gandhi on her explanations. Finally, if any set of banks seriously distort our priorities and trade structure, it is the foreign banks which do so and, therefore, should have been the first to be taken over on purely economic reasons. But the Government did not have the guts to displease its foreign supporters. If the demand for nationalization of foreign banks had come from the followers of the Syndicate, one would certainly not have failed to see the political reasons behind their demand. But to have ignored the economic force behind the demand amounted to nothing but self-denunciation on the part of the Government.

Left to himself, Morarji would never have nationalized banks, even though, paradoxically enough, those who owned and controlled these banks have always provided political support to Mrs. Gandhi against Morarji. But if ordered, either by the party or the Prime Minister, he would have carried out the measures. So in this respect, neither Morarji's protests nor Mrs. Gandhi's explanations carry conviction. Shrewdly anticipating each other's moves both have played to the gallery.

There is thus one simple question. If Mrs. Gandhi had not felt threatened or slighted at the Congress Parliamentary Board's choice of Sanjiva Reddy, who was selected contrary to her wishes, would she have struck the way she did? The simple answer is "no," if only because no one has said "yes" to that question. However, a more important corollary of that answer is that despite Mrs. Gandhi's overall strategy of keeping the whole power structure weak, amorphous, and hence at a low level of functioning, she can act desperately, ruthlessly, and unpredicably when threatened at the seat of power. One unpardonable crime in politics is failure. And no one has understood this point better than she has. Of course, such acts can bring her down as much as elevate her power. But her strategy, nonetheless, remains far superior to that of her rivals who seem to be fighting her with eighteenth-century methods. Among the players of the game, there is also the vital generation gap. Old men, out of power and on their way out, however desperate, cannot play for long the exhausting game of power politics.

Despite some considerable backstairs management, the act of nationalizing banks has been widely acclaimed, though the most informed and committed are highly sceptical about its economic outcome at the hands of Mrs. Gandhi. Besides the intrinsic merit of the act, its being a bold and massive act has made many an unwary proclaim on behalf of Mrs. Gandhi that she is a person of action. It is dangerous to build a theory or strategy on a single piece of action. Weary of political pragmatism, they gloss over the fact that for three and half years she remained a prisoner of indecision, so much so that the Central Government was reduced to its lowest ever governing functions since 1947. If Mrs. Gandhi can act and will act in a big way only when her job is threatened, then she is not only a most unsuitable Prime Minister but also has no future;

Introduction xvii

the inexhorable political forces will demand their price when the nemesis sets in. If with the defeat of the Syndicate a new era of non-decision-making sets in until new rivals and contenders of power emerge on the scene, neither the country nor the other components of the power structure will tolerate this situation for long. Mrs. Gandhi applied her strategy in a decaying situation and succeeded. But what she has given us subsequently is a post-nationalization self-portrait rather than a political statement.

The role, functioning, and drift of the static power structure of the Congress Party are unlikely to change very much with the exception that Mrs. Gandhi has added more options to her strategy. She has tasted blood as well as acquired a quasi-charismatic image and she can be relied upon to go to any length, no matter what happens to the polity, economy, or the nation, to retain herself in power. This is entirely a new element in her strategy. Pushed to the corner, she will play her cards close to chest, behave inflexibly, and react violently. She should also be relied upon to patch up temporarily with her rivals for tactical reasons if she is convinced of the futility of her desperation. Both possibilities are present in equal measure and add up to a new strategy of Mrs. Gandhi.

Much, though not all, will depend upon the strategy of her rivals too. Notwithstanding the disarray and total humiliation of the Syndicate, it appears that, caught in a political maelstrom of their doom, the men of the Syndicate have reacted defensively to her attacks. They, with the exception of Morarji, seem to have learned, as if from Mrs. Gandhi herself, the technique of waiting and watching, if judged against their internal divisions, distrust, and organizational and tactical weakness. They should be trusted to attack again at the point of their own choosing. It does not have to be a Syndicate of the same old men. So long as caucus principle and control are accepted in the Congress and so long as Mrs. Gandhi does not reshape the Congress Party into a full-fledged cadre or constituency party, the power struggle will be fierce and bloody with every new round. With the exit of Morarji, i.e. the disappearance of a catalyst, battle lines are going to be drawn more sharply from now on. Another reason is the likely elimination of such weak links as S. K. Patil and Atulya Ghosh from the

Syndicate not only because of their last hobbling performance in the Congress Working Committee but because these people had enjoyed, far too long, disproportionately more power than their base justified. They are unlikely to figure meaningfully in any future struggle for power.

It is in her moments of victory that Mrs. Gandhi enters the most crucial and difficult period of her political career with her overall strategy having survived intact. Had the deadlock between her and the Syndicate been resolved completely in her favour or against her, she would have had to face a serious vertical split in the Congress Party, totally polarized politics, and the task of forming before 1972 a definite coalition of her supporters in the Congress with some parties in the opposition. Now she can continue until 1972 with the old technique of locating support for her both inside and outside the Congress, while remaining herself at the head of the Congress Government. By agreeing to compromise with her opponents at a time when she could have totally eliminated them, she has revealed the strength of her strategy as well as the weakness of her political position in national politics.

It is the very nature and magnitude of Mrs. Gandhi's victory over the Syndicate and the way it was achieved that have pushed her into the most difficult and dangerous period of her political life and brought the nation to an even more difficult and dangerous phase. Mrs. Gandhi's strategy so far had succeeded on the stated premise of static power structure and political balance, which implied no serious clash or conflict with all other political forces except the party caucus, i.e. the Syndicate. In other words, the strategy was based on a stable but static cleavage system, which left most of the nation's problem untackled and so much as unattended. Within such a cleavage system, neither the leadership struggle could translate itself into a new party system nor the existing system stand the strain of old as well as new dilemmas and problems created by Mrs. Gandhi's victory. If the system is not purposefully dynamized and results shown within a reasonable time, she will no longer be able to make the public believe her alibis of blaming others. Therefore, her strategy requires a little further discussion.

Introduction

Mrs. Gandhi is the leader of the party in power at the Centre, but seldom has she accepted that role in full. On the contrary, she has always attempted to cast herself in the role of a national leader and has sought to create a consensus around her. Superficially, she still remains by far the most acceptable choice to disparate factions and parties. Her acceptability is due more to her known political pliability, notwithstanding her strength shown in the act of bank nationalization, than to any special political qualities. Not that her rivals are strong by any means; their much-trumpeted strength has proved to be nothing but a cover for their lack of political courage. No leader in the Congress can truly be called a strong leader. Thus, what appears as her weakness and the cause of her acceptability is also the source of her strength, in so far as her struggle against the old leaders of the Congress is concerned. This is a paradox, the resolution of which perhaps will require the whole set of present leaders to disappear by their mutual attrition.

Over three and half years of her rule or non-rule, Mrs. Gandhi neither developed charisma nor was she accepted as a national leader of consensus. She was not even considered powerful by any standard, despite the tremendous power and patronage that went with the position of the Prime Minister in India. Now for the first time she has emerged as a semi-charismatic leader, with lot of courage to her credit. The real question is whether or not she grows into a full-fledged national leader. Doubts arise because of the recent deal hatched at the last Congress Working Committee meeting, which has left many foci of power in the party out of her control. Moreover, this semi-charismatic position has been earned through a razor-thin margin by which V. V. Giri won.

A leadership of national consensus is coterminous with one-party dominance. For the multi-party system of today, the concept of a national leader is contradiction in terms. Before one can make oneself accepted, by persuasion or/and coercion, as national leader, one must first satisfy the minimum condition of becoming the unquestioned leader of the largest party. Mrs. Gandhi had never been accepted as such nor has she tried to win over the loyalty of several leaders and factions constituting the overwhelming majority in the Congress Party. On the other hand, she always tried to locate her support inside as well as outside the Congress Party, particularly of late, as the forces and parties against the Congress have become exceedingly active and powerful. Contradictorily she tried to have it both ways. The paradox is that the more the Congress is weakened and the more Mrs. Gandhi relies on the opposition parties and factions for support, the less, contrary to expectations, will be her credibility as a durable national leader when the elections draw near, because the ultimate struggle is not between different elites but between different parties.

The Congress Party has always permitted factions within itself to maintain its legislative majorities. In the early period, it kept factions within the limits of its overall functioning as a ruling party. Now it is not the party or its leaders who control the factions but factions which control leadership and party organization. Factions in the party are so much at loggerhead with one another that they make it impossible for the party to function or to rule. On the other hand, the opposition parties have grown more in number and some of them in strength. The system is not strong enough to allow both types of opposition. Either the opposition parties must be reduced to pre-1961 level or the Congress must shed some of its incongruent factions to become a little more coherent.

Even during the period when the opposition parties were weak and could not challenge the supremacy of the Congress, there were informal pairings, on loose ideological bases, between the opposition parties and the factions inside the Congress. Nevertheless, so long as the centralization of leadership and policy mechanism existed in the Congress and symbolized some ideology, the pairing was weak. During Mrs. Gandhi's rule, and significantly more recently, the pairing has become sharp, open, and defiant as a consequence of the ideological ambivalence and absence of policy frame or decision-making that go with Mrs. Gandhi's strategy. Consequently, the only consensus among all factions that seemed to survive in the Congress Party till a few months ago, namely, the consensus on survival in the party itself, is fast disappearing. No individual, group, or faction inside the Congress Party feels safe from being altogether eliminated by another.

So long as such pairings were confined to the area of parties only, cooperation and conflict were restricted. With the formation of the non-Congress Governments in several States, particularly of the United Left Front, the area of competition and conflict has been widened and the nature of cooperation changed. Never before this change occurred did the non-Congress parties seriously involve themselves in or influence the alignments, conflicts, or understanding among members of the Congress High Command and the bodies representing it such as the Congress Parliamentary Board, Congress Working Committee, and the Congress Parliamentary Party. Today the picture is completely changed. Mrs. Gandhi has more dependable and firmer allies in the DMK, Akalis, BKD, and the Communist parties than inside the Congress Party, particularly among groups and factions controlled by other leaders. It is, quite understandbly, unacceptable to men like K. Kamaraj, S. K. Patil, Atulya Ghosh, and Sanjiva Reddy that Mrs. Gandhi should be allied with their respective enemies outside the party. An entirely new dimension has been added to the struggle for power, namely, the cross-cutting of inter-party and intra-party conflicts.

The massive cross-voting that was organized by Mrs. Gandhi in defeating Sanjiva Reddy has paved the way for the split in the Congress, laid the ground for the type of coalitions that are likely to be formed, and knocked off a crucial part of her own strategy. The last-mentioned effect did not come to materialize soon as a result of the compromise she had entered into with the Syndicate to call off the struggle. The opposition groups and parties which supported her are bound to get disillusioned with her strategy unless and until the coalition based on her supporters every where emerges.

Mrs. Gandhi is said to have found a new weapon in her strategy to defeat her rivals in the Congress Party—the weapon of policy, more appropriately radical policy. This weapon was used for the first time, and most successfully, when banks were nationalized. It would seem, however, that there is nothing new about it. Such a step was quite consistent with and logically an inevitable consequence of the expansion of the areas of conflict and cooperation between leaders, parties, and groups as analyzed in the preceding paragraphs. It is the awareness about the new weapon and its conscious use by Mrs. Gandhi in the struggle for power that is new, and also an entirely new element in her strategy.

Here a distinction must be drawn between two strategies, both of which may appear to be the same but, in fact, one is exactly the opposite of the other. The first strategy, which is newly adopted by Mrs. Gandhi, centres on the use of policy or policies, spectacularly as well as opportunistically, to defeat her rivals in the power struggle. Nationalization of banks, long overdue and quite useful for economic planning, falls in this category. Its motivation, timing, and procedure had no economic relevance and will perhaps defeat its very purpose. It is generally not realized that bank nationalization was probably the most readily available weapon to be used. Mrs. Gandhi could defeat Morarji with radical policies but not Kamaraj or Chavan. For the latter, there must be some other policies, which cannot be radical, and certainly not in relation to the known economic imperatives. The Syndicate has never been an intellectual or ideological seabed. Nor has Mrs. Gandhi revealed over three years of rule any coherent ideology. Despite all the fanfare of socialism, her overall strategy remains patently anti-ideology.

The second strategy is to carry on and accelerate the struggle for power, not once but continuously, with economic objectives and imperatives clearly in view, by the use of relevant policies consistent with those objectives and imperatives, by advance preparation of the machinery and personnel to implement those policies and by holding together all those who are natural partners in the alliance. This strategy has certain disadvantages in the short run. The element of surprise in it will be smaller than in the first. Besides, the rivals will have time and opportunity to prepare their counter-strategies for slowing down the struggle. It will require, more than anything else, a strong coherent party organization, cadre, and functioning elite at all levels. If the leader of the party does not happen to be charismatic, a real sharing of power at the top will be essential to avoid internal dissension. Mrs. Gandhi has set herself against all these requirements and thereby opted against the latter long-term strategy in favour of the former short-term strategy. But, in the long-term, it is the second strategy which can be more effective, durable, and also yield definite positive results in contrast to the first strategy which can also boomerang on her. Moreover, the first strategy can slow down economic growth, depreciate party's power, lead to radical romanticism, and anti-intellectualism, all of which instead of crystallizing political forces will make them more amorphous than before and replace the politics of the parties by politics of populism more than ever before. This effect is already noticeable in Mrs. Gandhi's undue reliance on the Communists and Nijalingappa, in turn, hobnobbing with the Jana Sangh and Swatantra for acquiring support. By relying on the first strategy, Mrs. Gandhi is emerging not as a leftist but as a populist leader. The opposition parties are already indulging in populism on a vast scale.

The aforesaid state of affairs is unhealthy, destructive of the party system, and finally inimical to the interests of the Congress Party and its leaders, though a short-term bonus has been earned by Mrs. Gandhi on that account. The one chance the Congress had of removing the contradictions between its policies and its structure had been lost in the defeat of Sanjiva Reddy. Had he won the Presidential contest, the Congress may have had the chance to consolidate itself by narrowing the gap between its policies and its structure, by eliminating its extreme Left and Right and, paradoxically, reducing itself from a majority to a minority party. But that chance is gone and with that has also gone the chance of stable coalitions appearing after 1972 elections. The Congress Party, which is not a party of socialism, is once again stuck with adopting a programme which it cannot implement effectively and purposefully. The word "socialism" falling from the mouth of a Congressman sounds some malapropism. A situation of unending political and economic crises is likely to remain with us during the time that passes till the financial collapse of the Congress Government and system of power or till the Congress removes its internal contradictions.

Our experience of the last two decades is that the actual rate of growth of the economy has been far below the potential rate required by the actual resources input. But the actual as well as potential growth rates have been lower than the growth rate of the big business. So much so that even in years when the economy remained static, the big business multiplied its assets almost at the same rate as in other years. These relationships should normally have produced a higher rate of savings, which they have not. I am not suggesting that the big business does not save. What I am suggesting is that the rate of savings in the economy is unrelated to the growth of its most crucial part, the big business, which neither saves enough itself nor allows others to do so. This is a highly dangerous situation. The Licensing Committee's recent report has sharply focussed attention on the big business' successful attempt to pre-empt most of the licences and then not use nearly one-third of them. It is well known that, along with controlling licences, the big business exercises still tighter pre-emption on foreign exchange and bank credit. The low rate of growth and low rate of savings both reflect this basic malady. The questions the ruling Centrist party must debate are whether or not the big business has ceased to be the proper instrument of growth and whether the party needs big business as its ally.

The recent nationalization of large banks has partly answered the question. But only partly and that also as a half-truth. The Congress Party is not a party of socialism in the classical sense of the word. It is essentially a party of the Centre, more appropriately Left Centre. Its programme of nationalization is and has to be an organic part of its Centrist character. Otherwise, it will make no sense. Its natural class allies are medium-size business in the industry and peasant proprietors in the agriculture with a large bulk of middle classes thrown in. It is with neither the big nor the so-called small business that the interests of the Congress Party coincide. The medium business is totally squeezed between the power of the big business from the top and the politically oriented pressures of the outdated small ones from below. The anti-technological bias of the small business, which is properly speaking no business at all, is as inimical to growth as the pre-emption of resources by the big. The growth of the big and the small business has been faster than the medium business, a fact which lies at the root of the political crisis of the Congress Party and economic stagnation of the country.

V. V. Giri's victory has not increased the chances of parties and politics being streamlined on their most natural basis. Mrs. Gandhi's Centrist allies outside the Congress, such as the DMK, Akalis, and BKD, and her supporters of the same hue within the Congress Party, will remain divided over several political parties. The same will be the fate of other ideological groups. The problem of Indian politics today, based as it is on unlimited, corrosive pluralism, is how to bring about polarization between two Centre parties, one more or less Left oriented and the other similarly Right oriented. The real danger is that through a widespread use of radical demagogy, the Prime Minister and her supporters as well as opponents will unleash on the nation a new wave of populist politics in which all parties will merrily participate. Populism is organically opposed to stable party structure, political principles and ideologies, secondary political institutions, economic development and rationality, and a whole lot of other components of the political structure on which a stable system depends. This has been discussed at some length in Chapter 9.

The new element in the politics of today is that Mrs. Gandhi, head of the federal Government in India, has entered the populist fray. To go over the head of political institutions and appeal to the masses for support may be good tactics once in a while. But if Mrs. Gandhi continues to follow the same, as she has threatened to do, she would be responsible for putting India on the dangerous path of Soekarno of Indonesia, Joa Goulart of Brazil, Nkrumah of Ghana, or Peron of Argentina. Comparisons are odious just as the Indian conditions are different from those of the countries just mentioned, but it is the common principle which they all believed and practised that has great relevance for us today. They were all populist leaders who were utterly ineffective administrators, and destroyers of political institutions. Mrs. Gandhi's "populism in reverse" may be judged as a balancing factor of the populism of the opposition. But between the two, the Congress Party will be ground to nothing and the Government will become a victim of a widening gap between radical professions and poor performance, resulting in increasing violence in the streets. The forces of the Right, which are not yet fully populist, will have to take the same course to survive. Jana Sangh is already fast on its way to become populist. The Swatantra is on its way out, precisely because it has not developed populist techniques and has failed to realize that populism is the surest method of defending the *status quo*.

It is in the light of this accelerated politics of populism and the autonomous sharpening of the struggle between Mrs. Gandhi and other leaders that one must judge the relevance and worth of Mrs. Gandhi's promises about principles. Radical ideas are freely available. It is their economic administration that is rare and costly. The line of division between radicalism and populism is drawn on the level of administration of ideas and policies and the organization of the people behind these policies. The attempt to maintain unity in the Congress, which is a mixture of all types of ideologies, strengthens our fears of populism becoming victorious in the end. Populism also has the habit of devouring its creators. That is why I said earlier that Mrs. Gandhi has entered the most difficult and dangerous period of her political career. If she really believes in principles, she must organize under one banner all those, whether outside or inside the Congress, who have faith in those policies. She has so far clearly avoided this type of alignment because, in this approach, the risks of retaining and losing power are nearly the same. On the contrary, she has more than once preferred political expediency to principles like a true populist leader anywhere else.

It is not inevitable that Mrs. Gandhi should remain populist and not change her strategy, purposes, and class and non-class allies. The only relevant indication for such a change will be found in her changed attitude to, and decision-making about, all those institutions which have been set up to make our politico-economic system function but are not doing so. Not only is it important that the procedures, norms, inputs, and outputs of these institutions become operative, it is also required that she initiates similar changes at the top in the structure of leadership of the party and the Government. Leaders and ministers around her or in her group do not arouse confidence and have proved themselves very poor instru-

Introduction xxvii

ments for making any big advance towards policy implementation. The single most important criteria is whether she transforms the Congress Party into a coherent, functioning, and adequately and rationally structured party. Otherwise, Mrs. Gandhi emerges nothing but a populist leader, and a very dangerous one at that to contend with. She has temporarily secured popular legitimacy. She may either reinforce it by institutional legitimacy or simply fritter it away by manipulating old balances. The "people" may be with her but they do not support the system as such.

It is no use pre-judging Mrs. Gandhi's future performance. A wise and powerful leader often uses a wide variety of strategies and tactics to retain power, influence behaviour, and serve national objectives. If she proves unequal to the task, this opportunity she has got now to make use of her adroit, flexible, and expanding strategies may turn out be the first and the last, because solutions to the mounting problems the nation faces cannot be postponed. Part of her strategy has revealed itself to be narcissist, exclusive, and inflexible—the strategy of a populist leader. The least that she must do now is to stop the rot from growing further and to launch an organization and develop a policy process first inside the Congress itself in such a way as would keep authority and control in her hands and also permit her to make use of her authority for mobilizing organizational power towards national goals. If this much is not done, she will have no political future.

Mrs. Gandhi has quite legitimately raised three other important questions of principle. Without going into the motivation and timing for opening these questions, both of which raise doubts, those who are concerned with the growing rot in our polity must pay full attention to them. Mrs. Gandhi has demanded, quite legitimately in principle, (*i*) the primacy of the Prime Minister over the entire political structure particularly in relation to the organizational wing of the party in power, (*ii*) that she would want a President of the Republic of India with whom she could get on harmoniously, and (*iii*) that there must be obtained a national consensus on the choice of the President. There are obvious contradictions between (*ii*) and (*iii*). National consensus of all major parties could have converged on a candidate who might not have been to the liking of the Prime Minister. Nevertheless, these three principles require careful examination.

Let us take the second proposition first. We are not concerned here with all aspects of the powers of the President; only political aspects will be dealt here. The Indian Constitution nowhere mentions that the President will be acting all the time on the advice of his Council of Ministers nor does it restrict the President's powers to that of his being merely a constitutional head. If the Constitution is vague, it is inescapable that the party political structure and party competition, which were not taken into account by the founding fathers of our Constitution, will and should now be the determining force for such major decisions as the election of a President. It is even more difficult to focus on the criteria, the principles, and the methods of the Presidential election by restricting oneself to any definite constitutional provision. How the new or next President will exercise his powers, within the present constitutional ambivalence, will depend upon the political strength of the Central Government and the party or parties that man it. It will also depend upon the relationship of the ruling party with the Opposition in Parliament and the States' legislatures. It cannot and should not depend upon the wishes of the Prime Minister. It cannot also depend upon the wishes of the President because the demand for the primacy of the Prime Minister can be countered by a similar demand from the President himself or on his behalf, for neither the Constitution clearly states the principles of primacy nor is there a precedent to go by. It is essentially a matter of the combined force of constitutional, structural, and power relationships between institutions and not a simple one than can be reduced to mere personal relationship between the Prime Minister and the President; it would be quite illegitimate even to do so. In asserting this principle what Mrs. Gandhi obviously desired was that she must have a President who would agree to her demand for the dissolution of Parliament in case she was defeated in the Congress Parliamentary Party, a situation which an unobliging, ambitious, and shrewd President could always exploit to his own advantages. In getting Sanjiva Reddy defeated, Mrs. Gandhi has won a political victory, but she has not established any principle or precedent about the primacy of the Prime Minister *vis-a-vis* the President.

Harmonious and smooth functioning relations between the President and the Prime Minister are a matter of great importance. But to say in the same breath as well as to assert that the President has no real powers given to him by the Constitution does not make a convincing piece of argument. Harmony has never been Mrs. Gandhi's strong point because she never bothered about the need for harmoniousness of much more meaningful relations, namely, those between the Prime Minister and the President of the ruling party. Here, Mrs. Gandhi, unfortunately, is on a very wet wicket and her manoeuverability on principles increases or declines more by the logic and consequences of her own strategy and by the manipulation of others.

What about the consensus? There were powerful reasons behind her demand that the choice of the next President be made through consultation with Chief Ministers and other political parties. In that way she wanted to forestall entirely the possibility of the Congress High Command forcing their candidate on her. Therefore, no one in the Congress Party, or outside it, had taken the consensus proposal seriously. On the contrary, the members of the Congress High Command, as believers in majoritarian democracy, had unequivocally expressed themselves in favour of a Congress Party candidate in respect of all important elections, for the party still has an edge in voting strength over the combined strength of all other parties and groups. Though the demand for arriving at a consensus was in itself admirable, there were enough reasons for its not being accepted in the particular case for which it had been put forward.

First, there were ample chances for making the late Dr. Zakir Husain, in 1967 election, a consensus candidate but Mrs. Gandhi forced the issue on personal and party lines to the complete undermining of the very concept of consensus. The opposition parties knew all this too well and that was why they did not show any interest in consensus politics for the Presidential election this year.

Second, the very consensus which put Mrs. Gandhi in power in the first place has completely disappeared and in its place no new consensus has emerged. Nothing of significance is derived today from the principle of consensus. On the contrary, Mrs. Gandhi and other leaders are more deeply involved than ever in factional politics.

Third, it is quite elementary to understand that to create a national consensus on any subject, it is incumbent on the leader of the largest and the ruling party in the country to produce first a consenus within his or her party before any dialogue can be started with other parties. Who can claim a consenus inside the Congress Party on any vital issue, including the acceptance of its elected leader? Mrs. Gandhi had nearly succeeded in dividing the party into two equal halves in the recent crisis.

Fourth, Mrs. Gandhi had no mandate, if she was at all serious about consensus, to sound non-Congress parties and their leaders before getting a clear mandate from her own party to do so.

Finally, the most relevant consideration with Mrs. Gandhi was that consensus, if ever arrived at, would truly be on a politically weak candidate, far weaker than herself. And nothing would have suited her better. But all the forces involved in the power struggle do not desire a weak candidate. Only some do. No wonder, consensus, a very useful technique in a deeply plural society, became a dirty word at the hands of the Congress Party. The selection of Sanjiva Reddy by CPB and his defeat at the hand of Mrs. Gandhi buried the Congress system of consensus once for all.

However, Mrs. Gandhi's demand, despite all the spurious arguments put forward by her, that a Presidential candidate should fulfil the condition of being acceptable to the Prime Minister in office should not be lightly dismissed. It was a matter of profound importance because, if accepted, her demand would have established, in principle at least, the primacy of the office of the Prime Minister. She tried to push the same demand through the compromise resolution of 25 August passed by the Congress Working Committee. Mrs. Gandhi has not left the matter there. She has raised it again and again since then. However, since the Indian Constitution is a halfway house between the Cabinet and the Presidential system the primacy (or lack of it) of the President or the Prime Minister does not depend upon the wishes of Mrs. Gandhi but will result from the power and party balance operating in the polity. No such stable balance exists today as would decide

Introduction

the matter one way or another. Mrs. Gandhi cannot seriously insist on having the two principles of consensus and the primacy of the Prime Minister accepted simultaneously. The primacy of any one office may be desirable in itself but it cannot be had for the asking because such a primacy will enable the person holding that office to twist the whole power structure in his or her favour. To enjoy that position, the holder of that office must first be so acceptable to the existing power structure. Obviously, Mrs. Gandhi cannot seriously make that claim and if she does, there will be many opportunities in future to test that claim. Her recent victory, gives some, though yet insufficient, strength to the claim and it should be recognized. The crucial question is where does she go from here.

The aforementioned principles will stand confirmed or rejected by the type of relationship or balance obtained between the Government and the organizational wing of the ruling party. In principle Mrs. Gandhi is correct in her insistence on the independence and precedence of the parliamentary party, otherwise the Government can neither pursue its accepted programmes nor rule effectively if it is subjected to continuous pressures or nibbling from the organizational wing, all the more so if the bosses or caucus control the party. Under no circumstances can a Prime Minister, however weak and pliable, can accept dictation from the party bosses; he or she must have freedom of action. But the issue is not resolved by insisting on principle only. It can be resolved (*a*) by institutionalizing the relationship between the two wings of the party and not merely reducing this relationship to establishing good personal rapport between two individuals, one at the head of the Government and the other at the head of the party organization; (*b*) by establishing norms of conduct, recruitment, and performance of both wings; and (*c*) by the balance of power in the Government and the party conforming to each other. None of these methods or arrangements are obtained in the Congress Party, hence the perennial crisis. So long as the existing uncertain state of affairs continues in the party, the only way two wings can work smoothly for the next year or so is by the Prime Minister herself becoming the Congress President. By simply having her nominee elected to that high office in the organization will only further intensify the contradictions and crises in the party, as happened twice before in the cases of Kamaraj and Nijalingappa.

Setting-up of formal and correct institutional arrangements is only part of the job. The more important and arduous job is for the Prime Minister to adhere to and improve the governing functions of the Government, if she seriously desires to tilt the existing balance of power in favour of the Prime Minister. This improvement cannot come by empty slogans and raising to a pitch the still unfulfilled and unrealizable revolution of rising expectations. In India, the Prime Minister, as correctly pointed out by Mrs. Gandhi, has federal and international responsibilities which cannot be subservient to the Congress system and its balance of power or its underbush. But a Prime Minister cannot dictate to the organization wing any more than she can allow herself to be dictated by the latter. A functional division of power between the two is essential. The organization must work towards instant articulation, organization of mass support, vote-structuring, and winning elections. The Government wing must implement the programmes laid down by the party and by effectively performing its other governing functions.

Mrs. Gandhi cannot perform these functions satisfactorily by continuing her meandering policies of the last three and a half years. Her Government is dangerously weak in relation to the national tasks. Power in the case of Mrs. Gandhi has remained a potential except when used to safeguard her threatened position. This way of using power is called static, i.e. the replacement of one set of elites by another set, without fundamentally changing any of the existing balances. Unless its use becomes dynamic, the power centres in the Congress Party and Government cannot but remain in an uneasy and unchanging static balance. By and large, it is within the static power balance that the disputes concerning choice of alternative policies is subordinated to unending conflicts between competitors for power at the top while leaving the party weak and dysfunctional.

Ever since the day the Congress assumed power, it has gradually lost the character of a mass party, and has slowly evolved itself into an elite party. In between sometimes it did call for mass contacts, but the call was just a slogan. For any change in the Centre, the

Introduction xxxiii

role of at least four elite institutions must change. Each one of these institutions has turned into a cockpit for the struggle for power and thereby has remained largely divorced from its real functions. The Congress Parliamentary Party (CPP) takes up issues of policy only after there is enough controversy or crisis about them. It meets infrequently and generally for less than an hour. Its executive, ECPP, is a forum for carrying by others the struggle for power on behalf of leaders. The Congress Working Committee (CWC) acts more like ECPP than as the highest body of the party; it seldom takes up issues of party organization unless it is forced to intervene in party affairs which when it does, it normally does most clumsily. The Congress Parliamentary Board (CPB) is there generally to balance various interests when conflicts arise over such matter as nominating and selecting candidates, formation of governments, coalitions, and ministries.

It is really the super-elitist character of the last-mentioned institution that brought the crisis in the party to a head. Nevertheless, were the leadership struggle confined to these organs, some rational compromises were bound to have emerged, but Mrs. Gandhi has carried out the struggle simultaneously at two other levels, namely, in Parliament where she keeps and gets her support from the opposition parties and groups, and in the administration where she effectively uses the governmental machinery against her rivals. Because of this multiple and unequal struggle, it is but natural that other leaders and groups should attempt to get larger influence, weightage, and representation on these elite institutions and organs. She can never get hold of them, or dominate them, so long as she carries the struggle for power inside as well as outside the party. That probably is also the reason why Mrs. Gandhi has had to challenge at many occasions the authority of the ECPP, CWC, and CPB instead of carrying them along with her. However, the bosses' recent challenge to Mrs. Gandhi and their subsequent defeat at her hands has not only provided Mrs. Gandhi with a chance to change the character and composition of these institutions but also to make the Congress a "mass" party. Whether or not she accepts the challenging task, the power conflict in the Congress has now irretrievably become open, clearly identified, and unresolvable.

This conflict can no longer be carried purposefully through groups and factions which are labelled as Right or Left in the Congress and which find support from similar groups outside. This strategy of dependence on the distribution of power between groups rather on the power of the institutions, i.e. the integral power, will destroy the possibility of any consensus emerging either in leadership or on policies.

No other factor seems to have brought nearer the impending eclipse of the Congress than the breakdown of its party organization almost at all levels. The depth and degree of organization of a party directly determine its capacity to function. Barring the States of Maharashtra, Gujarat, and Mysore, the party organization is in shambles everywhere else and nearly extinct in those States where stable opposition Governments have come to stay. It is misleading to count on the very large vote polled in the general elections for the Congress, for it is the capacity of the Congress organization to influence future vote-structure, not its past prestige, that is going to matter most. In almost every other aspect, except vote-catching at a diminishing rate, the Congress is losing legitimacy as a party.

It is recognized that the increasing grip of powerful caucuses and bossism have cut the roots of the party from the masses and from those activitists who would have been attracted towards a centrist-democratic party functioning. It is as well true that there is no mutual responsiveness between the various structural components of the Congress Party organization. What is probably not fully appreciated—and this is the new and most crucial new factor—that the local power structure, which had long remained largely insulated from the impact of the power struggle at higher levels and which had provided a solid base to the Congress Party, has been effectively pierced through by all sorts of forces. Even till after the last general election, the Congress was right in claiming that in its local power structure, particularly at the rural level, no party had made a serious dent. The mid-term elections, the Telengana movement, the phenomena of the *Senas*, the confrontations arising out of the new agricultural strategy, a perceptible and uninterrupted decline in the growth rate have all contributed to cause the Congress lose its unchallenged dominance at the local power

Introduction

structure. And if this process is accelerated the defeat of the Congress at the polls will also be hastened. Briefly, the Congress Party organization today is fast breaking down at all levels. For the Congress to retrieve its position, the process has to be quickly reversed, beginning at the highest level, the caucus.

The defeat of the Syndicate, the top caucus of the party, can be traced as much to its internal contradictions as to the power and superior strategy of the Prime Minister. Its composition remains uncertain. And on its composition depends its strength. There are no permanent "ins" and "outs" and this fact alone reveals its inherent weakness. But its real weakness arises from its numerous internal contradictions just as its strength depends upon neutralizing them. The internal contradictions of the Syndicate must be properly understood because the final outcome of the struggle between Mrs. Gandhi and the members of the Syndicate will largely depend how vitally operational those contradictions are.

Caucus by its very nature is an anti-thesis of the strength of party organization. The survival of the undiminished power of the Syndicate as such is a threat to the party, the Government, and its leaders, whenever the two are in conflict. The Syndicate often enjoys power without responsibility. Between Mrs. Gandhi's populist tactics of supporting the non-Congress parties and Governments, on the one hand, and the destruction of the internal structure of the party at the hands of the Syndicate, on the other, the Congress cannot possibly survive.

The first contradiction arises from the conflicting political-interests of its members: those who have got a solid base in one or more States and those whose base is very narrow. The hard core of the Syndicate today consists of those whose political base has shrunk so much as to have reduced them into their being no more than regional leaders. In this category are K. Kamaraj, Atulya Ghosh, and S. K. Patil. Their very survival depends upon Mrs. Gandhi's reversing her present strategy of finding for herself support from and giving support to non-Congress parties which have defeated the Congress and thereby these leaders in their respective States. Their hostility to Mrs. Gandhi remains complete and implacable, since she is most unlikely to oblige them by reducing her widely distributed base of power. The "fight-to-finish" slogan is quite relevant here, when given either by Mrs. Gandhi or by her opponents.

The other members of the Syndicate or their temporary associates do not depend upon Mrs. Gandhi for their survival and are powerful by their own right. Y. B. Chavan, Morarji Desai, C.B. Gupta, and Nijalingappa fall in this category. Their relationships with Mrs. Gandhi are of flexible nature, of cooperation as well as conflict, depending upon the circumstances. Chavan's refusal to resign on the day when Morarji was dismissed can be explained by the peculiar position of the "associate" members of the Syndicate. Since the interests of the two groups do not always coincide, their conflict or strategies sometimes run parallel. The Syndicate's capacity to create firm unity or dynamic common strategy, as a durable dynamic element in its power struggle, is ruled out.

The second contradiction, which was more pronounced in recent crisis, is the vital differences in the ideological positions of its members. S. K. Patil and K. Kamaraj have little in common between them regarding the economic programme of the party. It is argued sometimes that these ideological differences are not real and, if any, are very small; all leaders are essentially centrist. This may be so. But their opposing ideological postures, which are overwhelmingly important to the politics of populism, are enough to deny them homogeneity and to their common leadership credibility. Since the line of division in the Syndicate on ideological lines cuts across the division that is determined by political strength, its membership, whenever enlarged, paradoxically, reduces instead of increasing its effectiveness as a power group. This contradiction allowed Mrs. Gandhi to evolve a flexible strategy. But now with Morarij's exit, there is no one left of any significance whom she can fight on ideological grounds. Chavan and Kamaraj can go one up on Mrs. Gandhi in making radical professions, without meaning anything more than what Mrs. Gandhi does.

The third contradiction flows from the first two. As the struggle between the Syndicate and Mrs. Gandhi becomes fierce, those who have vulnerable power base are attacked first by Mrs. Gandhi. There is no point in attacking those, such as Ghosh and Patil, who, whether vulnerable or not, have no real base. She dismissed Morarji because he was most vulnerable—not because there was any shrinkage in his political base—and because his removal brought rich dividends to her. The removal of Chavan will have similar effects when the time comes and he is found most vulnerable. Since Mrs. Gandhi, quite correctly, attacks them one by one, they are left each to pursue his own effort more for individual than for collective survival. Patil's recent acrobatics are a case in point. Despite appearances to the contrary all the members of the Syndicate have not shown the same degree of concern on Morarji's dismissal.

Fourthly, the Syndicate's power or the power of some of its members is disproportionately larger than their actual support in the party as well among the citizens in general. As political caucus, the Syndicate's power rests on the reduction of the power of the numerous sub-organizations of the party at different levels. It is through these organizations that a party can establish confidence and support among the people. The fiercer the struggle for power, the narrower becomes the base of operation of the Syndicate. A populist leader who can demogogically appeal to the mob can always successfully exploit this contradiction of the Syndicate, namely, its divorce from the lower echelons of the party and the masses.

Fifthly, the Syndicate acquires power, consolidates itself and attacks only on specific occasions and in relation to specific problems. Once a problem is resolved, whether in their favour or against them, the Syndicate members start flying at one another. S. K. Patil, Atulya Ghosh, and Ram Subhag Singh let down their senior colleagues at the meeting of the Working Committee which was called to discipline Mrs. Gandhi but ended in the Syndicate agreeing in principle to the primacy of the Prime Minister and thereby disciplining itself.

Finally, as a consequence of these contradictions, the Syndicate cannot produce a leader who combines in himself minimum of these contradictions, command full loyalty and support of other members and develops a strategy equal, if not superior, to that of the Prime Minister. Not one among its present members, including Morarji Desai who for all practical purposes is now with the Syndicate, can claim to have these qualities. It is this weakness of the Syndicate which gives Mrs. Gandhi a powerful edge over everybody else. Besides, the combined power of the Syndicate, which is now left with only one of its members as Cabinet Minister, in the sense of the use of governmental power, patronage, and personnel, is extremely small in contrast to that of Mrs. Gandhi. This is as vital a factor in the struggle for power as it is dangerous. Mrs. Gandhi was able to turn minority into a majority in her favour by the use of these powers.

It will be a gross mistake to conclude that its total humiliation and the impossible victory of Mrs. Gandhi have caused the final demise of the Syndicate. So long as the Congress Party remains structured as it is now, a new Syndicate or caucus will emerge to challenge her authority. The new Syndicate will have to be more powerful to do so. Its likely membership will come from strong Chief Ministers and powerful survivors from the last debacle. To avoid the rise of such a centre of power, Mrs. Gandhi will not only have to get control of the party but also to reorganize it on a completely different basis.

It is broadly true that all politics is the struggle for power. But it is certainly not true that all power is meant to play politics only. There are some, no matter how few, public purposes for which people in power have responsibility. In a parliamentary, as distinguished from a presidential system, parties really govern as well as grow as instruments of change. Nobody will suggest today that the Congress, despite Mrs. Gandhi's taking a couple of bold steps, has become an instrument of development and change. The Congress has ceased to govern: so much so that its governing functions came to a complete standstill during two months of recent political crisis, without Mrs. Gandhi or any other leader feeling responsible for this national waste. The Congress can no longer even be called an active element of *status quo* in the broad social sense. These two functions cannot be given back to the Congress now by any set of intellectual formulas, political gimmicks, or backstair management. In fact, the unit of analysis is no longer party but functions. Mrs. Gandhi would probably be best suited for a Presidential system in which parties can be loosely organized, are factionally composed and separated from power to govern—all the more in a federal polity which also has a socially federalist structure. Her strategy and the present system, however, stand in sharp contradiction to each other.

It is generally not realized that the fall of Mrs. Gandhi's Government, if and when it comes, will come largely from its non-governing character and the loss of legitimacy and not from the attacks of the Syndicate. Whatever the majority a party may have in Parliament, it can look forward to stay in power for the full term on the basis of legitimacy, its governing character, and the adequacy of its policies. The pathology of Mrs. Gandhi's Government is unique; it refuses to govern as it becomes increasingly irresponsible. And the more it becomes ineffective, the more it relies on gimmicks, slogans, and political farce. The techniques, strategies, orientations, and capabilities of her ministers are most deplorable. Legitimacy in the final analysis is the recognition and acceptance by the people of the authority of the Government to rule and rule effectively. The effectiveness of a Government has a direct relation with its legitimacy; the ineffectual character of a Government, like that of the present one at the Centre, is an expression of its illegitimacy and vice versa. The only way people get their demands, reasonable or unreasonable, accepted is by breaking law and order and destroying institutions which are precisely meant to articulate and nationalize their demands. The new popularity earned by Mrs. Gandhi is not based on any effectiveness of her Government but on her wild promises, coming in the wake of bank nationalization. On the one hand, there is an air of general defiance, resort to mass agitation, breach of law, unconcern for public property, and hatred and disgust for politicians. On the other hand, the public is fed on either wild promises or total cynicism and practical unresponsiveness to their rational demands and pressures. In brief, there is growing deep down alienation of people from politics and politicians despite some occasional outbursts. No Government can long survive these corroding influences on the polity.

Briefly, in straight functional analysis, the leaders of the Congress Party are divorcing themselves from Congress Party as a system, as an organization, and even as a party. The Congress Party can accommodate many factions, interests, groups, and ideologies but it must clearly exclude some. Besides, there are standard functions that a party must perform for pattern-maintenance, adaptation, integration, and goal attainment. None of these functions are being performed at that minimum level at which the Congress can remain as a party. Even during Nehru's days, all these functions were not performed as a mix that could take the party forward. But Nehru could (*a*) provide leadership which guaranteed the minimum performance of some of these functions and (*b*) separate the functioning of the Government from those of the party through depoliticizing certain institutions and functions. Thus the Government could perform these four functions at some critical level, higher than the level at which the party was functioning. The policies of Nehru's Government, despite appearances to the contrary, were always more coherent and precise than those of his party. Mrs. Gandhi has, on the contrary, gradually brought both the government and the party at an extremely low level of functioning and cohesion, almost to the complete absence of these four functions. Before 16 July 1969, there were doubts as to whether any one was running the country. Conflicts within the ruling party today are inseparable from conflicts with or within the Government itself, as are their respective levels of functioning, each slowing down the entire economic and political apparatus. No leader can survive for long this situation.

It was stated earlier how the confrontation of the States with the Centre was skilfully diverted by Mrs. Gandhi towards other top Congress leaders. Now that it will not be possible for her do so. We must explore the dimensions of this struggle and its consequences upon the Congress Party itself, irrespective of as to who bears its main brunt. However, even the worst-ever confrontations before 1968 did not degenerate into prolonged crises; they faded out without being fully resolved. But all those Centre-State conflicts which began after the mid-term polls totally refuse to leave the political stage, particularly the conflicts between the Centre and the Communist-led States. It may be the question of CRP, Governor's power, Plan allocations, Telengana controversy, or the new tax measures, whatever the issue, unless the Centre yields, the issue remains unresolved. And the more Mrs.

Introduction xli

Gandhi keeps up her individual dialogue with the State leaders for acquiring personal support, the more implacable and serious becomes the States' opposition to the Centre. This is as much a result of the Centre's inability to take a counter stand against the demands of States as of the failure of the Centre to formulate rational policies to meet half-way their rational demands. The situation requires compromises of understanding, not of convenience. Giri's victory largely depended upon the support that came from the States. This support was acquired by Mrs. Gandhi by making promises and further pandering to the States' bosses. She will have to face a difficult situation from now on with these bosses consciously wielding their newly acquired power and demanding, with fanatical audacity, of Mrs. Gandhi that she fulfil her promises.

There is a certain amount of false hope entertained in Mrs. Gandhi's camp that the adventurism of the Left-controlled State Governments will be cancelled by the conservatism of the Right-led Governments. That may be so in some matters. But where political survival is at stake—and this is at the mercy of the most unpredictable voter—all State Governments, Right, Left, or Congress, are of one mind in demanding their pound of flesh and thereby weakening the Centre. The real danger lies in the double strategy of the State Chief Ministers. They are all sweet and persuasive when they are negotiating with the Centre to get whatever they can. But as soon as they go back to their States, the call for confrontation is heard everywhere, if only to divert the attention and anger of the people towards the Central Government. It is difficult to see how any Government at the Centre can survive by building bridges with those who are bent upon destroying it.

However serious the factional and leadership struggle inside the party, one real force working behind the break-up of the Congress is the deepening economic crisis in the country, and total absence of its political management, despite the appearance of stability on the surface. By and large, the Government's policies are straight leading the economy to the deepest pits of stagnation. Crises often occur; but it is the political will and mechanism to fight them that matters. So long as a certain minimum level of public and private investment programme remained in operation the economy, and hence the polity, was able to withstand temporary shocks. So long as pipeline projects and investments, current as well as past, in their combined effect kept up a high rate of capital formation, employment, and output the economy, the polity, and the Government remained stable despite occasional crises. That situation has basically changed now.

Four factors are of crucial importance here. Firstly, the perpetuation of a low rate of growth, which means smaller economic surplus, whether for further growth or for distribution for political purposes. In fact, it was the unnecessarily and disproportionately large diversion of the economic surplus towards meeting politically oriented demands that has reduced the growth rate. It has been a vicious circle. The lower the surplus available for investment, the slower was the growth in the next period, and smaller the the surplus for distribution in face of steadily mounting political demands. The Government could not do what it had promised. On the top of it came the growing imbalance between the Centre and the States, generating a newer demand for distribution of resources which inevitably further reduced the share of productive investment. Transfer of a rupee worth of resources from the Centre to the States *ipso facto* reduces capital formation. So much so that the firm rate of savings in India today has become the lowest ever since 1953-54. Mrs. Gandhi's jubilation and wild promises following her recent victory are going to add more fuel to the fire. A successful management of political crisis is no substitute for efficient economic management.

Secondly, the economy has been left without any cushion of pipeline projects to absorb shocks of considerable magnitude. Even in the worst period of two successive droughts, the capital formation remained at a fairly high level by a large number of pipeline projects. The draft Fourth Five Year Plan, if it can be called a plan, leaves few of the old projects or creates new projects in the pipeline. Of course, we may be lucky so as not to face any serious shocks but there is a natural cycle of weather we have to live with. Another drought will, to be sure, cause not only an unprecedented economic but also a first class political crisis, particularly because between 1965 and now the Government's

Introduction xliii

governing, planning, and management capacities have further deteriorated.

Thirdly, as a consequence of the above two facts, there is a strong possibility of a further growth of the violent, populist, and extra-legal politics overtaking normal political processes. For example, while the rate of increase in unemployment, according to the Employment Exchange registrations, has gone up by 10 to 15 per cent annually, the net increase in new jobs, as indicated by the same agencies, is less than 2 per cent. Growing unemployment, particularly of the educated youth, along with mounting demographic pressures, rising tempo of politically oriented demands, and the inability of the Government to either articulate them or to satisfy them will increasingly take such violent forms as they have in Telengana. Violent agitations are the direct product of economic stagnation, which sometimes passes as stability and of struggle for power, which is called either political development or progressive politics.

Fourthly, it will make all the difference whether Mrs. Gandhi adds to this populist politics or subdues it by matching her popular slogans with a massive attempt at resource mobilization, improving the public sector, reorganizing the public bureaucracy, and, above all, by canalizing people's support for a massive national productive effort. If all this is not done, the political imperatives of Mrs. Gandhi's strategy and her struggle for power will set the printing presses into motion, leading to massive deficit financing and spiral inflation. The common man instead of benefiting will be worse off. A great disillusionment will set in, bringing in its wake total con tempt for the existing political system. A good monsoon can only postpone the day of reckoning.

The so-called ten-point programme and Mrs. Gandhi's latest note on her stray thoughts, both unanimously and ceremoniously approved by the AICC, do add up to a radical programme, which in terms of professions, make the Congress Party's economic programme not very much different from those of the SSP, PSP, or CPI. And yet the structure of the Congress Party, which spans a wide spectrum of interests, groups, and ideologies, is not even mildly radical. Nor can Mrs. Gandhi's Government be described radical, if judged by its performance over the last three and a half years. Nowhere was this contradiction more openly brought out than in the slowing down of growth rate while the demands on the economic cake showed no let-up. So far the radicalism of Mrs. Gandhi has revealed practically nothing by way of so changing the economic structure as to put the economy back on the growth path. On the contrary, following bank nationalization, she has begun with more non-productive spending which is likely to be accelerated as she enters the new phase of winning friends and splitting enemies.

Take another example—it is about the Government's attitude towards the demand for enquiry against the Birlas. Although the groups involved in the controversy make it out a straight ideological issue, most informed people know that it is nothing of the kind so far as Mrs. Gandhi is concerned. It is not a mere coincidence that in every crisis Mrs. Gandhi has faced, she has found the big business, particularly the Birlas, lined up behind her, either through their willing cooperation or by being subjected to governmental pressures or both. The way the enquiry has now been ordered reveals that the Government has nearly bailed out the Birlas. The real facts behind the controversy on the Birla enquiry are: (1) attempts on the part of some groups of big businessmen who are hostile to Birlas to keep up the pressure; (2) the political leaders' attempt to woo and use Birlas as instruments for their struggle for power; and (3) the efforts to ignore, if not to deny the real question— apart from its known corrupt practices—what is left today of the big business as an instrument of economic growth? These factors are seldom brought out in the open. To imagine that the Congress Party will get polarized over such issues as inquiry into the Birla empire cannot be called a good analysis, to say the least.

How far Mrs. Gandhi will be able to fulfil her economic promises depends how she tackles the political problems facing her and the Congress Party. It will be agreed upon that the present political situation, the aftermath of recent crisis, is confused, uncertain, and incapable of yielding unfailing predictions. However, there are some inescapable tasks, if not inescapable choices, before Mrs. Gandhi.

Mrs. Gandhi has before her three difficult tasks to fulfil: (1) How best to get control of the party? (2) If control over the party is

Introduction xlv

established, what strategy will ensure victory at the next elections? (3) If complete victory is not possible and coalition seems inescapable, what sort of coalition Mrs. Gandhi should look for, either before or after the next elections? These are all inter-connected tasks and for each task there will be number of overlapping choices or options open to her. Of course, each choice will require a different measure of struggle to grasp it and all the choices will be subject to the overall constraint of her adequately fulfilling economic promises to the people in general, and weaker sections in particular. The outcome of her efforts given to fulfil these three tasks will partly answer some other questions regarding polarization, party structure, future governmental set-up, etc.

The discussion of all the three problems will be taken together but we shall begin with the question of her acquiring control over the party organization. If she is really successful in getting complete control of the party by an almost total elimination of the old guard and serious rivals, and, thereby, emerges as the unchallenged leader of the party as well as the Government, Mrs. Gandhi would have done two things. She would have made the party really coherent, programmatic, and united behind her. But as a result of that she would have also, perhaps, reduced the party to a smaller size. This paradox, which the Congress and Mrs. Gandhi have been avoiding so far, overshadows all possible choices before her.

After acquiring control of the higher organs of the party, such as the CWC and CPB, she will have to expand somehow her base in the party to remain in power. To do that she can follow one of the two paths. She undertakes a massive radical programme for higher growth rate, for changing the structure of the economy, and for reshaping the character of the party. To do all this seriously and not spuriously is very difficult and fraught with the danger of some of her none-too-radical supporters leaving the Congress Party and thus further reducing her base. She could make up for all these losses by entering into a firm alliance with some or all parties of the Left. In this way she would genuinely polarize politics and lose all her non-radical supporters like the BKD, Akalis, and DMK to the Opposition, which would become a very formidable combination, if they all could join together. For Mrs. Gandhi to emerge as a successful leader in 1972 on the basis of this method will require turning her own part of the Congress into an entirely new, functioning, and cadre party with some definite programme all the time kept hot on the anvil. But a more crucial requirement is to win over the major portions of the existing State and local power centres, which exist on cross loyalties, vague programmes, and fully entrenched local bossism. Mrs. Gandhi cannot but face tough opposition in this method of acquiring control of the party, and she is shrewd enough not to try it. She has not got time, personnel, apparatus, resources, and even well-thought-out programme to accomplish this task, hence this path must be ruled out. A United Front of the democratic Left or all Left parties under her leadership is wishful thinking. She is not made of that stuff to set about doing it.

The other course for her to broaden her base, if she is in full control of the party, is not merely to enter into an alliance with other centrist parties like the DMK, Akalis, and BKD and also invite some mild radicals like Ajoy Mukherjee's rump, the PSP, and similar assorted groups to join that alliance but also to have a straight and complete merger of these parties with the Congress. This arrangement for merger will have to be worked out well in advance because Mrs. Gandhi cannot hope to go to the polls at the head of a truncated party and win majority by opposing her opponents as well as erstwhile supporters in the Opposition. Whereas an alliance or an understanding does not guarantee Mrs. Gandhi's return to power in 1972—on the contrary, it may bring about her defeat—a merger fully ensures such a comeback. Superficially, she will still require to keep a semblance of radicalism, which she should be able to manage by carrying the struggle against the Jana Sangh and the Swatantra more determinedly than against the Communists and the SSP. And if the public enthusiasm for Mrs. Gandhi is maintained, and also if the timing and strategy of going to the polls happen to be correct, she should be able to impose a crushing defeat on both the parties of Right and Left, except probably in one or two States. This situation will amount to a return to the system of one-party dominance. However, such a neat outcome, though quite logical, least costly, and most beneficial

Introduction

for Mrs. Gandhi, is neither feasible nor consistent with contemporary politics. Neither the Congress can ever return to the old conglomeration of every conceivable interest and ideology existing under the same umbrella, nor are the opposition parties, which have emerged stronger by defeating the Congress in several States after a hard struggle, obliged to destroy their most cherished identities and commit suicide to save Mrs. Indira Gandhi or her party. This second path is also ruled out.

Therefore, the more likely approach that Mrs. Gandhi is expected to adopt is to enter into massive and numerous and even mutually contradictory alliances and compromises with various factions in every State Congress Party or Government. Except for well identified opponents, everyone who is prepared to jump on to her bandwagon may be taken into the fold so as to build maximum support behind her in the Congress Party. Such an amalgam has to be so loosely knit and amorphous as will give her a broad based support and also suit her supporters outside the Congress Party. The general character of this amalgam, once again, will be centrist, like that of the Congress now, yielding much the same type of politics but heavily weighted in her favour in terms of intra-party power balance. The new forces and allies of Mrs. Gandhi will be led by different men but no essential structural change is likely to follow. All that Mrs. Gandhi has to accomplish is to become herself the Congress President and pack with her own men the Congress Parliamentary Board, the Working Committee, and the Pradesh Congress Committees. No structural or constitutional change will be needed in the party set-up. It would be a bloodless coup and superficially cheap because it would have led to no grand solution except keeping Mrs. Gandhi in power for some time. In fact, any major attempt to restructure the party may not allow such an expansion of her political base. Pressures for polarization will not be strong, because up to 1972, the economy will be stagnant but not in depression, politics fragmented but not yet in anarchy, and the people will be catching up with slogans but not yet hysterical.

If Mrs. Gandhi can afford to go slow on programme implementation—the public can always be cheated—she can enter into an understanding with the centrist parties like the DMK, Akalis, and BKD, on the basis of a promise of a future coalition at the Centre, depending upon the electoral performance of each party, as well as entering into an electoral adjustment with all or some of them. The combined strength of Mrs. Gandhi and her allied parties should be enough, though small, to put her back into power after 1972. This alternative allows Mrs. Gandhi to play all her strategies with no commitment to any one or to any programme. It will require no great adjustment of the existing power balance either. However, the victory may be so small that the future coalition may not come off, or if it does, it may not stay on for long. Yet this alternative enjoys maximum probability.

It would seem that the clearer and sharper the choice, the more difficult and risky it is to be translated into the immediate imperatives of power, and, therefore, more unlikely to be made by Mrs. Gandhi. Unless power balance in the Congress Party does not shift at all in Mrs. Gandhi's favour, a vertical split in the Congress on the basis of ideology, factions, territory, or pure power should be ruled out and with that also any significant change in the programmes, policies, and instruments of their implementation. However, if power struggle in the Congress takes some new unexpected sharp turns and twists, new changes should not be ruled out, but it is safer to conclude that the pattern of power struggle will follow its by now very familiar course.

Therefore, expectations about polarization are likely to be belied so long as Mrs. Gandhi remains in power. The deepening crisis inside the Congress Party and a more serious crisis in the economy accompanied by new attacks on the party from outside it have to be in unique combination to bring about polarization. It is impossible to predict such a combination emerging in the near future. Nevertheless, the Congress will face all the time prospects for its breakup because of its old and new internal contradictions, analyzed in the following chapters, remaining unresolved. If the break-up really takes place, its consequence may not be polarization of the party system but further party fragmentation.

Were the present static power system to undergo some change, polarization may yet not come off because the real nature of factions in the Congress is changing in the direction of individual members of the Party getting disillusioned with their respective factional leaders, particularly if defeated. The decline in the support for the Syndicate among the legislators between 20 July and 25 August was staggering. Much more important is their disillusionment with the system, their growing sense of insecurity and uncertainty about the future and the risk they run in closely aligning themselves with leaders whose own future is uncertain. Therefore, there is no chance of polarization either through ideology or through combinations of factions. The Congress is squarely set on the path to either fully maintaining the *status quo* or breaking-up into several pieces and in a manner which depends upon the series of crises that will overtake it. It is to these crises that serious attention must be paid.

If the pressures from outside the party were to ease or to remain at low level, the present system has a better chance of continuing. But the anti-Congress forces, including those which are paired from outside with factions or leaders inside the Congress, are unlikely to oblige. For example, the Left opposition parties, with whom Mrs. Gandhi keeps a continuous rapport, shrewdly play the double game of supporting her and opposing the Congress in order to strengthen themselves, as indeed they must. But no leftist will ever support Mrs. Gandhi except when she is juxtaposed against her colleagues for mutual annihilation. It is, therefore, the ferocity of the opposition attacks and the strength of other more vital forces in the polity and economy which will determine the rate and the shape of the disintegration of the Congress.

The alternatives or paths suggested above posses enough logic to be accepted or rejected. But choices and alternatives in politics cannot be reduced to mathematical abracadabra. Could the politicians see as to where their bickerings and chicaneries, their intrigues and alliances were leading them and the country, some logical and rational possibilities could be discovered even within the present static power structure.

In search for easy and ideal solution, a lot of effort, largely speculative, is being expended on bringing about polarization, coalitions, and mergers. The future of the Congress Party does not depend on any pre-meditated alliances or ideological sharpness, because the Congress does not face any serious challenge at the

Centre from alliances or ideological groupings. The impending defeat of the Congress is to be seen in the light of new emerging party forces which have the characteristics of (1) party fragmentation, (2) decline of the all-India parties including the Congress, and (3) extremely pluralist and unpolarized multi-party system. Of the various choices open to Mrs. Gandhi and discussed above, not even one may be allowed to become operative if these factors or characteristics come to dominate party politics in the immediate future. In case this happens, her downfall will come sooner than later.

Indian democracy has given birth to unlimited social and political pluralism which denies political parties, even the most well-bound ideological parties, the scope of having a solid social and economic base. This phenomenon has been accompanied by a rapid party-fragmentation—the number of parties at all levels having crossed the three dozen figure. These developments militate against the formation of stable coalitions much as they thwart polarization that would be consistent with the democratic system.

Therefore, the prospects the Congress faces is not only the obvious one—end of its dominance—but also the difficulty of arranging for prospective coalitions well in advance of the 1972 elections. On the other hand, the more the Congress delays its decision on the future alliances, the greater will be the nibbling at its strength by the opposition. A talk of polarization in the Congress may be unrealistic, but it cannot conceal the breakdown of the old consensus or the uneasy, fragile alliances among its numerous intra-party factions. Each faction enjoys today much lower level of legitimacy in the eyes of its own constituents.

Therefore, on the basis of feasible and not idealistic or logical alternatives that are available to Mrs. Gandhi and her supporters on the one hand and to her opponents inside and outside the Congress Party on the other, only three models emerge for the Indian body politic in the immediate future. Mrs. Gandhi is not the only one to pick up alternatives and implement them; there are others who can frustrate them equally.

Firstly, populist politics may come to dominate the entire political life of the country, with all the attendant consequences, if the

Introduction li

power struggle in the Congress Party is not so decisively resolved as to make it a coherent, united party. For all practical purposes *status quo* will be maintained through the widening gap between radical professions and actual *status quo* politics. This is the Nasser-Soekarno-Nkrumah-Goulart path mentioned earlier. Inflation, recession, large income disparities, public and private corruption, inefficiency will all become common features of the system, resulting in total party fragmentation, violence, massive extra-constitutional politics, and contempt for political institutions. Superficially, politics will appear to be getting polarized, though in reality it will get pulverized. Mrs. Gandhi will inevitably be caught in the populist maelstrom and in the absence of powerful, well-organized revolutionary forces emerging as s countervailing factor, the entire political structure will collapse, resulting in the rise of Right-wing authoritarianism. Populism is Mrs. Gandhi's as of the country's worst enemy, though both are increasingly being pushed into that direction. If she is serious about her claim that the people have given her a mandate to go socialist, she cannot but carve out a powerful Left United Front to fight populism. Otherwise, her attempts to go above the institutions and appeal to masses for support will only accelerate populism. Alternatively, she could also establish a strong centrist coalition or alliance, as suggested earlier, and complete those stages of capitalist economic and political development which, of necessity, must precede socialist transformation. There is no third way out of galloping populism.

Secondly, Mrs. Gandhi may follow a mixture of strategies and choices mentioned earlier and go to the polls at the head of a Congress Party divided against itself and by making all sorts of alliances and compromises with groups and parties inside and outside the party, but leaving intact the existing political balances of the system as a whole. In that case, the elections of 1972, if projections from the past are carried forward, will yield innumerable parties both in the States legislatures, as witnessed in 1967 and 1969 and in Parliament at the Centre. The Congress cannot possibly remain a majority party in such circumstances. The decline of the all-India parties and the existing regional parties will take place in favour of new regional parties, splinters parties, personal parties, communal and caste parties, and Independents, as was unmistakably demonstrated in the mid-term poll of 1969. A new era of unstable coalitions will begin at the Centre, resulting in instability, dysfunctionalism, and anarchy. The party structure will become so fragmented as to become completely divorced from all major national tasks. Once again the system will have to go down without having created a rational alternative. Here, too, the only way out will be for the Centre and Left Centre parties to coalesce and if they are able to muster enough majority, the system may survive. Mrs. Gandhi could lead such an alliance. The chances for such a revival are not bright though. An authoritarian alternative will have greater chances to emerge.

Thirdly, before the system is finally pushed, either by populism or party fragmentation, to its impending collapse, some new combinations of political forces may rise to stop the rot. After all the Indian polity and economy can be sharply differentiated from other populist countries by her having established a strong industrial and agricultural base, developed political and economic infrastructure, a powerful bureaucracy, and host of institutions which can be pressed into service by a conscious and determined political leadership. The rise of these forces will have to take place long before the critical moment of collapse comes. However, since populism and party fragmentation will get accelerated in next three or four years, the stabilizing forces that could combine will be (1) bureaucracy, (2) military, and (3) politicians of some national and regional standing. Those who say that India cannot be ruled by a military dictatorship have strong reasons behind their assertion. But if the law and order problem becomes serious and extra-constitutional politics gets further impetus, military will certainly become *one* factor of power among several others. Every stable nation rests on a stable balance between some major macro factors of power. In India that balance has yet to emerge because the sort of balance which Nehru wanted to create lost its chance even before his death. The new balance between military, bureaucracy, and a few political parties and groups is the only one that has a chance to survive out of the growing anarchy. Balance between these three powerful forces cannot possibly remain stable in the long run. But whether it can be stable

Introduction liii

in the short-run will depend upon the nature of the distribution of power among the three and their functioning capacities. They will find their support in the basic strength of the economy, local political power structure which runs parallel to local bureaucracy, and vast proliferating intelligentsia. They will be opposed by both extreme Right-wing and Left-wing parties, more so by the latter. But the internal weakness of these parties will make them collapse under their own weight. Anyway, it will put an end to populism, party fragmentation, and political anarchy. Mrs. Gandhi may not be acceptable to this combination because it is by defeating her that such a combination will come to power.

None of the aforementioned alternatives were discussed in relation to normative political categories such as democracy, socialism, welfarism, national and unity discipline. It would appear that, except the alternative of Left Centrist forces coalescing among themselves, all others are antithetical to norms and ideals that the nation has set before itself. But *real-politik* and ideals do not always go together. The way they are combined is a function of political leadership. Mrs. Gandhi owes it to herself and the nation to bring about a proper combination and save the country. Otherwise, she has no future.

So far as the task before a political analyst is concerned, I can only say with Christopher Serpell that "when public figures do something which is apparently inexplicable, they create an unbearable situation for those whose job is to interpret their actions. Immediately general hunt starts for some secret and subtle motives which will make sound sense of what seems to be unsensibal." It is for the readers to judge the analysis presented in the following chapters.

PART ONE

1

THE NEW PRIME MINISTER

IT WOULD BE churlish not to wish good luck to the new Prime Minister as she settles down to her onerous responsibilities and for the first time faces Parliament in her new role. She would need a lot of it in the coming months and years. But what she would need most is a detached understanding, independent of both her supporters and opponents.

It seems, therefore, utterly unrealistic and unfair to her as well as to the nation to attribute to her, encomium-wise, those high-sounding policies and pristine qualities of performance from which she stands yet at a good deal of distance. The danger is that she may either be driven into adopting such impossible policy postures under high-pressure advice from young ideologues and noisy clamourers around her or be so modelled into a star image by political ad-men that her most dedicated accomplishments may ultimately appear to fall too short of expectations and thus lower her prestige and authority.

Although there is almost nothing in her past that goes against her, yet all that the image-makers are digging up from ever since the days of the "doll brigade" do not add up to anything quite clear or predictable. On the other hand, there are people who have completely dismissed her in advance.

In terms of problems, time is running against her, and she may not have ample opportunities to show and even develop her mettle while in office. It would be more than cheap politicking and sham amateurism to pre-judge Mrs. Gandhi either way. Let us not in this case follow the Chinese practice of improvising seasonal gods and by force of habit demolish them if their performance is less than godly.

It is quite interesting to note that the word "socialism" does not appear in Mrs. Gandhi's first national broadcast. If it is not a mere slip on the part of the speechwriter, the omission augurs well. It is high time that this parlour game of self-deception about socialism should come to an end: both the socialists and the Congressmen should realize that the Congress Party, as constituted at present, is anything but an instrument of socialism. Whether socialism is practicable or not is another matter; but this word has been bandied about so meaninglessly and almost dishonestly and for so long that its use today almost sounds pejorative. There is no shortage of words in political parlance by which the policy and the reality of the Congress Party or the Government can be more appropriately defined. My fear is that this word would be hustled back in speech-making without a single tycoon losing his sleep over it. This would reveal not the strength but the weakness of the Prime Minister unless she means to move radically towards socialism, both in the Government and the party.

The purpose here is to study and analyze, while eschewing all prejudgments, the dynamic forces in the power structure of the Indian polity, particularly of the Congress Party, and determine their relationship with the Prime Minister in office. There is bound to be a struggle in which the forces of the power structure that have installed her in authority would attempt to control and strait-jacket the new Prime Minister in their favour, and the Prime Minister on her part, one would assume, would try to utilize and modify the power structure to strengthen her own authority. This is quite natural, but the outcome of this struggle will largely determine the sort of Prime Minister Mrs. Gandhi would make or emerge.

It is very tempting to reduce the study of power mechanism to the level of alignments and realignments of innumerable factions inside and outside the Congress. Factions are important; respective personalities or ideologies that go with them are also not irrelevant. But in the functioning of the total power structure, an undue emphasis on factions yields a distorted view of politics and sterile conclusions.

I shall instead proceed differently by asking a rather simple question: if Mrs. Gandhi was not considered a serious candidate for Prime Ministership after Nehru's death, what was there so remarkable and compulsive that happened during the next eighteen months, either in her performance in office or in the political consolidation of her base in one or more States or in the Congress Party, that she could score a landslide victory over Morarji Desai? There is certainly no positive evidence for anything so remarkable a result. I would very humbly submit to Mrs. Gandhi that if she puts the same question to herself, her long-term perspective about her future role in relation to the formidable forces she will have to contend with (in other words, the whole reactive mechanism between her and the political structure) would emerge quite clearly.

Let us first merely recount some of the forces (not factions) that constituted the power-structure in the election to the office of the Prime Minister. (1) The Congress President Kamaraj by himself or in the Congress Working Committee, (2) Chief Ministers of various States, (3) the Congress Parliamentary Party, (4) the Syndicate, (5) communal, linguistic, and other sectarian forces inside and outside the Congress, (6) organized business, and (7) external forces, particularly the USA and the USSR. This is not a homogeneous but a heterogeneous set of forces. It would be shown below that the only thing common between all of them, in relation to the office of the Prime Minister, is that they will all decisively vote for a weak Prime Minister to retain and increase their own respective strength. There is nothing so startling about this because this must happen in the sort of democracy we have adopted. The role of these forces need further analysis.

(1) During Nehru's rule, there had been no conflict between the party and the Government wings of the Congress. The only exception was Purushottamdas Tandon's election to Congress Presidentship and Nehru made a swift job of it. Since Nehru's death, the Congress President has become a real force for any Prime Minister to contend with, even if there is no conflict between the two. Any Congress President would by virtue of his office plump for a weak Prime Minister.

However, conflict, cooperation, or struggle must be seen only as a new dynamic relation and not as once-for-all balance or imbalance between the two. Kamaraj cannot forget that Shastri, an erstwhile weak Prime Minister, very cleverly reduced the Congress President's importance during Kamaraj's re-election to the same office. Mrs. Gandhi may be on the best of terms with him as the new Congress President, but if she is to assert she will be up against a powerful force, depending upon the Congress President's personality.

Besides, once a very powerful personality occupies that august seat, and unless he keeps occupying it, he cannot go back to his earlier job in the State he comes from. He must go forward either as a contender for Prime Ministership or for Presidentship of the Republic. It is widely believed that Kamaraj refused to accept the job before it was offered to Mrs. Gandhi.

There could be good reasons for it and one need not go into them. But the million-dollar qustion Mrs. Gandhi must address to herself is: Where does Kamaraj go from where he is? A weak Prime Minister could be easily brushed aside by Kamaraj.

Paradoxically, it is precisely by her own performance that Mrs. Gandhi would increase or reduce her own stature and thereby reduce or increase that of the Congress President; but her very performance would be constantly overshadowed by the powerful Congress President. (The other question whether Kamaraj would be a better Prime Minister than Mrs. Gandhi or vice versa is completely irrelevant here.) Herein lies the real difference between Morarji's candidature and Mrs. Gandhi's and not in the fact that the former is reactionary and the latter progressive.

(2) Partly as a result of the peculiar working of the federal Constitution in India over the last eighteen years, and partly as a result of the weakening of Nehru's hold on the politics of the country in the last phase of his rule, a considerable shift of power has taken place from the Centre to the States. The Chief Ministers, as a combined force, are more powerful than any of other forces, even if put together. Their role in Mrs. Gandhi's election marks the culmination of their power. It would hardly serve any useful purpose to delve into the semantics of the constitutional exercise of power. Only the fact of power is to be recognized.

No Chief Minister in his senses would vote for a strong Prime Minister and get his own power clipped. Having their peculiar local difficulties, instabilities, and dissident oppsition, the Chief Ministers could deal with them according to their own wishes only if there were few external checks on them. Almost every Chief Minister faces charges of real or imaginary misdeeds and would tremble in his shoes at the sight of a strong Prime Minister who must act one way or another at least to show his strength. Since 90 per cent of the Centre's policies depend for their implementation on States, strong State Governments could make mince-meat of any Central policy that is considered inimical to their political power. There are innumerable examples of this and the sabotage of the national food policy by the States is the latest reminder of this fact.

However, what appears to be the strength of the Chief Ministers also happens to be their biggest weakness and a shrewd and bold Prime Minister could very skilfully exploit it. But Mrs. Gandhi should have no illusions about the reasons for their choice; they expect her not to interfere in their affairs which they could not expect from Morarji Desai.

(3) Congress Parliamentary Party is not an independent force, although in theory it should be the strongest. In most European democracies from which we have borrowed our democratic structure, parliamentary parties are the strongest force. The Congress Parliamentary Party has no effective say in the selection of the candidates for the General Election, plays little part in policy formulation except broadly stamping the official policy, and is riven with irreconcilable factions which find support in opposition parties of similar thinking rather than inside their own party. Its members are increasingly divorced from their local political base and thus remain at the mercy of State bosses and the Congress Parliamentary Board.

A Prime Minister by strengthening the Parliamentary Party could strengthen his or her own position, but the factions constituting it today suggest that most of them, though not all, would prefer a weak person rather than vote into power a strong Prime Minister who would curb their factionalism or balance them in such a way as to utilize them for his or her own power.

(4) The Syndicate appears to be a very strange and ugly body. Its influence may not have been as decisive in Mrs. Gandhi's

election as it was in Shastri's, but its role and importance must be clearly understood. The Syndicate provides the missing and final link in the creation of the party political caucus in the Congress for ruling the party as well as the Government.

The growth of this caucus, consisting of the Chief Ministers, the Congress President, and the Syndicate, is marked by the reduction of the power of the two democtatic bodies, the AICC and the Congress Working Committee, in whom alone power is legitimized. In the face of a strong Prime Minister, the Syndicate would just disappear—there was no such body during Nehru's days.

The Syndicate, therefore, by the nature of its inception and definition could do no better than vote for a weak Prime Minister, and it would always remain a threat to the authority of any Prime Minister. In Europe the democratic parties could not grow until the political caucus which preceded them was completely destroyed. Of course, a shrewd Prime Minister can always reduce the power of caucus, but it will require great courage and intensive decision-making.

(5) It was once commonly believed that after the completion of the linguistic division of the country, there would be no force or power left in the linguistic groups for political agitation and participation. More or less a similar facile optimism prevailed with regard to communalism and casteism when communal practices were legally banned.

Unfortunately, all these sectarian forces have come back to life through political activity, almost with a vengeance. Today their members do not go to national political parties for the redress of their grievances, if any, but to their respective groups. They have become a vital political force, and not only do they constitute a significant section of each political party including the Congress but also cut across political parties. Some of the groups may not be as highly developed as others, but each major internal crisis strengthens them one way or another.

Their role in the election of a Prime Minister may also not seem very clear, but their power in Cabinet formation is unmistakable and Mrs. Gandhi's Cabinet is no exception. The image of a strong Prime Minister of a unified nation should frighten these sectarian forces, and it is not surprising that most of the minority communal and caste groups in the Congress have sided with Mrs. Gandhi in the hope that she would not take drastic measures against them.

Of course, one communal group may desire a strong leader who would stamp out some other communal group, but when it comes to choosing an utterly uncompromising leader in relation to sectarianism, they would really waver. As such groups cut across political parties, the jubilation of their respective counterparts outside the Congress is another indication of their calculating Mrs. Gandhi, a secular leader, to be a moderate if not a weak Prime Minister.

Communalism of the majority did not show its claws completely but its instinctive reaction cannot be misunderstood. It is not enough that a Prime Minister should be non-sectarian; he or she should put down such forces with a firm hand and at least should refuse to make a Cabinet by pandering to these interests. Nehru talked against communal, caste, and linguistic forces and yet the actions of his party in Government resulted in considerable appeasement of the same forces. It is not very instructive at this stage to know how many votes of the scheduled castes or communal groups were shifted from one candidate to another; what is to be recognized is their continuous dead-weight which would inhibit any new Prime Minister from adopting national policies.

A more sinister tendency, which has not yet burst out into the open on a vast scale but has become a strong underlying force, is reflected in the division of the votes cast between the North and the South. Few commentators seem to have bothered to note that almost the entire support for Morarji Desai came from the North except for a few diehard dissidents who would have voted anyway against a candidate whom their respective Chief Ministers were supporting. A person who would tolerate no nonsense about North or South and would upset this accumulated balance between the two would not be acceptable to the South. I am not suggesting that Morarji Desai would have done so. He was only unpredictable whereas Mrs. Gandhi is likely to follow, by her own admission, Nehruite policies which amount to total appeasement. Divisive tendencies from the South will only encourage fascist tendencies from the North.

The perpetuation or growth of this conflict, as for example so brazenly reflected in economic policies, would suggest a vote for a weak Prime Minister and would even weaken a strong one.

(6) The role of organized business, particularly of big business, in the essential political processes of this country, is either flatly denied or tremendously exaggerated. One often hears the grumbling and whining of businessmen about their interests being neglected by politicians, and one also comes across such assertions as this or that business tycoon having scores of Members of Parliament and several Ministers in his pocket.

Such wide off-the-mark assessments hardly help analysis. We know that big businesses have multiplied their wealth several fold over the last 18 years of "socialism"—a tribute to political hypocrisy from economic toughness. But we also know that there were a number of top leaders in the Congress, any one of whom as Prime Minister would have gladdened the hearts of businessmen. But they were not seriously considered.

Yet business played its hand most shrewdly by changing its support as the prospects of candidates changed and ultimately came to support Mrs. Gandhi. Now it is infantile to assume, as the Leftists do, that the new Prime Minister would or should be at loggerheads with business; it cannot be so in a mixed economy. However, one may ask: do not the businessmen calculate that the old policies will be continued?

To this Mrs. Gandhi is saying yes. She talks about grim economic problems the country faces and yet expresses her devotion to past policies and their implementation which have caused the emergence of these problems. Her total faith in past Nehruite policies is the weakest crutch on which she is leaning and she at once exposes herself as a Prime Minister who will not bring about any radical change in the *status quo* and hence will be a weak or a temporary incumbent.

(7) The two super-powers, the USA and the USSR, overshadow all major decisions being taken in this country. There is no other Prime Minister in the world on whom both powers, who

are still enemies to each other, would lavish such praise as they did in the case of Mrs. Gandhi. They approved her with their smiles, whatever their own assessment of the situation. This great-power posture would prove a source of both strength and weakness, depending upon how she manipulates it. She is obviously looked upon by each power, and by her own admission, as a Prime Minister who would not make any radical change in India's foreign policy which has been in uttter doldrums in relation to our national security; nor would she tilt the balance in favour of either power.

It serves both commonsense and national interests to remain and work for friendly relations with our neighbours; but it takes two to make friends. It is possible that a new military crisis may appear on our borders sooner or later, and we may be forced to create new balances rather than rely on ineffective neutralism.

This is the most urgent and important question about our relations with great powers: would they permit and help us in making some recognizable pattern out of the seamless web of our foreign policy in relation to national security, or would they prefer us to remain glorified in our faults?

Our war with Pakistan has shown clearly that modern defence inevitably means attack on the economy. Also, the decision on the atom bomb one way or the other has to be made straight on issues of national security and not on ideology of foreign policy or some sanctimonious principle.

In terms of these and a host of similar problems, it seems the big-power appreciation about Mrs. Gandhi, at least, is that she is not going to be a great decision-maker. One unmistakable sign of this appreciation would be that for every non-decision or pseudo-decision, an increasing amount of aid from both powers would pour in. There is another theory which is quite current, namely, the election of Mrs. Gandhi was a temporary choice and had been made in her capacity as a great vote-catcher for the next General Elections which are not very far off.

This theory may or may not be true, but it does not in anyway require the modification of the preceding analysis of the political forces that matter. These forces and their power and interests would be relevant for the election of any other person as Prime Minister. A person who has the image of making a strong Prime Minister would be seriously resisted.

However, the validity of the theory is doubted on two grounds. First, with the given dynamics of the political structure, any other contender would not only have to be nationally more popular but also be the one who would stand in better appreciation of the demands of the electing political forces, that is, he or she has an image of greater weakness. Nobody important seems to satisfy these criteria.

Second, it is possible that Mrs. Gandhi may so upset the balance between of some of these forces as to make it necessary for them to topple her down. This could happen. But if she has the capacity to upset political forces, she could, by virtue of the same reason, manipulate them in her own favour and relatively strengthen herself. That, of course, will be the real test of her political sagacity. However, if she proves to be a weak Prime Minister, she is unlikely to upset any such balance.

What has been stated in preceding pages certainly does not add up to a very complimentary or a reassuring image of politics and politicians. But the purpose here is not to pay compliments or reassure anybody. The purpose is to lay threadbare the naked or hidden forces of the modern political life in India. This brings us to the second part of the question that was asked in the beginning: the modification and the manipulation by the Prime Minister in her own favour of the same political structure that has put her into power. Whether she would be able to do so or not would at once amount to prejudging her and falling into subjective valuation.

It was stated a little while ago that if Mrs. Gandhi attempts to modify the political structure in her own favour, in any drastic manner, until the next elections, her re-election could be threatened. Therefore, she will have to resort to a considerable cautious peddling until then. But if she does nothing of significance and only talks and talks, she would also have done herself a great harm, for the problems the nation faces are too pressing.

Her first year in office is going to be very difficult if she has a boldly imaginative programme for the long term and is determined to become a Prime Minister commensurate with the destiny of India. However, she can certainly give her full attention to few urgent issues of national importance which, if adroitly and realistically handled, could dramatically improve her prospects and relatively reduce those of her potential rivals. On the other hand, if this formative period is lost in groping and dithering and procrastination, then she would only have strengthened the political structure against herself.

It is not possible to go into a detailed one-year programme here but she could undertake the following steps. First of all she must renounce the built-in approach of tackling problems as they take serious proportions.

Her experts will have to forecast for her any serious crisis that is likely to come in the next few months and prepare the strategy in advance to meet it, instead of being caught unawares and unprepared. The last phase of Nehru's rule was full of unpleasant and stunning surprises. A body of experts whose one and only one job would be to forecast and prepare relevant strategies should be immediately appointed. She would make a serious mistake of depending on easy-going officials or on persons of narrow political manoeuverability.

Second, on the food front, she cannot do anything substantial in one year which would remove the fundamental causes of low production in agriculture without coming into clash with the Chief Ministers, and yet not to show a major change in the past policies would be disastrous. Therefore, apart from the one-sided programme of Subramaniam, which is not effective from the long-term viewpoint, she must boldly abolish at one stroke the food zones, remove other restrictions on food movement, put teeth into the Food Corporation, and give general direction to the States to protect tenancies.

Some Chief Ministers would not like these steps while others would wholeheartedly support her in adopting these. But in no way these steps seriously modify the States' political *status quo* in the overall political structure and hence the resistance could be broken.

This would also be the opportunity to create a wedge in the solid front of the Chief Ministers by working out a framework of new alignments behind the scene. Open frictions will have to be avoided.

Third, she must initiate a popular movement for administrative reform and not leave the matter to be deliberated by the Commission. It is here she could also win the support of the Opposition by directly associating it with the movement. She must take the matter in her own hands and encourge popular response at various levels.

Fourth, since we have reached the lowest rate of growth in industry ever since planning started—half the industry is working at less than half the installed capacity—Mrs. Gandhi cannot afford to let this go on and not face serious inflation very soon. She will have to drastically cut down the establishment for the next year of those low-priority industries which have a heavy import content not only in machines but also in raw materials. Available foreign exchange must have a top priority in increasing the utilized capacity. Mrs. Gandhi would face opposition to this policy from doctrinaire socialists and planners but any other course could bring the whole house down on her. Of course, this cannot be a long-term strategy.

Fifth, if India is to become a nucleus of a big-power system and not a satellite—and that is the only way she can remain as a united nation—she will have to have an entirely new foreign policy in the long run. But for the short run, Mrs. Gandhi would not be able to make any serious changes.

However, she will have to build for herself an image of a tough person, for she cannot seriously negotiate from a position of weakness. Shastri to some extent accomplished this. She may by being tough irritate some foreign powers, but within the country she would find a solid support for nationalist and not pseudo-ideolgical policies.

This is by no means an exhaustive list. There are many more issues on which a short-term strategy, as distinguished from long-term strategy, must be fully worked out within the next few weeks.

On the assumption that Mrs. Gandhi would be re-elected as Prime Minister after the next General Elections, in what way can she modify the political structure in her own favour in the long run? It would be very rash to predict future events for the long run and therefore it would also be unrealistic to suggest all, or even major, possible modifications that could be usefully introduced. Only a few important directions can be pointed out. Many new opportunities will also open as the future unfolds itself. There is also the need to realize that the suggested modifications have a time dimension; a hasty or unduly delayed step could also bring a lot of harm.

(1) Mrs. Gandhi must redress the balance between the Centre and the States in favour of the former. There are constitutional barriers but it is the extraconstitutional powers the Chief Ministers have acquired that must be broken down first. It is doubly important because an increase in the strength of the Centre not only increases correspondingly the strength of the Prime Minister, it also improves the chances of the Centre's policies to be more effectively implemented and not sabotaged by the States.

Besides, the Centre must set up some of its own implementing departments and agencies. The system of Centre's loans and grants must be abolished in due course and in the meantime administered according to the standards of performance set in the Centre's directives. The Planning Commission should be strengthened instead of gradually allowing it to become an impotent body. Persons with strong States or regional loyalties should never sit on the Planning Commission.

It was a sad day when the National Development Council came into being. It is a body which seldom deliberates but very forcefully acts as a pressure group at the Centre; it must be abolished. The Centre must also operate more effectively through IAS and other high-ranking officers working for the States. Decisions about important projects must be made on technical rather than on regional considerations. Examples can be multiplied.

It is the big failure of important policies which is both the cause and the effect of the Centre-State power imbalance. There are certain subjects of national significance on the States List, for instance, agriculture, which will have to be constitutionally transferred to the Centre, because the State Governments are largely manned by people whose interests basically clash with the national policies on such subjects. No wonder, the States undermine rather than implement such policies. Several progressive Chief Ministers may be willing to pass on such subjects to the Centre rather than face hostility within their own party; others who might feel power slipping from their hands may resist the change. Over a period, constitutional changes could be introduced. The Finance Commission, a constitutional mechanism which leaves little discretion with the Centre, must be abolished.

Many Chief Ministers feel insecure for one reason or another, but particularly for their acts of omission and commission and corruption. The Prime Minister must keep a very strong man at the head of the Home Ministry, who must not have such State loyalties as to remain in fear of being driven out for lack of political support while dealing with erring and scheming Chief Ministers.

(2) The second suggestion is only a corollary of the first and follows straight from the last paragraph. Increasingly the Prime Minister must man her Cabinet with persons of least State, communal, or regional loyalties. The current practice is the most absurd and is a great limitation on the powers of the Prime Minister. On the other hand, if she chooses men who do not have such loyalties, she must be strong enough to support them and create some other base or support for their political strength, for Ministers must be political species, not technocrats only.

(3) It also immediately follows that the power of the Congress President must be reduced. Since he could be in office with the support of the State Congress bosses, the new Prime Minister cannot afford a conflict between the Government and the party wing. It is not a question of who is the Congress President, a friend or an opponent; it is a question of power-relation. Shastri temporarily performed this task very skilfully, but only temporarily. The fact that the Congress President is to be elected after every two years and he may not always be the same man gives some scope for manipulation to the Prime Minister.

But this is a narrow way of looking at things. The best way to reduce the power of the Congress President and also that of the Congress Working Committee is to increase the power and status of the CPP and AICC. A determined Prime Minister can always go back to the AICC and get a broad and democratic support for the Centre's policies than remain forced to resort to compromises and appeasement of small groups. It may not seem very clear to many people but the strengthening of the AICC would both lead to and require the strengthening of the Congress Parliamentary Party. Both heavily overlap and their effective power is reduced by the political caucus. It is the caucus whose strength must be eliminated.

(4) The Syndicate, as analyzed earlier, is a part of the caucus and Mrs. Gandhi should try to completely eliminate it as soon as she can. She should not forget that if the Syndicate had its real way she would not have been the Prime Minister.

(5) What is argued above finds its logic in the changed structure of the Congress Party. Only two relevant aspects deserve mentioning. The Congress was at the time of independence a party organized downward in the sense that its fulfilment and development came under the direction of the national leadership of a previously established national movement constituting numerous local groups and spontaneous movements.

Over the last decade or so, however, this party has come to be increasingly characterized by being organized upward, that is, through the amalgamation into nation-wide alliance of powerful State, local, and ideological groups, and its composition and structure has come to be affected considerably by the composition and structure of the States' organizations which have more often than not conflicting interests between themselves and *vis-a-vis* the Central leadership. In a society like India structured on unlimited pluralism political caucus suffers from the weakness of not being able to recruit its members and constituent units on supra-local and categorical basis. Only parties organized downward draw the bulk of their support from among all persons throughout a nation who are part of a particular social class, have similar occupation, adhere to common ideological position, or are of a common religious persuation. That is why the Congress Party being upwardly organized has no such solidaristic local units. The same is true, by and large, of other opposition parties which makes it difficult for them to compete with the Congress colossus.

The absorption or bribing by the Congress of the various protest movements without regard to principles and policies has accelerated this shift from downward to upward organization. Consequently, though the Opposition parties were continuously sliced off and the Congress became big and bulky, no coherent policies or leadership emerged. Unless the Congress Party is organized downward as a homogenous body under the leadership of a strong Prime Minister, it will remain the biggest stumbling block in the way of political and economic progress of the country. Mrs. Gandhi cannot afford to ignore this long-term problem.

It is weak structure of Indian politics that the new Prime Minister really faces. And no amount of group realignments and narrow, dirty manoeuvring can change this structure. The Congress Party is bent upon staying in power, but also has a sub-conscious maniacal desire to commit suicide and scuttle the ship of the nation by ignoring pressing issues. The only way the structure can be both strengthened and modified in favour of the Prime Minister is by bringing into the forefront all major national problems to the exclusion of local problems and meeting them determinedly through realistic policies and programmes.

India needs a leader who can boldy face issues in the face and does not shirk from dropping any number of sacred cows, whether persons or policies. If Mrs. Indira Gandhi thinks she has the making of that leader, there is nothing that can stop her from becoming a great Prime Minister; if not, then her election leaves only a big question mark.

February 1966

2

CONGRESS LEFT AND INDIRA GANDHI

MRS. INDIRA GANDHI has no mistaken notion of being a great Prime Minister yet. It is also true that the economic and political mess in the country keeps multiplying despite some decisiveness and courage she has unmistakably exhibited in taking unpopular measures. It is another matter whether those decisions will ultimately turn out to be right or wrong, for they relate mostly to the category of long-term problems. Besides, this election year is likely to be full of unsavoury and barren politicking, and Mrs. Gandhi being the weakest although the most crucial link in the power-structure of the Congress Party, even the most raucus criticism of her, from opponents both inside and outside the party, should not appear surprising.

But what about the politics of fitful rebellion? The Leftists, who hailed her election to Prime Ministership only a few months ago as a dawn of a new era, have changed first to caustic, accusatory, and then finally to the most violent attacks not only on Mrs. Gandhi's politics but also on her personality. Of course, the Leftists are not unknown for dropping large bricks but their new ferocity needs some explanation and several hypotheses would be worth examining.

First, the Leftists accuse the Prime Minister of having proved unfaithful to Nehruism. They arrogate to themselves the role of true interpreters and custodians of the Nehru doctrines. During Nehru's life-time, the Leftists praised Nehru profusely in season and out and blamed his so-called Right-wing colleagues for the failure of his policies. Ironically in the process of defending him, they have all but destroyed their own chances of becoming an alternative political force to the Congress.

It would require a big argument to analyze Nehruism, which cannot be fully taken up here. As a theory or a grand design,

Nehruism represented in politics, economics, and international relations an arithmetic compromise between extremes. But, in practice, except for some spectacular but illusory successes in the early years of Nehru's rule, Nehruism has been reduced to a vast political waste-land. It has bequeathed to India an ugly situation of multiple and apparently insoluble crises with increasing melancholic and cynical political effects. Policies were piled upon policies as ineffectual compromises, so much so that there do not seem any more policies left which can be turned into actions.

The Leftists are making a desperate bid to make defunct Nehruism survive these inconvenient facts and thereby impose on the nation the cruel choice of throwing away the baby with the bathwater. Great men of history have never been belittled by the succeeding generations discovering their faults or wrong policies, for nations cannot afford to live on false history. It is always healthy for a nation and its historians to have a frank look at their heroes.

The refusal of the Congress Left—which in effect belongs to a class within a class—to re-appraise past policies seems, therefore, motivated by their desire to hold on to whatever position they have got in the Congress Party, for if the Party rejects that large part of Nehruism which has become unoperational, there would be little reason for the Leftists to remain inside the Congress Party, a party which has unmistakably proved itself as totally divorced even from highly diluted socialism. The rest of the debate on changers or no-changers, pragmatism or fundamentalism, theories and empiricism, alignment or nonalignment, etc., is meant to conceal their real motives, for the Leftists cannot be so crass as to ignore that policies cannot be valid for ever, particularly if such policies have proved unworkable compromises.

It is quite legitimate to argue that there is nothing basically wrong with the policies; it is their execution which has gone perverse. This implies three things: first, the Congress Party and its different sections, ideological and other conflicting power groups, are so balanced that despite the consensus on policy, their respective interests pull them so wide apart that operationally they make nonsense of accepted policies.

Secondly, there is enough working consensus both on policies and their execution inside the Congress Party, but the opposition to the party, its policies, and their administration is so strong and widespread, people's distrust so great and social and economic milieu so unamenable that even the best efforts go waste. In brief, the nation has lost its perspectives and purposes.

Thirdly, the balance of groups inside the party, so precariously sustained by Nehru, has been badly upset by a mad scramble for power. A new ideological struggle has been imposed on the party on the assumption that it is possible to bring it back, through internal struggle and external pressures, to the path of socialism.

There is some truth in all the three aforementioned contentions but there is also a large measure of illusion. If the first point above is true, then it logically follows that no major policy, Nehruite or otherwise, can ever be of operational significance. The nice but tight balance of groups destroys the effectiveness of policies, and, therefore, Nehruism is rendered as irrelevant as any other policy.

If the second proposition is valid, the position becomes worse, because both the party and its policies become totally irrelevant and jejune. Leftists have no business to belong to it or be a party to its collective incompetence. Consensus about policies and ideals is not enough; it must also be about the norms, conduct, and purposes of political activity within the society.

Regarding the first point, taken together with the other two points, it can be safely predicted that it is next to impossible for the Congress Left to snatch control of the party machine from the hands of the caucus that controls it. When men and issues become totally incongruent, as they have become in the Congress, it is the strength of the former and not the validity of the latter that keeps a party alive. Besides, the Left inside the Congress has never been so weak as it is today. One of the characteristics of the Indian political party spectrum that has originated from the non-homogeneous character of the Congress is that, by and large, each opposition party can be paired to a corresponding group inside the Congress Party. The opposition parties do not support or oppose the Congress as a whole but only a part of it. And what pangs of debunking: only the other day Krishna Menon and Hiren Mukerji were saying, short of rhetoric and vituperation, the same thing while one opposed and the other proposed the no-confidence motion against the Government.

In this pairing, the strength of a group inside the Congress depends on the corresponding group outside it. In recent years cleavages have appeared in the Communist camp followed by general disarray, and this fact has weakened the Left inside the Congress. Thus, there seems hardly any change of the Congress being "brought back" to the path of socialism. (The non-Communist Left and Left Communists have no or a weak pairing with groups inside the Congress and hence have, as a result of that, been both secularly declining and adopting postures of total opposition to the Congress. Their position has been one of consistent opposition to Mrs. Gandhi and hence does not require any analysis.)

Although the execution of policies remains ineffective, this fact has nothing to do with Mrs. Gandhi's alleged turning away from Nehruism. Never before has the rattling unreality of Congress policies and politics been revealed so sharply as witnessed in the unbridgeable gap between policy and performance, between ideal and behaviour, and between leaders and the masses. It makes an eloquent commentary on the so-called integrating character of Nehruism that after Nehru the Congress Party has been left neither with a consensus nor an expertise to sort out intra-party disputes. No wonder, Leftists are accused of adopting double standards and sheer opportunism by both those supporting and opposing the Congress Party. The Leftists are not only turning out to be myth-makers but also unfortunate and willing victims of their own myths, which leads them into sharp opposition to Mrs. Gandhi.

The second hypotheses relates to Leftists in the Congress having been left out completely from the seat of power. The current relationship between the Congress Party and the Leftists is like the one between political capitalism and its have-nots or dispossessed little kings. Nehru at least attempted a balance or created the illusion of such a balance between the so-called Right and Left in the Union Cabinet. The Kamaraj Plan, according to one of its interpretation, was the last act of balancing by Nehru. Neverthe-less, from the Leftist viewpoint, such a balancing could not and should not have been looked upon as something solid and proper because no such balancing existed at the States' level to which the real power continued to shift from the Centre. This formal balance, which was not structural, had already become nebulous during Nehru's life-time and is facing a total collapse now. The Leftists have very little strength in the States Congress organizations.

Another shift in the power-structure has been the increasing concentration of power, both at the Centre and the States, in the hands of tough political cookies on whom the Leftists have always poured scorn. Yet, again, at the still lower level, Leftists do not control more than half a dozen district Congress Committees out of several hundred such committees.

Sometimes a questionable assumption is made that Mrs. Gandhi made a tactical mistake in not having some Leftists in the Cabinet. But her difficulty can be appreciated if one realizes that the top leaders of the Congress Left had been discredited in rapid succession and neither the party nor the nation has been seriously expecting them to be included in the Cabinet. Their position in the party has been reduced from self-appointed oracles to that of noisy gadflies. The Leftists have themselves to blame for it, for they should have long ago brought forth new dynamic leadership. The Leftist leaders of today are a motley crowd with not even mutual rapport found among them; even at the personal level they lack any equation, not to speak of homogeneity.

Third, behind their ideological pretensions and moral indignation lies the deep malaise in the entire Left movement which has passed through a series of crises and internecine factional fights. The movement on a national scale is in disarray despite the localized big strength at a few places. The Left Communists have been fast trying to suck the strength of their Right-wing brothers who, in their current predicament of being both for (Nehruism) and against (Mrs. Gandhi) the Congress, face the prospect of obliteration unless they are ready to open an all-out attack on the Government of Mrs. Gandhi and join electoral alliance with parties opposing the Congress, whether they be socialist, communal, or semi-fascist. This is an election year and it has added some nagging new dimesions to their entire movement.

Were it not for this excruciating factor of the coming General Elections, it would be difficult to explain entirely the Leftist outcry against Mrs. Gandhi's Vietnam proposals. The Vietnam war has reached such an impasse that it would be a miracle, and against all principles of international power diplomacy, for India, in her present weak and vulnerable position, to produce peace proposals which would be acceptable to most parties to the war and be significantly meaningful as well.

What Mrs. Gandhi attempted to do in her Vietnam proposals was to relieve the increasing pressure on India from both powers and give herself a breathing space by suggesting a set of proposals which were certainly not very meaningful. As a matter of fact they were not meant to be so. Have our Leftists become so divorced from a national approval that they cannot possibly see India being saved from an embarrassment abroad. It is a pity that India is passing through a temporary phase of decline in the collective conscience and inarticulation of national interests, thus making it possible for the Leftists to get away with their blind and suicidal policies.

Fourth, the seed for the Leftist disarrary lay in the original bifurcation of the movement into groups inside and outside the Congress Party. As a result of this and the heavy constraints imposed on their militant activity by their willing commitment to Nehruism, the Leftists gradually lost the three fundamental sources of their strength, namely, workers, peasants, and intellectuals. All the three classes have become increasingly depoliticalized. At no time in its history has the trade union movement been so well-organized and yet so apolitical. The Leftist influence has been largely destroyed among the peasants because the major fiscal policies of the Government are orientated in favour of the farmers.

Despite an overwhelming majority of the intellectuals individually swearing by Marx, the Marxist theory of alienation applies to Indian intellectuals in full force as they are completely divorced from active political life. Occasional and withering outbursts among the university professors against the USA or the Prime Minister and her Ministers arise from their guilt complex of simultaneously swearing by Marx and feeding from the hand that doles the dollars for educational programmes.

However, this political void did not reveal its force so long as there were no major economic and political crises in the country. But as crisis after crisis burst, as surely they did in recent months, and there did not exist organized political channels for their resolution, the void came to be increasingly filled by mass and spontaneous violence which the Leftists tried to capitalize to the maximum. The Leftists could not, in all honesty, simultaneously show sympathy and participate in *bundhs* as well as participate in struggle for power inside the Congress Party. To get out of this contradiction, they found the convenient ruse of attacking the Prime Minister for all the ills of the country.

Fifth, the Leftists have come to live for quite sometime now on the tenterhooks of their own decaying leadership and some top Congress leaders under whose cover they, as mandarins of socialism, could camouflage themselves. Their growing disillusionment and disappointment with Mrs. Gandhi forced them to search for a new leader and they soon found him in Kamaraj who has, apparently, fallen out with the Prime Minister. They jumped on the bandwagon of Kamaraj for whom they earlier showed little enthusiasm, and made out that the quarrel between the two leaders rested on principles and policies and not on power struggle. Kamaraj has become for them a new saviour of defunct Nehruism despite his (*i*) calling for a small plan, (*ii*) allowing the feudal elements to be brought into the Congress, who stand in contradiction with the Leftist policies.

The Leftists have chosen him as their candidate and from now on whatever Mrs. Gandhi may do to support the so-called socialist policies, they are not going to lower their banners against her. By doing so they are simply rejecting the Leninist and proving the Hobbesian hypothesis that political insecurity seeks resolution in an unprincipled submission to changing leadership. Of course, the Leftists are fully entitled to a calculated manipulation of the irrationalities of the Congress leadership, but by doing so they are also revealing themselves as pseudo-socialists if they believe that they can stage a comeback through Kamaraj. As a realist, Kamaraj has to take the party and not its weakest group with him to get to power and the Leftists are sure to be dropped like hot potatoes once he is in power. Despite the Leftists plodding Kamaraj to go ahead, there is no surety whether he would succeed at all in his bid for power or even choose to contest. In that case the Leftists would have only ruined themselves. This is also an early warning to Mrs. Gandhi that she cannot undertake realistic and nationalist policies while clinging to old, battered, and pseudo-socialistic slogans of the Congress Party because Kamaraj can always do one better than her in this game.

Thus, once again the Leftists are making the same mistake, which they have repeatedly made, and to their continuous disadvantage, of shifting their loyalty to another Congress leader in the vain hope of reviving through him Nehruite policies which have irrevocably become irrelevant, and non-action compromises and complacencies. Nehruite policies had ceased to operate in Nehru's last phase, and since he was, in a sense, his own opposition leader, the Leftists were reduced to playing second fiddle.

Shastri headed a team of equals and worked on the principle of joint responsibility and, once again, the combined force of the Congress caucus rendered the Leftists ineffective.

Mrs. Gandhi is unfortunately almost entirely on her own and hence quite vulnerable. No other person could be more suited to put into action Nehruite policies, but having been caught between old romantic loyalties on the one hand and cruel and pressing crises demanding new policies and realism on the other, she has become the target of the combined hostility of the Right and Left forces. Old and tried leaders inside the Congress have also refused the principle of joint responsibility by joining the most vicious struggle for power, because, for most of them in their late age, it is now or never.

If Mrs. Gandhi is ultimately unable to extricate herself from this morass, she would have clearly failed to twist the power structure in her own favour and in the interest of the nation.

The Congress Party in its present set-up has become so decomposed and functionless that it is incapable of appreciating and responding to elementary realism, much less of ushering in socialism which the Leftists so keenly desire. The so-called latency of its political resilience and its traditional strength have disappeared.

In fact, its entire transition from a movement to a party has totally misfired. The Congress today cannot mobilize public opinion, formulate policies, articulate popular demands, and even as much as state its objectives clearly. It is caught between the adventurous rhetoric of the opposition and total futility of its past policies. A party which works for long on the basis of conflicting and mutually hostile loyalties as well as kaleidoscopic coalitions, and yet functions on the theory of collective legitimacy, as distinguished from consensus, is ultimately bound to be frozen into immobility.

The Leftists may genuinely believe that in their opposition to the Prime Minister they are sharpening issues of politics and parallel diversification of interest, but they cannot be blind to the fact that they have been attempting this approach for the last two decades with the worst possible results for themselves, the Congress Party, and the country. The entire politics of the country has become pseudo, fragmanted, disorganized, and violent without purpose.

The Leftists as well as the Prime Minister have become prisoners of words because they swear by the same ideological slogans and yet are mutually irreconcilable. At the hands of the Congress Party these slogans not only defy straightforward description but have also become arid and jejune. Being abstract generalizations and at the same time completely out of focus with the crude reality of the political landscape of the Congress Party, they have come to be manipulated by whoever wanted it. Ideology is not irrelevant but it, particularly Leftist ideology, has come to play a distorted role, especially in the Congress Party. Instead of its changing from dogmatic statement to solutions of problems, it has reversed its role. The Leftists share their blame of ambiguity in their futile attempts at rationalizing irrational policies, in the name of some highly abstract generalizations. Politics is a difficult art; slogans, however, radical, do not make it in any way easier.

It is not that socialism has become irrelevant. It is the Congress Party, as constituted at present, which has ceased to be an instrument of its adoption or to provide a link betwen actions and fundamental beliefs. The content of socialism in the context of our problems, the stage at which that content becomes valid, the movements that will carry its burden, the organizations that will put it through, etc., are all the missing links in the contemporary political process in India.

The Congress Party is essentially a party of the Centre or at most Left Centre, and unless it throws out its traditional Leftist and Rightist weeds, it would be difficult for the party to give content to its policies.

The only honourable course for the Congress Left is to join the ranks of other Leftists outside the Congress, to clarify national issues and rationalize the political party structure in the country. An independent, progressive Government cannot grow on or as weeds. The speed with which Mrs. Indira Gandhi can build a new structure of policies and remove the impasse to discarding policies worshipping the past would hasten the process of cleansing the Augean stables of the Congress.

August 1966

3

STRUGGLE FOR LEADERSHIP

ANY ONE CAN BE wise *ex post facto*. A political analyst must say something definite and positive *ex ante* and hazard prediction (and sometimes face the prospects of being proved foolish), though not by way of fanatic political crystal-gazing, and not necessarily about the so-called sixty-four thousand dollar questions but the crucial questions that face the Indian polity. These are three immediate questions on which the nation's attention is concentrated.

Firstly, what is the margin by which the Congress Party will win at the Centre and what is the significance of this margin? Those who were rash enough to suggest a defeat for the Congress Party on grounds of deep-seated public indignation and hatred against that party or some mythical multiplier, or opposition alliances, etc., have sadly come around to accept the Congress victory. It does not need a great gift of prescience or sophisticated use of statistical techniques or estimates of individual fortunes to understand the crux of political change or lack of it. So long as the number of candidates per seat remains on an average between 4 and 5 per seat, the Congress could be voted to power with as low a vote as 30 per cent in its favour. The more things change the more they will remain identical under the existing electoral system. Except in the event of an internal explosion in the party, neither now nor in the foreseeable future can the Congress be defeated so long as the disproportionate ratio of candidates to seats is not rectified.

Of course, there will be some nasty shocks and the Congress is likely to be battered in many States. But that will not change victory into defeat at the Centre. Nonetheless, the margin by which the Congress wins will have a good deal of influence on the struggle for leadership; the struggle will become more acute, the smaller the margin; machine politicians like members of the Syndicate will have a disproportionately large weightage. S. K. Patil, not unnaturally perhaps, dislikes the prospects of the Congress winning more than 300 seats. Besides, after the elections a smaller margin will necessitate some horse-trading with non-Congress members to bribe them back into the Congress Party and this is bound to be the handiwork of the Syndicate and State bosses as well as a source of new accretion to their strength. A new sense of self-confidence and arrogance oozes out of their pronouncements as against their sense of defeatism at the hands of the Kamaraj-Indira axis a year ago. Consequently, no candidate can be sure in advance of his or her election to leadership.

And this brings us to the second and most exciting, though not necessarily the most important, question, namely, who will be the next Prime Minister? It is a difficult question to answer amidst an immensely amorphous power situation and the romantic confusions about it. The uncertainty of this choice has already been noted by the fact of the Congress having gone to the polls without being united under a single leader. Though by far the most acceptable candidate to static power structure, there is a facile optimism in the camp of Mrs. Gandhi in her insistence that she is a popular vote catcher and that she can directly appeal to the masses over the heads of the party colleagues, which fact in itself only reveals the uncertainty and weakness of her position within the party. I intend to show that the question who will be the next Prime Minister is not a very important one; how he or she is elected will be more important. Let me answer this question regarding Mrs. Gandhi on the bases of the twofold assumption: (a) the Congress Party wins about 300 seats with a margin of ± 5 per cent, and (b) the technique of her operation remains more or less the same, her re-election, if it comes about, will only heighten the irrelevance of that office in relation to the immense problems the nation faces. For that matter the election of any other Congress leader will be equally irrelevant.

There are three reasons for Mrs. Gandhi's inability to have grown in that job. (i) She has exhibited a lack of comprehension about the intensity and ferocity of the economic, political, and external problems of the country. There is not a single coherent statement of hers in which one can find a sensitive and intellectual understanding of these problems. Instead of having cons, upstart advisers, ghosts, and make-up men, she needed a disciplined staff systematically analyzing the problems and pondering over policies and their effects. She failed in this elementary political exercise and thus did not develop a policy or problem oriented image.

(*ii*) She has proved herself completely incapable of modifying and twisting the power structure in her own favour; if anything, she has emerged weaker and bruised from every attempt made to improve upon her position vis-a-vis this power structure. (*iii*) In her attempts to bypass the power structure, she could not stop the structure from becoming increasingly dysfunctional, because the conflict between the power groups has reached a point where it has defeated policies by creating a situation of total non-decision making. The Prime Minister enjoyed the unique position of providing a corrective mechanism to the growing dysfunctionalism. The functional relationship between the Prime Minister and all other groups could have been effectively keyed to the requirements of cohesion as a problem-solving instrument. Unfortunately, Mrs. Gandhi in her uncommon political ambition and impatience with the power structure only generated extra-group conflict.

The poignancy of these failures is heightened by the fact that she began her job with immense goodwill unlike Shastri who started with a considerable hostility against him but who, perhaps fortuitously, grew in his job. Although when she was elected nobody believed that the ducks of the Congress Party had hatched a wild swan, her performance has not been edifying to her in any way. Therefore, on the basis of the aforementioned assumptions, it is very clear that, if Mrs. Gandhi is elected, which she would be most probably, she would be unable to retain her job for long and her forced exist before 1972 will remain a strong possibility. The exit would certainly not be graceful because she would be the inevitable focus of the dissatisfaction over the Congress misrule.

Be that as it may, let us return to the hows and whys of the question. The form and content of political control in the Congress is dependent on the form and content of forces constituting its power structure as well as their degree and form of structure specialization.

One decisive point is that the choice fell on Mrs. Gandhi for Prime Ministership only because she was the weakest of all the aspirants to that job. Subsequent events have more than proved the truth of that conclusion. The real question now is whether the same factor will operate and force a similar choice irrespective of who the candidate is? I have my doubts. Logically, it may appear that the interests of all the aforementioned constituent elements, including those of the super powers, stand in inverse relation to the strength of the Prime Minister. But politics is not always logical. Something quite important in the sphere of State-Centre relation has happened to necessitate a possible reversal of that relationship. A weak Prime Minister and a weak Centre have both contributed to the weakness of the State bosses, particularly in the Hindi-speaking areas, who are mainly responsible for Mrs. Gandhi's election.

A weak Centre means (1) a low rate of economic growth from which States' plans suffer a good deal; (2) fewer resources become available for transfer from the Centre to the States, particularly because a weak Centre means a low level of foreign assistance; (3) weakening of the political hold of State bosses on the party and the government because of uncontrolled rivalry and opposition to them from within the State governments and parties; (4) emergence of virulent and uncompromising opposition parties almost united against the Congress and spreading violence and causing breakdown of law and order; (5) unchecked rivalry between States and thereby the mutual undermining of the ruling groups, etc. All these factors point towards the necessity of the States desiring not only a strong centre but also a somewhat strong combination of the Prime Minister and the Congress President. The power has been continuously shifting from the Centre to the States for almost a decade now and any further shift in that direction seems to have been checked for fear of national disintegration. Under the circumstances it is most likely that the opposite trend will start.

The organized business would certainly prefer a malleable, though not a weak Prime Minister because weak leadership cannot stop the growing rot in the economy in which the business has large stakes. Mrs. Gandhi's one-year tenure has been accompanied by more serious crises than in any 5-year tenure before. It is precisely for this reason and the absence of her hold on the government or the party that the money bags refused to contribute directly to the Congress Party election fund. Instead, they are either financing individuals and their own men or have put up purses for strong party machine bosses who control chunks of votes.

The third and apparently the most important question is what is going to be the character of the Congress Party and its ideology, for the party cannot remain permanently moribund and also remain in power. That the Congress is not a party of socialism is crystal clear. Essentially, its heart, like that of Barve, lies to the left of centre and that is where it should lie if it is to remain healthy. It is only in this posture that the Congress can grow into a homogenous political organization, a genuine democratic centre and a party whose right and left would only be of degree and not of kind. With forces of socialism being very weak, only a centrist party can give historical significance to our political development and adopt nationalist policies.

This is not the place for a full-scale analysis of the economic and political dynamics of contemporary India; nor can we here go deep into the study of scale, structure, culture, and degree of differentiation of the Congress. Nevertheless, to get a sharp focus on the Congress leadership the minimum must be said. The internal dynamics of the society is that India by and large is a capitalistic country; it is pressurized by a host of distributive ideologies and pressure groups from the left to the right which have made the functioning of capitalism difficult by reducing the rate of growth. On this situation rides the Congress Party whose organizational structure is utterly feudal with capitalist interests holding the flanks and the left, as gadflies and symbols of its guilt complex, nibbling at some parts. Besides, the trend is towards further infeudiation. On the top of it all has been imposed some sort of a vague socialist veneer which makes for the worst possible confusion. The real and genuine forces of socialism are weak, divorced from power and hence outside the radius of the operation of the power structure. This situation has to go and the internal struggle in the power structure is helping it towards some clarity.

Unfortunately, some of the external forces are forcing the party to the right of the centre, an equally unstable position. The USA has learnt that it can turn and twist the Indira government to any position towards the right and the Russians faced with the only alternative of Swatantra-Jana Sangh are also likely to plump for the Indira government as lesser of the two evils. In brief, if the USA and the USSR can exert their decisive influence in the choice of the leader, they are likely to converge from two opposite angles on the side of Mrs. Gandhi. Both Morarji and Kamaraj will have no chance with the super-powers. No wonder Birlas are not supporting Morarji against Mrs. Gandhi.

After Nehru's death the Congress President became one of the most important elements in the power structure. A firm alliance between any Prime Minister and Congress President could become the most dominant and unchallengeable force of the Congress as well as of the whole of Indian politics. Their rivalry could not only weaken both of them but also shift the balance to other elements in the structure. It is the latter which has occurred, creating a balance of weakness between Kamaraj and Mrs. Gandhi and adding uncertainty to the choices for both these posts. As I have argued earlier, it is neither the temperamental nor the ideological differences between the two but the struggle for power that has created this balance of weakness.

The struggle between Kamaraj and Mrs. Gandhi is par excellence and naturally a power struggle in which issues are used as convenient weapons. If one asks oneself just one question and tries to answer it, the force of this struggle would be as clear as daylight. Where does Kamaraj go from his present position? He cannot remain permanently in the post of Congress Presidentship. And he has to make his choice very soon because postponement of the decision until after the new government is formed may be too late. He may (*i*) go back to Madras as Chief Minister and become just one among the several Chief Ministers who are quite powerful; (*ii*) like to step into the august and otherwise very powerful post of the President of the Republic; or (*iii*) join the Cabinet as number two or make a bid for the Prime Ministership.

Going back to Madras in any form would surely amount to his political down-grading besides his facing other hurdles, particularly those which could arise if the Congress gets heavy battering in Madras.

Second, Kamaraj is not yet a tired politician and conceals his immense common-sense, artfulness, and realism behind the cloak of simple-mindedness and non-theoretical positions. Kamaraj may feel himself unsuited for that job or be uncertain about the power that could be wielded from there so long as the present state of the working of the Indian Constitution continues, and the pressures and pulls of political forces and traditions and customs, which have reduced the President of the Republic to a figurehead, remain in force. Constitutionally, the President enjoys immense powers. But for any person, however, dynamic and strong, to resurrect and wield those powers would be possible only under conditions of a total national crisis or upheavel or the breakup of the Congress Party or prolonged external aggression. Maybe Kamaraj could wield those powers in inverse relation to the weakness of the Prime Minister, but Mrs. Gandhi is unlikely to oblige him.

Regarding the third choice, it should appeal to reason that Kamaraj would accept the second position in the Cabinet only if he is certain that he cannot compete for the first position. The Congress Party's fortunes are dwindling, but if the loss Congress suffers in the next General Elections is properly distributed in different regions, and also if the new alignment and shifts in the political power structure, which are bound to come about once Kamaraj makes a bid for Prime Ministership, do not tilt over whelmingly and decisively against him, I think Kamaraj would not like to lose the prize job by default.

Of course, if he is totally sure of not collecting enough votes, he would not hesitate to make the second best choice, particularly when he has been told in so many words by the USA and the USSR that he is not their candidate. He is no more or less a socialist than anybody else in the Congress. If, however, he is defeated at the polls, he will be out of focus for a long time.

Morarji Desai is powerful but a static personality. No other Congress leader has carried himself with so much dignity and rigid loyalty to the party and its avowed principles as he has. Despite his growing stature and declining age, his relative position vis-a-vis other elements in the power structure has not improved. Nevertheless, if there were a triangular contest, he would perhaps win. He remains a candidate whatever the odds may be and if ever elected, he can be relied upon to twist the power structure in his favour and make it functional.

Thanks to Mrs. Gandhi's disastrous inept interventions, the Syndicate which was considerably weakened a year ago has now emerged apparently as the strongest force in this power structure. Yet it must be realized that its strength lies in (1) the weakness of the Prime Minister, (2) rivalry between the Prime Minister and the Congress President, (3) declining margins of majorities for the Congress in the Centre and the States, (4) dysfunctional character of the party and the government, (5) lack of well-defined policies of the party, (6) its control of money bags, etc.

It should not be difficult to see that the aforementioned factors, individually or collectively, do not, with the exception of (3), add up to anything that is structurally or functionally relevant to the power system. The colossus has feet of clay, but it needs someone to discover and strike those feet. But no one has yet appeared on the political scene. Therefore, the members of the Syndicate, mostly desperate men who are in the last phase of their political life, would not tolerate a strong Prime Minister. It should not be surprising if some of them aspire for the leadership of the party. Nevertheless, to them a weak Prime Minister, if their experience of Mrs. Gandhi tells anything, becomes a liability and source of corrosion of their power via the growing functionlessness of the system. Their proclaimed loyalty to this or that leader has no meaning for purposes of the election of the future leader. It is nothing more than rehtoric of public relations. Mrs. Gandhi, by far still the weakest candidate, cannot draw on their support with any certainty.

What is the final picture of the power structure emerging then? It is obviously one of contradictions and paradoxes. First, on the one hand, Congress Party's "circle" keeps shrinking and thus pointing towards the possibility of increasing political conflict inside the party, while, on the other, the state of dysfunctionalism has reached a point where the leadership must look for a consensus and decreasing political conflict. Second, while theoretically the interests and the strength of the constituents of the power structure stand in inverse relation to those of the Prime Minister, in practice very cruel relativism operates; a weak Prime Minister weakens, nationally, every other element of the power structure. Third, while the Prime Minister's job remains the prize job and there are any number of aspirants for it, the main contestants are in such a mutually exclusive position that they can only wreck their rival's chances without improving their own. In a triangle, the two sides are greater than the third, and that is how Mrs. Gandhi was elected in 1966, but now it appears to me that this method is ruled out.

These contradictions could be resolved in either of the two ways. Either the Congress Party will face, internally, increasing political conflict along with the growing dysfunctionalism of the system. In that case, the party must break up sooner or later, with rival groups being forced to seek alliances with the Swatantra or other opposition parties. Or, the party will have to work out at the top a new consensus on policies and on leadership. The party cannot afford to be bogged down all the time in structural questions; it must ask the relevant functional questions. Both types of consensuses will have to be evolved together, for one without the other will not work. It fits very well into the character of a centrist party like the Congress that it can function through an ideological consensus alone. A consensus on leadership, in light of the available spectrum of leaders and their groups, must lead to a collective leadership. The present pattern is very anomalous. There are leaders spread all over but there is no leadership provided to the nation. Some sort of a super-cabinet of persons in strategic command-posts of political power structure could be formed among these leaders on the basis of division of power. And this theory of division of power is quite flexible and not mechanical. Such an arrangement could be inclusive of dark horses waiting in the ways, such as Chavan and Jagjivan Ram. Besides, the smaller the margin of Congress victory, the greater will be the pressure for a collective leadership or a sort of a political directorate. There is no other way to set in motion the articulative, integrative, and communicative functions of the structure which are now marked by their conspicuous absence.

It was on the strength of availability of only two alternatives that I suggest that whoever is elected new Prime Minister on old balance of weakness in the power structure will be a temporary if not an irrelevant choice. A new stable leadership can emerge only on the basis of a new balance of strength in the power structure through which the Congress Party can also adopt coherent, integrated, and realistic left of centre policies. This proposed collective leadership cannot emerge and successfully work simply as an aggregate of elements, it must evolve itself as a grouping of inter-related elements possessing a boundary or limits of each elements, internal and external principles, and mechanism of integration and above all a measure of functional unity. Depending upon the relative weights of the participants, in this cluster of postures and positions will lie the real authority and not in any one office or person. With the passage of time a person may emerge stronger than others, but that person would be an extraordinary one, and in the present set-up no one seems to possess that calibre. Therefore, unless, the Congress Party is hell bent on committing harakari and scuttling the ship of the nation, she has to adopt the latter course.

There is no guarantee that a collective leadership fully aware of its responsibility will emerge from the complex power struggle. Its growth is limited by the level and nature of technique and means of power struggle. Nor is there an assurance against the same pressing problems unsuccessfully repeating themselves to the reshuffled pack. Nor is there any certainty of the emergence of consensus on policies and programmes because of external loyalties and pressures on leadership and the pseudo-collective emerging as a result of temporary cease-fire between mutually hostile caucuses. Finally, there is no certainty about the new top leadership developing into a ruling leadership, partly because the most formidable opposition to the collective will come not from the Prime Minister or the Congress President but from the Chief Ministers who may now desire a strong Centre but would not like to be dictated by several bosses in their ruling of the States.

Despite all these obstacles, the emergence of a collective leadership is the only alternative to chaos and national disintegration and the only chance of survival of the present leadership. The hope of an alternative to the present superannuated structure of the leadership lies in the Congress Party throwing up new, youthful, and imaginative leadership from below. This hope has been belied by the Central Election Committee having enforced the *status quo* and Mrs. Gandhi, the youngest leader, having failed to improve her position.

Mrs. Gandhi is the most probable political choice. If she is ever re-elected, it would be due to one or more of the following reasons: (*i*) deadlock in the party over the choice about the pattern of leadership; (*ii*) when there are only two candidates in the field; (*iii*) as a compromise choice of the collective leadership but with her powers sufficiently clipped; (*iv*) influence of the USA and the USSR; and (*v*) unexpected defeat in the general election of some of her powerful rivals. Whether she or the nation will benefit from her election on the strength of these factors is doubtful. The only case in which this benefit could accrue, in the absence of a collective leadership emerging, will be that of her firm alliance with Morarji Desai. Things will change then, but then this step itself will mark the beginning of a collective leadership. Kamaraj then would have no choice but to join the collective to the exclusion of the Syndicate.

To conclude, the struggle for leadership can at present be resolved by two choices: either collective leadership of some sort will emerge or total dysfunctionalism will prevail. The days of politics of pressure groups or ideological confrontation are over, for highly organized pressure groups can work functionally only in a highly organized party structure, and without a powerful Left there can be no ideological battle. There is also a moral for the Left. Power will always allude them, unless they develop (*i*) institutionalized leadership, (*ii*) genuine social base, and (*iii*) effective organizational structure.

February 1967

4

CONSENSUS AND ALL THAT

THE DECLINE AND fall of Kamaraj has brought into disrepute the consensus method, both as a political concept and as an operational technique. He battered the word out of all its meaning. His last act of selecting his own successor by consensus was an anticlimax. Nijilangappa was elected in a manner in which Kamaraj was practically bypassed or outmaneouvred. He has left behind no good fabric of consensus.

Yet, in a society such as the Indian, which is complex and undifferentiated in the sense that it is not marked by a natural division of classes, the consensus technique, encompassing action and ideology, remains indispensible for conflict-resolution. Consensus-conflict balance implies that various competing groups are allowed to fight for their own respective interests through constitutional and recognized extra-constitutional methods up to a point beyond which consensus must prevail. In brief, consensus is the twin problem of creating a dynamic equilibrium in a democratic mass society and of developing collective techniques which make rapid social transformation possible while retaining the pattern of an open society.

Consensus can be practised at various levels of group behaviour. We are concerned here with its operation at two levels only: national and party. In India, where the party political structure is not yet streamlined, intra-party consensus is as important as national consensus. Nehru attempted and extensively utilized the consensus technique at both levels, although that consensus broke down in its critical forms during his own life-time.

Failure of the Nehruvian consensus can be traced back to several factors, the analysis of which does not lie within the scope of this chapter. However, some relevant ones can be mentioned without being dilated upon. First, Nehru's technique heavily tilted towards an "over-consensus" at the top and "under-consensus" at the bottom, which left multiple unresolved conflicts at all levels. Second, policies and objectives, such as planning, nonalignment, etc., around which consensus was created, failed in the end because of their invalidity, faulty implementation, or the absence of a corresponding political infra-structure. Third, he confused national consensus with party consensus leaving little scope for balancing various conflicts. Fourth, the consensus on policies remained inseparable from the consensus around him as a national leader, a juxtaposition that naturally could not survive him. Finally, the Nehruvian consensus ended up by subtly enforcing conformity in thought processes and adjustment to his omnipresent personality, while neglecting integration between values, norms, facts, and policies relevant to our society.

Kamaraj, on the other hand, concentrated, and rightly so, on intra-party consensus. However, neither did he have the stature or power nor did it probably lie within his functions to attempt a new national consensus. His efforts for total party consensus also lie in ruins and have sunk the party in complete paralysis. His only success, and that should not be exaggerated, was marked by the selection or election through consensus of two successive Prime Ministers. Why did he fail in the final analysis?

After Nehru's death the crucial problem was not that of selecting Prime Minister but, after having selected him or her, to structure a consensus about the proper division of power and functions within the Congress Party by which the Prime Minister, though a first among equals, was to share power with others until he or she grew in national stature, or failing that, could be replaced by another and better contender. For that it was essential to build a political collective at the top which was to work on defined functions of power and also evolve and implement vigorously suitable policies. At the time of both successions it appeared that some such system was being evolved. But soon after each of the events it became clear that Kamaraj's interest in the consensus and collective method was strictly limited to the duality or dichotomy of power, not essentially between the Congress organization and the Congress

Parliamentary Party, which was a valid dichotomy, but between himself and the Prime Minister, which was an invalid dichotomy and which proved to be a disastrous one. Such tactics were bound to end up in Kamaraj's disadvantage partly because of his own profound inadequacies and partly because all the real power and patronage lay with the Prime Minister. Kamaraj never understood this point, which should have gone home to him at a very early stage when his re-election as Congress President was made possible only by the last minute intervention of Shastri. In many devious ways he tried to undermine the power of Mrs. Gandhi who obliged him by the use of the same technique against him. Consequently, the consensus technique never came to be affectively used at the level of top leadership despite all appearances to the contrary.

It was much beyond Kamaraj's comprehension and power to create on his own even a facade of consensus on policies within the party, though he could have started a proper debate about them. He was no intellectual mandarin. No one expected Kamaraj—least of all he himself—to understand the philosophic nuances of the consensus theory except as a tripped down version of rugged reality. Policies once initiated by Nehru, whether relevant or irrelevant in the post-Nehru era, became the catch-all for every leader and faction in the party to protest, honestly or dishonestly, its adherence and loyalty. No attempt was made to revaluate those policies. All the top leaders of the Congress put together were not equal to Nehru and hence no one, least of all Kamaraj, dared raise the question that Nehru postponed for seventeen years, namely, the reorganization of the Congress as a Party with a coherent internal structure and with policies matching that structure.

The Congress Party never stopped arrogating to itself the role of a national movement simply having transformed itself into a national party. Weak opposition was accepted only as a matter of formal democratic courtesy. We were told, with full backing from foreign starry-eyed experts, that the loose nature of party organization was in consonance with the cultural pluralism of our society and that for reasons of stability it was justifiable to permit the Congress to become an overlapping kaleidoscopic amalgam of all sorts of ideas, persons, factions, etc. Factions are understable, but factional tolerance to the point of causing party disintegration should have been checked. Serious cracks appeared in the party organization during Nehru's life-time and he saved the party from disintegrating not by dynamizing the consensus but by either employing personal vassalage relations or downgrading his colleagues via such techniques as the Kamaraj Plan.

On the strength of its internal structure, and not on its paper resolutions, is the Congress not a party of socialism. An analysis of its natural class allies, the pattern of its voters, the character of its cadre, Members of Parliament and legislatures, etc., will show that it is essentially a centrist party despite the attitudinal hetoregeneity of its leadership. It can no longer afford or even survive to remain a party of generous shelter for everybody from saints to crooks, for factions that take subterfuge under slogans of the Left and of the Right that conceals itself in the garb of pragmatism. For the Congress Party, the two problems of consensus on policies and on organization were, as they are today, really one and the same problem. Kamaraj misunderstood or misapplied the consensus method and failed. After all, the great grass-root realist and organization man from Madras turned out to be a poor one at that.

Kamaraj applied the consensus technique in two contradictory ways. At the Centre or national level he applied it, as discussed earlier, as an instrument of establishing a particular power spectrum. At the States' level he outdid even Nehru by simply insisting on a hundred per cent or omnibus consensus in every matter without going into local power alignments or even into the merits of the case. Nor did he realize that coordination is the inevitable tool of a functioning consensus. Beyond a point the role of accommodation and apparent political integration conflicts with organizational integrity. Instead, he developed a neo-feudalism in politics which was unknown before and thereby left every State Congress organization in complete shambles. He almost completely eliminated the ballot from the party at every level. It is true that an undue use of the ballot in a loosely knit party may threaten the effective operation of consensus. But total consensus can also stifle the dynamic elements in the party, destroy the credibility of the consensus promotor, and make the party lose sight of its objectives and functions. In one word he gave the party a consensus of political stagnation. His growing divorce from problems of State parties weakened the political legitimacy that lay behind his holding that office. A shrewd leader, while rightly insisting on lower echelons for creating a consensus, would rely, behind the scenes, on the technique of implicit mediation. Instead, behind the polite fiction of consensus, he worked towards its destruction by completely ignoring its working at deeper levels. And whenver a true consensus did emerge as for example on Nijilangappa for Congress presidentship, nobody felt more embarrassed than Kamaraj himself. The real question that still faces the Congress organization is whether the party will control the factional groups instead of the factions controlling the party as at present.

The inability of post-Nehru leaders to create consensus lies partly in each one of them being committed to one or the other section, regional, or group interests. Kamaraj was too heavily committed to Madras for his own survival to have played the grand wizard of the consensus. Mrs. Gandhi has so far been exceptionally successful in building a national consensus around herself but at an incalculable cost of denying the nation a consensus on policies, and the party a consensus on organizational needs. For her it is the end of the beginning, because either she fills these gaps in the near future or her own strategy will recoil against her. So far neither she nor anybody else has satisfactorily solved the most crucial aspect of party consensus, namely, a functioning division of power within the party at the top and the adoption of policies that correspond to the party's internal structure at the bottom. Such a consensus to be effective would require to institutionalize itself as well as create physical sanctions against those who would break it for their own selfish group interests. The Congress Party at present is nowhere near it.

Finally, the consensus of political stagnation, *a la Kamaraj*, has made it impossible for opposition parties to develop their own consensus. Non-Congressism is a politics of one amorphousness against another. Every internal crisis within the Congress or every Congress attack on the opposition with its diametrically opposed constituents sends the latter rolling into an abysmal mess. One should not misjudge the health of our polity from the contemporary hectic political activity. Politics may develop in a country without either increasing its power, capacity or growth, etc., or strengthening its substantive consensus. The basic function of active political consensus is the recognition of problems, the formulation of issues, the controlled deliberation of issues, the resolution of issues, and finally the solution of the original problem. Kamaraj failed in this task and Mrs. Gandhi is nowhere near even comprehending it.

October 1967

5

THE STRUCTURE AND DIVISION OF POWER IN THE CONGRESS PARTY

THE CONGRESS PARTY stands today at the threshold of a new role and purpose, including perhaps its possible extinction. Any analysis of its internal power structure can be made only on the assumptions of an entirely changed situation. What are these assumptions?

The era of one-party dominance is over, not merely because the Congress has lost control of several State Governments but because it has, in its total amorphousness and organizational paralysis, outlived its original functions. It appears like the passing away of an empire. For example, the old consensus and its technique which remained inseparable from a charismatic leader are gone for ever, and are being replaced not by a new consensus as inevitably demanded by the altered situation, but by massive political divisiveness, threatening India's unity and the Congress Party's very existence.

The end of one-party dominance, however, has as yet not led to the rise of a clear and balanced alternative to the Congress. A fragmented party structure of several small, internally unstable and inconsistent parties has seized national politics. Within this party structure, clearly, it would be difficult for the Congress to gain any significant weightage in its legislative strength in excess of its popular vote. It was through this weightage that the Congress enjoyed in the past a near monopoly of power.

The Congress Party may have suffered grievous losses but it is not yet defeated. If its decline is to be called a defeat, it is a calculable defeat. All said and done, Parliament does not yet have an official opposition party of fifty members. The overall decline of the Congress gets exaggerated by the convulsive struggle of power within the party itself. One has only to look at the fact that, during the fourth general elections, no opposition party was able to make any decisive dent in the traditional rural votes polled for the Congress anywhere except in Orissa. Of course, it is not inconceivable that the Congress Party as such may be decisively defeated in the next elections, for the Congress vote is no longer immutable. But the Opposition vote is even more precarious, although, contrary to appearances, it is the uncertainty about the Congress and not about the opposition which has set in motion the politics of instability and economics of immobilism.

At the same time it would be a mistake to underestimate the decline of the Congress in the functional sense. Its greatest asset, which no other party can claim, is its elaborate party machine at the States' level. Its greatest liability is its weak national organization. This weakness is singularly reflected in its insecure and divided leadership, the narrow range of national political action, and the corrupt and inefficient government authority.

Whether the Congress Party survives or collapses will depend upon its ability to resolve two sets of contradictions: (*i*) the contradictions between its party machine on the one hand, and weak national organization and leadership on the other, and (*ii*) the contradiction between its policies and its inherent structure. The persistence of these contradictions would make any further decline or even downfall of the Congress just about as plausible, as their resolution would enable the party to stage a comeback, even if it is temporarily voted out of power, largely because it still happens to be the only all-India party. But the choice is not so absolute as to force the Congress either to make itself into a totally cohesive party or remain a kaleidoscopic amalgam of factions. Nor does the choice lie between its being a fully programmatic or doctrinaire party (such as a class party) and its arrogating to itself the role of a national movement which it once was. Any attempt to make the Congress absolutely cohesive soon by imposing on it the choice of one or the other ideology could split it right through at all levels. The Congress organization is sustained on a certain balance between cohesiveness at higher levels and a deliberately contrived looseness at the middle and lower levels among caste, communal, linguistic, and other groups. For example, the Congress would face the danger of complete extinction in States like Kerala, Madras, and Orissa, if it were to be too cohesive on such issues as language, Centre-State relations, etc. The resurgence of local, caste, economic, regional, and communal groups demand a very flexible strategy to encompass such groups as well as to constrain them. On the other hand, in the absence of some critical minimum coherence, cooperation, and mutual trust among its national components of power, nothing ever will get done, least of all keeping the attacks from the opposition at bay. It appears that the Congress will remain unstably poised somewhere between these two positions for some time. There is no sign yet of the party moving in the direction of resolving the aforementioned contradictions and, hence, there is a strong possibility of new, rather nasty, shocks being administered to it.

The end of one-party dominance, the breakdown of the old Nehruvian consensus, and the rise of scores of small parties have all thrown up an entirely new factor of a syncretic power, namely, coalitions between parties, factions, and groups. These coalitions are not based on principles or on workable programmes but on the desire for power and the negative politics of non-Congressism. It is impossible that the Congress, which has also developed sufficient traits of a negative power, should not be caught in these inter-party groupings. It is only a matter of time. Since, for some time to come the coalitions are going to be devoid of the critical minimum stability, uniformity, and generality, the struggle for their institutionalization is going to be replaced by a struggle for the arbitrary and opportunistic struggle for power, as has most conclusively been revealed by the experience of the formation and break-up of coalitions in quick succession in the States of West Bengal, Haryana, Uttar Pradesh, Punjab, Bihar, etc. Nevertheless, those who expect the coalition parties to disappear completely are going to be disappointed. Coalitions are going to replace each other with slow or rapid speed, depending upon how soon the most crucial coalition pivoting around the centrist hard core of the Congress is formed and returned to power. The gravitational pull of the Congress is the key to the problem and power of coalitions, particularly with regard to the necessity of a coalition transforming its specific political programmes into a common national programme without which there can be no prospects of a meaningful coalition at the Centre.

For two decades the in-fighting of the Congress Party was conducted, presumably, on varied and alternative programmes by its respective groups, factions, and leaders. Each opposition party was paired with one or the other faction in the Congress. That situation no longer exists and the process is reversed. Now it is the turn of the Congress to look for allies in the opposition parties, its second line of defence, as a hedge against political defections from its own ranks. The real political strength of any Congress leader depends on his or her support derived from the opposition parties or groups as much as is obtained from within.

The rapid rise of non-Congressism and its equally rapid decline has thus created new areas of friction as well as cooperation between the Congress and non-Congress parties. At least two facts are of utmost importance in this situation. First, the Congress Party as well as the non-Congress coalitions are losing ground to non-party elements and forces. Second, the Congress is the pivot around which an intense and fierce battle for power is and will be waged. These facts offer a challenge to the holders of power in the Congress and also throw up the possibility for creating a less amorphous structure of power. At present, however, it seems there is a growing vacuum of power about which the leaders of the Congress do not seem particularly worried. But it should be sooner than later that this ugly reality imposes itself on their easy going ways and habits.

The current in-fighting and leadership crisis may be the last but inevitable phase of the place system of power and its instability. But this struggle will remain for sometime more a crucial factor of power in this country. The Indian political power structure never developed a built-in mechanism to throw up new leadership continuously. It must be a measure of the exhaustion of its leadership and programmes that the most urgent organizational tasks are left unattended to and postponed day by day. Nonetheless, the functioning or non-functioning of a structure has its own force and logic which impels new power alignments to take place, however unplanned and imperceptible for a time they may be.

No other factor has so profoundly affected the internal power spectrum of the Congress as the shift of power from the Centre to the States. And no other cause for this shift is more relevant than the inability of the Congress to marry its unitary non-federative organization with the Federal Constitution and its politics.

This shift began during Nehru's life-time. Nehru increasingly came to rely on the personal loyalty of strong Chief Ministers instead of institutionalizing the relation between the office of the Prime Minister and that of a Chief Minister. These State satraps, in turn, consolidated their power, by all legal and illegal means, and through virtually taking over the States' administration and Congress Party organizations and ignoring the Centre's, the High Command's, and the AICC's directives on policies that did not suit them and their supporters.

Ultimately, this shift of power engulfed the Centre also, more decisively after Nehru's death. For example, the Development Council became more decisive than the Planning Commission in the making of economic policies and programmes of the Centre as well as the States. The Chief Ministers' conclave became more important than the Central Cabinet, and the Chief Ministers' power was never more decisively deployed than in the elections of Mrs. Gandhi, who was nowhere in the picture and was probably the least important member of the Shastri Cabinet. The abdication of the Congress High Command in favour of its State Committees to select candidates not only for the Assemblies but also for Parliament marked the rise to power of States' satraps at the level of party organization. Finally, at the Centre a bifactional or multifactional situation became more and more a reflection of opposing alignments in the States than of different ideological standpoints. The internal power structure of the Congress has been profoundly affected by these developments. This is the milieu in which one has, of necessity, to study the structure of power in the Congress Party.

How has the overall decline of the Congress in recent years caused the shift in the balance of power among the constituent units of its structure? Power, in the sense of command and influence

Division of Power in the Congress Party

over men and resources, mainly rested with the following: (1) the Prime Minister, (2) the Congress President, (3) the Working Committee, (4) the Syndicate, (5) the Congress Parliamentary Party, and (6) the State Chief Ministers and party bosses.

This classification illustrates the scope and limits of power to power relations of political leadership and political balances between specific components. The choice for this as against any other classification finds justification for itself in the following two special circumstances of the Congress Party. First, over the years the Congress Party has gradually evolved itself, for none too sufficient reasons, from a mass party to a skeletal organization in which really a handful of leaders, including candidates for public office plus a number of retainers, are all that matters. This process is still going on and the party's periodic exhortation for mass contact, as also its frustration reveal the agony of this change. The narrower the base of the party, the more acute and intense becomes the struggle for power at the higher echelons of the party, and the less is the function and purpose of this struggle in terms of national as against personal or group politics.

Second, the structure of the Congress is not federal but "national," which does not synchronize with the federal character of the Indian Constitution. The word "national" is being used here in a special sense, namely, in contrast to the word "federal." So long as the Congress had the unquestioned authority of a single leader or an authoritative collective, its being a national party was a factor of importance in mitigating the strains and stresses of a federal polity which was imposed from above on an inhospitable social system. As soon as that unique leadership disappeared, the effects went into sharp reversal. The unsolved problems of the federal polity came into their own, engulfed the weak national party and, as a consequence, disproportionately sharpened the struggle for power in the Congress Party. The new role of the Chief Ministers must be evalued in that context, as must the problems of the Centre-State relations.

Of all the listed elements of power, the Prime Minister, Mrs. Gandhi, has apparently emerged the strongest, not only in relation to the other five components but also absolutely, i.e. over the entire national power structure, which, though, itself has considerably weakened and depreciated. It is maintained that Mrs. Gandhi is a weak Prime Minister. The story of her first accession to power, still fresh in many a mind, and her two years of bewildered performance are unmistakable evidence in support of that contention. Her emergence at the surface as the strongest element in the power structure does not *ipso facto* turn her into a strong Prime Minister. One represents a position in the strucure and the other relates to functions of power: the two cannot be equated by definition. She still remains a weak Prime Minister, not in the sense that she suffers from a paralysis of will but in the sense that she lacks strength and capacity for continuously twisting the power structure in her favour in such a manner as would lead to a successful tackling of the pressing national problems and for creating a strong party by resolutely opposing the forces which undermine these objectives. Whatever the ideology, the Congress Party in the days of Nehru accepted his views on all important matters of policy without a showdown between the conflicting constituents of the party. Never again will there be another leader in the Congress to perform the same role, certainly not Mrs. Gandhi. Nor has she evolved a suitable machinery by means of which she can realize the objectives of the party in normal ways, through consensus or any other method, but without a showdown.

On the contrary, she manages to gather power in her hands by softening these objectives to a very dangerous level. Although she has so far come out unscathed from every crisis which this softening of objectives has created, it is most certain that this contradiction between the concentration of power and the recession of national objectives will explode one day. Maybe that Mrs. Gandhi has firmly clarified in her mind the reversal of this strategy at some later date, but one does not get its proof anywhere. In two recent statements she has ventured, boldly if not immodestly, to say that she is made of a sterner stuff and that her government is today stronger than ever. No one surveying the political scene over the last two years will be impressed by such claims.

A strong Prime Minister is expected to stand up to conflicting pressures which nibble at national power and bring about a more rational allocation in the distribution of power and privilege. Morarji Desai to some extent fitted that twin role and that is why she, as the least important member of the Shastri Cabinet, was preferred to him. The same applied to Y.B. Chavan.

A more positive and direct indication of her weakness is that the power and prestige of the job of the Prime Minister have continued to depreciate unabated ever since she took over. She has become totally dependent on ICS officials, make-up men, and party hacks. The clearest indication of this weakness was the way she was hustled into devaluing the rupee and abandoning the Fourth Plan. In both these decisions, as also in several other subsequent ones, a marked degree of unresisted external pressure was widely noticed and believed, leading, paradoxically, to a continuous strengthening of her position internally. It is not difficult to suspect that this borrowed strength is a real weakness of the national power of India and therefore of her leaders. Besides, it is not Mrs. Gandhi's shrewdness but the voters' taste for blood which eliminated, like a potato queue, many of her strong rivals in the party. Nevertheless, her newly acquired strong position in the party structure offers her a unique though final opportunity to prove that she is not so weak a Prime Minister.

She revealed her powerful strategy in the very first operation of making a clean sweep of every other element in the Congress Party's power structure which counted in the making of a Prime Minister. Her emergence as a leader is the result of a masterminded political operation never heard of or seen before in this country. The defeated stalwarts, who tried to rehabilitate themselves through the party loyalty of Desai and who had nearly succeeded in their bid to weaken the position of both Desai and Mrs. Gandhi, were removed through a technique of her which would be the envy of party machine-men in the developed world. All this could have been interpreted as a lucky coincidence or a fluke rather than the beginning of a new Indira technique. But she repeatedly applied with resounding success the same technique on several other occassions such as in the election of President Zakir Husain, the elimination of Kamaraj, in the dissolution of coalitions, and, above all, in the creation among the opposition parties her own second line of defence. For example, all opposition parties are avowedly and violently anti-Congress but they are not all against Mrs. Gandhi as a Prime Minister.

Nevertheless, she remains on an appallingly slippery wicket. The first minor shock, which though she was able to absorb, came at the Hyderabad session and its echoes have not yet died down. That she withstood the shock is important; but it was not a major one is even more important. She would certainly be worsted in the long run by her own strategy and is unlikely to survive it if it turns out to be an overplayed trick or a simple sleight of hand that bypasses the problems of having a strong united party, a united leadership, and a functioning system which could meet the national challenge, the problems which get more and more complicated as days and months pass by.

This is all the more important because it appears that probably the most significant objective of her technique is to acquire for herself an edge over her rivals through projecting herself as a national leader by appeasement of anti-Congress forces causing embarrassment to her colleagues, excessive drift, inaction, and even sabotage of the party's accepted programme and policy. This is typically a Nehruvian technique, which, of course, failed in the long run.

The following are some of the known facets of the technique applied by her. (1) She tries to remain on the right side of the non-Congress Governments in general and their Chief Ministers in particular. The same is true with regard to some opposition parties and leaders. (2) She has tried to capture the overwhelming support and confidence of leaders of the minority communities, more by appeasing them than solving their problems. At the same time, to keep in potential reserve the support of parties like the Jana Sangh, she has not campaigned consistently against the communal politics of the majority community. (3) She discarded some of her closest supporters when it was felt necessary to do so for her image-building. The so-called kitchen cabinet seems to have been disbanded. (4) She has completely stopped taking ideological positions on almost all issues, because the ideological conflict of today divides not only the nation against itself but also the sources of power against any one who has set his or her eyes on ultimately acquiring supreme power, whatever that be. She has certainly travelled a long way from a strong anti-communist position to ideology-free postures. Of course, in this newly acquired position she has also run the risk of being called a leader without ideas. (5) In foreign policy matters also her stand is largely noncommital. Whatever the impressions created, she is not nonaligned in the sense in which Nehru was on behalf of this country. She is nonaligned more on her own behalf so as to remain acceptable to super powers. One simple manifestation of this personal strategy, as distinguished from a national strategy, is that no longer does any one speak today of what is called the structure of India's foreign policies. India's West Asia policy was the only exception. No wonder she is accused of having no foreign policy at all. (6) She has revealed a remarkable flexibility with rivals in the party. Not only has she tamed Morarji Desai by overloading him with work and giving him the impression that he shares power with her which he does not but she has also permitted a dangerous ebb and flow of Chavan's prestige and power so as to make him end up by making loud protestations of his loyalty to her.

In brief, Mrs. Gandhi must not be underestimated, however weak she happens to be, although her strength in the Congress is largely a byproduct of the political, moral, and intellectual exhaustion of its other leaders. She could certainly be relied upon to perpetuate herself in power at the head of the Congress Party or some coalition and also bring about a national disaster or a national breakthrough. The age of lions is over and is being replaced by an age of foxes. The only lion who still roars in defence of the Congress jungle is Desai who has left himself to be tamed by Mrs. Gandhi, presumably because of his age and a complete lack of any serious political strategy. It is neither his rigidity nor presumably the renunciation of the right to contend for power which make him so unacceptable. It is his total refusal to contend for power seriously and strategically for building a national collective on a proper division of functions which provides Mrs. Gandhi a powerful countervailing factor in her struggle against all other contenders, whether individuals or all put together, as also against Morarji Desai himself.

It is in relation to the new power acquired by the Chief Ministers that the position and power of the Prime Minister has become uncertain if not precarious. As stated earlier, the non-federal character of the Congress Party and a similar position of the Prime Minister as the leader of the Congress parliamentary party on the one hand and the Prime Minister as head of the federal government on the other are two non-conformable situations, which are attended by innumerable potential conflicts. Nehru could successfully paper over the fissures not because he built any new institutional links or bridges between the two opposites, indeed he himself was the only link, but by the particular role he was cast in by history.

Mrs. Gandhi was chosen as the late Shastri's successor largely through the combined pressure of several Chief Ministers who had sufficient reasons to plump for a weak centre and a weak Prime Minister. Those reasons are valid today much as they were then. Some Chief Ministers had tasted real, autonomous power during the last and declining phase of Nehru's life. Not so surprising, therefore, was the fact that in the very first year, the formative period for building strength and an image for herself, Mrs. Gandhi could not impose on the Chief Ministers, nor could she persuade them to agree among themselves about, any single policy decision of national importance.

Two new developments of the post-election period have imparted new sharpness to the role of the Chief Ministers. First, the Congress Party lost more than half the States during the fourth general elections and by subsequent defections from it. Second, the Congress generally lost heavily in States which had a weak economic structure and won in economically stronger States excepting Madras. These developments have broken up the old united front of the Chief Ministers and created peculiarly contradictory pulls but with much the same effects on the position of the Prime Minister.

It is naturally in the interests of the weaker States that the Centre must be strong, powerful, and resourceful, whereas stronger States prefer a weak Centre. This particular configuration of success and defeat of the Congress strongly suggests that the re-election of Mrs. Gandhi in 1967 as the leader of the Congress Party was definitely due largely to her assumed or real weakness. Strong Congress-led States and all the non-Congress States, whether weak or strong but naturally desiring a shift of power to themselves from the Congress at the Centre, have combined in their desire to have a weak Centre and a weak Prime Minister who can be coerced into yielding to their economic demands and political threats.

Yet, paradoxically, the control of the apparatus of the Government by the Congress and the non-Congress simultanously has given Mrs. Gandhi a real extra edge in combating her rivals inside the Congress Party in so far as she is more acceptable than other Congress leaders to the non-Congress Chief Ministers, though not the least for effectuating national policies. The more she hedges against the claims of her rivals in the Congress Party by collecting support from the opposition ranks the greater is the paralysis of her party, its national programme and, in the long run, its entire leadership. These are clearly the foundations of a weak and not a strong Prime Minister. The Government apparatus under the given circumstances is bound to, as it has indeed, become more and more inefficient and spendthrift. The motive power behind this system is not the rational allocation of power and resources but a populist maximization of the spoils and share in the shrinking national cake.

The aforementioned attempt by Mrs. Gandhi to walk on two poles has, of necessity, created a vacuum between herself and the Congress Parliamentary Party (CPP), upon which she must ever depend most for remaining in power. The CPP has become a new factor of power, as of right, since the death of Nehru, and it is in relation to it that the position of Mrs. Gandhi is of the utmost importance. This is entirely a new phenomenon in the power structure. The composition and structure of cabinet-making is one part of that relationship. The day of the rubber-stamp Parliament being over, any set or sub-set of ministers will find uncertainty hanging over their heads and their position strengthened or undermined by alignments in the CPP.

At the first opportunity she got after her first election, Mrs. Gandhi singularly failed to utilize the CPP in drawing from it strength for herself, taking and testing all the major policy decisions on that forum, preparing it to evolve a new structure of policies through its combined wisdom and experience, and building up a position of trust and confidence between herself and its members. To get over the personality crisis after Nehru's death that overshadowed all leaders, Mrs. Gandhi more than anybody else urgently needed the establishment of a two-way line of communication and confidence of the CPP to make it her main base. Her failure and incapacity to do so were pathetically revealed in the fact that she did not go to the electorate as the chosen leader of the Congress Party.

At the second opportunity she got, Mrs. Gandhi went to the extreme by completely ignoring and bypassing the CPP, so much so that not only could she get elected no more than six of her supporters to the CPP Executive, but also refused to attend its meetings. It would be a mistake to call that attitude wilful or impetuous; it rather seems to be part of the same technique of building a national image or mystique around her, or else she would not have gone to the extent of threatening the CPP with her going over their heads to appeal to the people in the country. The results, however, have been disastrous. Factionalist activity in the CPP has quite intensified and a new power vacuum created, which fortunately for her and the party has been partly filled by Desai. The much-needed cohesiveness of the party and rationalization of its policies have also been lost in this superfluous game of building a personality cult. The rumblings of the rank and file of the CPP asserting itself have been heard all too often; and if they ever get articulated, Mrs. Gandhi's position will become untenable. The same experience was also repeated at the AICC, which largely overlaps with the CPP.

Whatever may be the personal qualities of her new ministers, her choice of ministers has failed to establish the necessary confidence and communication between her and the CPP. And this remains the most important factor of instability not only in the Congress Party but also in its relation to other parties. Either she, in her assumed role of a national leader, should have decisively influenced the choice of candidates before the elections for this type of cabinet, which she obviously could not, or she should have, after being re-elected, had a cabinet truly reflecting the CPP.

The present cabinet is neither here nor there and if it ultimately proves her undoing she has nobody but herself to blame for it. Nevertheless, even now, with the present ministers intact, the CPP remains her most reliable and potent ally both for leadership and policy-making. If she fails in this latter task of making the CPP an instrument of evolving and carrying a new structure of policies, she would have only proved herself to be worse than inept.

The Congress Party can never return to the Nehruvian phase of lop-sided relationship between the Prime Minister and the Congress President. However, the eclipse of Kamaraj has created a situation of basic shift of power from the Congress President to the Prime Minister. It is quite certain that to maintain this preferred position Mrs. Gandhi will ever endeavour, so far as it lies in her power, to have in that post only one of her trusted men. The possibility of one or the other of the defeated stalwarts or some other strong personality filling that vacancy seems out of the question. There are good reasons for it.

For two full years it amazed every observer of the Indian political scene to see how a man like Kamaraj, with all his reputed efficiency, discipline, and years of successful political control of the party and the Government in Madras, could have so badly managed the affairs of almost every State Congress Party and Government in the States. It also surprised many as to why he was undermining the Government of Mrs. Gandhi in many devious ways in the name of some real or assumed differences of principles. It is generally believed that Kamaraj deliberately left the Congress Party in such an amorphous and fluid state and opposed Mrs. Gandhi simply because he himself wanted to become the Prime Minister.

But all this is history now and not very relevant. However, a problem upon which attention gets focussed is the absence of a clear demarcation, either in principle or in institutional arrangement, between the functions of the Congress Party and its Government wing. Such a distinction is absolutely necessary in a federal set-up, though, not unnaturally perhaps, it got blurred under the rule of one-party dominance and one national figure, Nehru, who was his own opposition leader. That phase ended with Nehru. Since then the Congress Party has falsely reduced the problem of institutionalizing this basic distinction into the existence of an equation or non-equation between the Congress President and the Prime Minister. Nijalingappa, the new Congress President, and Mrs. Gandhi together, with all the goodwill in the world, cannot be adequate substitutes for a principle and a mechanism which assures a clear division of functions and power. They can always drift apart for the same reason for which their functions and powers are not clearly defined or institutionalized.

A good example is that of the Labour Party of Britain. The organizational wing of the party, which really sustains the basic structure of the party, is not only more radical but is generally very critical of the parliamentary wing. But their respective functions are clearly known, and it is always the latter that has the final say in governmental activity despite occasional strains between the two wings. No political party in India has worked out such an arrangement which, no doubt, would be of little operational significance if the party in the Centre always ruled all the States or if India had a unitary system of Government. When different parties rule in the Centre and the States, the question of federal power and party responsibility impinge on the relationship between the Prime Minister and the Congress President.

The Prime Minister has improved her power position not only in relation to the Congress President of the future but also in relation to the Congress Working Committee and the so-called Syndicate. The Syndicate is a name given to a combination of few party stalwarts, each of whom is a potential contender for the highest power, next in line to the Prime Minister and her main opponent. The Syndicate exercises the functions of a caucus that commands a determining influence in all matters relating to power and its division in the party. The original members of the Syndicate were Atulya Ghosh, S.K. Patil, Kamraj, Sanjiva Reddy, all of whom were downgraded in one way or another by the results of the fourth general elections, though they were highly instrumental in the first election of Mrs. Gandhi as Prime Minister. At the time of her re-election Mrs. Gandhi created the impression of setting up a new Syndicate of her own consisting of Y.B. Chavan, D.P. Misra, Brahmananda Reddy, Nijalingappa, and possibly one or two more

States' bosses. This was an illusion, for a Syndicate essentially nibbles at the political power of the Prime Minister who could not be expected to agree to her power being clipped.

The Syndicate politics is not a perpetual phenomenon because of the illusive and shifting fortunes of its individual members. The role of the Syndicate often comes into the limelight only at some turning point after which it ceases to operate almost on its own accord or because those who come to control power through it do not let it function. How serious a threat the Syndicate can pose to the Prime Minister was revealed at the last session of the Congres at Hyderabad. The Working Committee, although technically alive, is almost dead in the sense of the Congress High Command that it once was. Its effective operation is controlled by the Syndicate and the Congress President.

In brief the new balance of power within the Congress Party is clearly a balance of weakness and it also rests upon the general depreciation of national and party power. With it all is enjoined the peculiar strategy of the Prime Minister, Mrs. Gandhi, the success of which so largely depends upon the further softening up of the system. Too many sharers of power have developed too much stake in the political weakness of the country. The survival of the Congress Party depends not on the continuation but on the reversal of these trends.

What is the final picture of the power structure emerging from the analysis of the preceeding pages? It is obviously one of contradictions and paradoxes, though blurred. Yet some conclusions seem unmistakable for the Congress leadership to draw for itself from it.

First, the Congress Party is caught up in a crisis of increasing political conflict inside the party as much as outside it with an opposition which is desperate and unobliging to agree to a let-up in its attacks on the Congress leadership. Including the Congress, all parties are becoming increasingly unpopular with the voters and losing political support on which they depend most. Any shift of relative strength between the Congress and the Opposition rests upon the depreciation of total national power, from which both the nation and the party system seem to emerge weaker than ever.

No party seems capable of improving upon itself, but all set great store by their attempts at undermining one another ever so often.

Second, while theoretically the interests and the strength of the constituents of the power-structure in the Congress Party stand in inverse relation to those of the Prime Minister, in practice very cruel relativism operates; a weak Prime Minister weakens, nationally, every other element of the power structure.

Third, while the Prime Minister's job remains a prize job and there are any number of aspirants to it, the main contestants are, more by volition than by necessity, in such a mutually exclusive position that they can, individually, only wreck their rival's chances without improving their own.

Mrs. Gandhi has every reason to be satisfied with her strategy in so far as she has successfully cut the size and power of her rivals in the party. She has no business to be satisfied with her strategy and power remaining nationally infructuous and destroying the party's strength and solidarity. The most common and durable of conflicts and factionalism in the Congress Party is the unequal distribution of power among equals. Mrs. Gandhi cannot be lightly persuaded to part with power or she may consider that she can ill afford to do so, but she must at least learn in her own interest to be so cooperative in its exercise as would create confidence in her senior colleagues who do not seem to feel quite secure at her hands.

The Congress Party cannot survive without evolving a double consensus: consensus on national leadership and consensus among leaders on policies and the division of power. A consensus on leadership, in the light of the available spectrum of leaders and their groups, must lead to a collective leadership. This is the crux of the whole matter. The present pattern is very anomalous and helps very little. There are leaders spread all over but there is no leadership available for the nation to make decisions on its behalf. And it is amazing that in our democracy of today the chances of taking a wrong decision are small while the fact of non-decision-making is written large on everybody's face. Some sort of a super-cabinet of persons in strategic command-posts of the political power-structure could be formed among these leaders on the basis of a functioning division of power. And this division of power has to be quite flexible and not mechanical to allow new leaders to emerge and grow at all levels.

This proposed collective leadership cannot emerge easily and work successfully because as an aggregate of elements it must evolve itself as a grouping of inter-related elements possessing a boundary or limit of each element, internal and external mechanism of integration and, above all, a measure of functional unity.

There is no guarantee that a collective leadership fully aware of its responsibility will emerge from the complex power struggle. Its growth is limited by the nature of the means and technique of the power struggle applied by each leader in his or her own defence. Nor is there any certainty of the emergence of consensus on policies and programmes because of conflicting loyalties and pressures on the leadership. However, a pseudo collective emerging as result of a temporary cease-fire between mutually hostile causes cannot be ruled out.

A fast deteriorating political situation, or the appearance of it, has made some well-meaning people to demand the establishment of a National Government. Such a Government has to be formed, theoretically, either by leaders of like-minded parties, though it would be difficult to identify even two like-minded parties, not to speak of many more, or by a non-party, hence politically nondescript all-talent team. The far-fetched assumptions behind such a Government are: (1) national consensus, (2) common minimum programme, (3) common development strategy, (4) ideology free ruling set-up, etc. But the more important and also more ludicrous presumptions are that men of talent, twice born in a sense, are more honest and less power-seeking for themselves than their less fortunate, less talented brothers. This argument is utterly false as is evident in the present-day administration of Indian universities. Above all, the demand for a National Government is a remarkable piece of political innocence inasmuch as it calls upon those who have acquired power democratically to hand it over to others who have no special claim upon it.

However, the demand for a National Government is truly a substitute demand for a united leadership of the Congress Party, which has a clear and comfortable majority in Parliament. It is a warning to the Congress Party that it can no longer depend for support on the voters if its mutually destructive leadership cannot be bound together or eliminated. The answer to the demand for a National Government lies in creating a collective leadership of the Congress Party before it is really too late.

Despite all the difficulties, road-blocks, inhibitions, and hangover from the past, the creation of a collective in the Congress Party is feasible, as of necessity it is inescapable. The problem boils down to taking two steps. First, the four top leaders, Indira Gandhi, Morarji Desai, Chavan, and Jagjivan Ram, along with the Congress President, should form a super directorate to run the affairs of the party and the central Government. This caucus can work triumphantly only on a clear understanding that (*a*) Mrs. Gandhi shall be unquestioningly accepted as the leader for a fixed period after which a new consensus or vote on leadership will be freely taken, (*b*) the same principle will be accepted in substance and not only in name for Morarji Desai as the Deputy Prime Minister, (*c*) there will have to be such a clear and equal division of power and functions as will permit each leader to grow in stature while at the job, and (*d*) the CPP will be the source for all governmental power as well as the testing ground for every leader's performance and position.

The second step required is to homogenize the leadership at the States' level where, in reality, the Congress Party is facing its toughest challenge of survival. The emergence of a new leadership in States, from which the national leaders of the future will have to be recruited, is annexed to the suggested collective upon which lies the responsibility of fulfilling the national tasks.

Mrs. Gandhi can perform the most urgent national tasks with the help of these leaders. Morarji Desai, whom she has apparently got at a very cheap price, is her second in command but does not share power with her in the real sense. Nobody in the Congress has done so much for party loyalty. The Congress Party needs him today more than ever before for imparting discipline and organizational efficiency to the party and the Government. But for him Mrs. Gandhi would have had to face a debacle at the last session of the Congress Party at Hyderabad. His adherence to Gandhism in practice from which flows his refusal to play politics according to its rules, his total lack of flexibility, and his age will always stand in the way of his reaching the top. Chavan is another able and efficient political leader who seriously contends for power and should be expected to do so as long as Mrs. Gandhi allows the power vacuum to persist. He has the capacity to grow in his job but as a national leader he is seriously handicapped. Whatever his limitations Jagjivan Ram can be employed to some tasks for which no other leader is well suited. At present these and other leaders carry on their struggle and in-fighting within a static structure and on a balance of weakness. On the other hand, working together on the basis of equal sharing of power and balance of strength, they cannot only hold the CPP together but, along with the CPP, they can triumphantly put up a formidable front against an equally formidable opposition. Above all, working together, and not each separately, they can resurrect and rejuvenate that centrist hard-core of the Congress and of other parties which remains the only guarantee for stability. Besides, all these leaders do not have any serious ideological cleavages that could seriously keep them apart. They are all centrists by and large.

It is almost axiomatic that with the spectrum of leadership available at present, it will be a collective and not one leader who can comfortably rule as well as carry out the national tasks. It is worse than useless to hope that there will take place a basic alternation in governmental authority and purpose between this competing and mutually suspicious set of leaders. If Mrs. Gandhi works on the assumption of "one leader, one party" and applies techniques of building herself up as a national leader by isolating herself from the functioning structure of the party and ignoring the claims of leaders who are more than her equals, she is heading for trouble, however clever a manipulator she turns out to be. The future of the Congress Party is also tied to the outcome of this struggle for power. It is more probable, however, that the centrist hard-core of the party may assert itself and raise itself as an autonomous factor of power, and, by new alignments, create an entirely new leadership and impart new and healthy dimensions to the power struggle to fill the currently growing vacuum of power. A fine example of this trend is the recent demand by sixty odd members of the AICC, cutting across all groups and factions, for calling a special session of the AICC to stem the tide of the growing political rot in the country. However, one sparrow does not make spring. The cue for the survival of the nation as well as the Congress Party in the next few years lies in the combined force of the centrist hard-core of the Congress Party and a collective leadership or the great imponderables which lie behind all politics.

April 1968

6

MRS. GANDHI'S STRATEGY OF STATIC BALANCE

MRS. INDIRA GANDHI has now ruled for nearly three years and most probably will remain in power for another three years, i.e. until the next general elections, although neither she nor anyone else seems to know where or in what direction she is drifting. In functional or goal perspective, she can be said to have reached a plateau or rather the beginning of the end of the first phase. There may or may not be a next phase because, in terms of her own otherwise very adroit strategy and tactics of retaining power, she has juxtaposed herself with forces and personalities who have nothing in common with her except their own functionlessness and lust for power. She has been a remarkable success in defeating her rivals at their own game, but, in that process, she has also bypassed national problems, the forces behind which should very soon demand a change of leadership or policies or both. It is a dangerous technique or theory to go by as the bases of political authority and legitimacy.

A possibility remains, although it has not yet been tested, i.e. in face of a really deadly challenge to her she may react in a way that may encompass changes in national policies, objectives, etc., and in her techniques. However, not even one of her supporter has yet claimed or foreseen such a possibility. The pattern of power of which she is both a product and a successful manipulator rests on static stability and balance of weakness and is unlikely to survive or be serviceable in the next phase. However, three factors must constantly be kept in view. First, a Prime Minister in India enjoys vast prestige and power, wields tremendous patronage, and can perpetuate himself or herself beyond the phase of relevance or even political legitimacy. Secondly, Mrs. Gandhi has always revealed unsuspected reserves of shrewdness, tenacity, and ruthlessness in face of serious challenges to her authority. She could be relied upon to dismantle a part of the present political apparatus or institutions if threatened seriously. Thirdly, she is characterized by a personality structure which is less dogmatic than that of any of her rivals, particularly in respect of ideology and political party affiliation. In fact, she never encompasses action and ideology at the same time. It will have to be an extremely powerful combine, of a kind which does not yet exist, that could decisively challenge her authority within the present static framework. It is a contradiction but a very important one; she can survive, in the long run, only by breaking the present static, dead pan balance of power and yet it is by the same balance and its weakness that she reigns supreme in the short run. There is another contradiction within that contradiction: the more fundamental the change required, as certainly it is, the more pressing is the time element and the more urgent the need for taking steps to remove threats to her authority. And yet every attempt she has made so far in that direction has fallen short of achieving this objective because she had to contend continuously with new challenges and pressures immediately following her actions taken towards those objectives. The power of decision-making is always limited by the nature and level of technique.

A sharp reversal, therefore, is called for in her double strategy of *limited clash* and *static balance*, which is made possible by double tactics of *involvement* and *detachment*—involvement in her acting as a magnet to centres of power, and detachment both in allowing delay and avoidance of decisions as tactics in conflict resolution and by keeping herself aloof from all other competing power struggles, thus allowing a natural balance to emerge among the remaining contenders or components or power.

To put it in bland terms, this type of politics is called politics by factions, which today is the *leit motif* of the Congress Party. Politics by factions is recognized everywhere as one of the several legitimate modes of political operation, more so in a largely undifferentiated and socially complex society like India. But politics of total reliance on continuous shift in *ad hoc* combinations of leaders and personalities is utterly ephemeral, though it may get headlines in newspapers or be a talking-point in upper society circles of class power. Mrs. Gandhi is involved, by the logic of her own strategy, in both types: factions which operate more or less as permanent groups in the party, and those connected with the most active conflicts around her personality in relation to other leaders. She has been unusually rewarded by her strategy. She has not permitted any other leader to soar dangerously high in reputation; she has also forestalled the emergence of any powerful combination against her. That is probably all that she wants but that is certainly not all that is expected of her.

While we are still on the subject of Mrs. Gandhi's strategy, it must be mentioned that this strategy, abstracted as it is from every other larger problem, is now likely to yield diminishing returns for several reasons.

First, she has communicated a sense of crisis at all levels of the party and society. No one in the Congress Party feels sure of his own position or about the fortunes of the party. Never before had personal politics seized such a firm hold of the political processes as now.

Secondly, her strategy vis-a-vis the party is increasingly failing her as well as the Congress President in working together for resolving conflicts within the framework of authority which remains unimpaired. The Congress Party's structure has grown increasingly unstable because control has been divorced from authority and fallen into pretended power. In brief, the Congress Party has destroyed all the means of social change. The net advantage that she and her few rivals or confederates derive from herding together is likely to become more problematic when output of the system declines, as most obviously it has to some extent. Her methods of conflict resolution by allowing conflicts to find their own natural course do not contain any identifiable creative aspect.

Thirdly, serious cracks have appeared in her second line of defence, namely, those opposition parties and groups which had proclaimed their support to her in many crucial matters. The spectrum of these groups runs all along the line from Left to Right. It is not that any other leader has emerged to command their loyalty. In fact, it can be that the opposition is facing a gradual or rapid, as the case may be, slicing off in its political strength. The opposition parties are increasingly making Mrs. Gandhi personally the target of their attack because she has to fight, as much as she supports, the opposition to maintain her position inside the Congress Party. In brief, her strategy of dependence for support simultaneously on the Congress and the opposition, almost equally, is yielding a new polarization from which she can neither escape nor benefit any more.

Fourthly, the most vital part of this strategy is the politics of ambivalence, which makes others indulge in a perpetual guessing game. This was also Nehru's method. However, the technique of ambivalence is truly serviceable for a charismatic leader to whom others look up to for new ideas, policies, and sources of strength. For a non-charismatic leader like Mrs. Gandhi, this is a self-defeating game because, while affording some manoeuvrability to her, this technique affords greater facility for others to do the same. The distinction between a charismatic leader and charismatic movement must not be lost sight of. The Congress was a charismatic movement. Nehru was a charismatic leader whose charisma survived long after it wore off from the Congress Party. His strength came not so much from the Congress Party as from his independence of it. Try as she may, Mrs. Gandhi cannot hope to develop charisma around her so long as the political structure remains static and without a national purpose. The bureaucratic elements have come to gain decisively over the charismatic ones, while ultra-traditional elements are presenting such ecological dislocation as would permit new horizons and practices of politics to merge. Slowly and gradually, power has come to reside outside the Government, much as it has moved to the bureaucracy within the Government. This reallocation of power threatens much more vitally the authority of the Prime Minister than the intrigues of her rivals. And in the light of this, her strategy is totally inadequate in meeting this threat. The effectiveness of her Government as an instrument of political and social change is all but gone.

Despite these four formidable reasons that reduce the efficacy of her strategy, there is yet no fear of imminent disaster or total failure overtaking her within the present static structure. A considerable amount of routinization of politics and policies has taken place through new and old bureaucratic structures as shock-absorbers of the system, though the impact has been very small if not entirely negative. Only when other demands of polity and economy press hard for a change, a serious threat could develop to her authority. She has every reason to feel safe, but she has no business to be complacent.

A real threat to Mrs. Gandhi, or more definitely to the entire Congress leadership, emanates from more durable factors or underlying processes which are overtaking the present structure of power. First, the State is not gaining power which other political units are losing and even those units, groups, or parties which are definitely on the way out are not turning over to the State their functions or power. However much the stopping of the opposition flood or the disintegration of some opposition parties may have emboldened the Congress Party, this confidence could be no more than an illusion because the struggle for power has not always been conducted through the party structure. Below a certain critical minimum level of functionalism and goal satisfaction, if allowed to persist, the present party structure itself could be eliminated or supplanted by some other arrangement.

The decline in the power of the State is today manifested in continuous incidents of riots, strikes, burning of public property, wilful defiance of authority, open and unchecked corruption in high and low places of power, etc. Beneath the occurrence of these outbursts, one could point to the need for the articulation of popular demands. But above that level, which seems to have been reached, these ugly happenings signify not only the failure of the demand-articulating and goal satisfying functions of the Government but also the inconsistency of these functions, and the breakdown of lawful authority, no matter who broke the law first, the government, the ruling party or its distractors, or people with long unfulfilled demands.

Another aspect of this decline in the power of the State is the way in which the reallocation of power has taken place between the federal Government and the States. States may appear to have grown stronger vis-a-vis the Centre, but their capacity to handle law and order problems or check violent outbursts seems to have declined. This inverse relationship between power and authority is the source of general instability in the country. In such a situation, the central Government, no matter who the Prime Minister is, cannot hope to remain in effective power for long within the limits of a static structure that produces increasing violence. Violence of any type within a static structure can serve no function, revolutionary or adaptive, except in undermining the power of the State and its leaders.

It is well known that without the support of Congress Chief Ministers Mrs. Gandhi would never have been chosen Prime Minister. It is also a matter of common knowledge that she assiduously cultivates State bosses. What is probably not so clear is that her entire strategy, particularly ambivalence and delay in decision-making, has added much to the power of the State bosses. She may have successfuly eliminated the chances of her rivals at the Centre threatening her position but by doing so she has also increased the potential threat to herself and to any new Prime Minister by permitting the States to grow in power at the cost of the Centre, particularly when the entire national power has depreciated. Her position as leader of the Congress Party in opposition to other parties and her power as a federal Prime Minister by which she won over to her side the non-Congress Chief Ministers are contradictory in nature and are bound to defeat her strategy ultimately, as indeed they have to some extent. The dismissal of opposition Governments in several States has disillusioned her erstwhile allies in the opposition. She is unlikely to find allies in opposition parties again because of their defeat at her hands. Besides, if in States like Uttar Pradesh and Bengal the Congress were to come back to power by defeating the opposition at midterm polls, power alignments would have changed in a definite way. She would have brought back men into power in these States who are hostile to her, and, consequently, lost her support in those as well as in other States. The continuous economic stagnation over the years, from which there appears no escape yet, is the counterpart of the static and, functionless political strucutre. No one with political stakes is prepared to opt for the hard way, and there is a general tendency among Government and opposition leaders either to allow a dangerous drift of the economy to new, unseen crises or to mount new distributive pressures on the shrinking cake. The drastic decline in investment programmes, drying up of saving potentials, foreign exchange difficulties, crippling labour problems, etc., have all converged on frightened policy-makers who are utterly busy in saving their own skin. Despite large-scale decontrol and substantial increases in agricultural production, there are no signs yet of an economic recovery.

Two crucial features of our economy today require special attention. First, within the present fiscal and monetary structures, it is impossible to raise resources for larger investment and hence for a bigger plan. The most sanguine estimates for savings do not go above 9 to 10 per cent for any year over the fourth plan, the lower figure being more realistic in view of large demands for distribution from politically vocal sectors. Foreign aid will be there but roughly about half the size of that secured during the Third Plan. If all goes well, the highest rate of investment will hover around 10 to 11 per cent, the lower ratio being more pertinent. Reallocation of fiscal resources between the Centre and the States, if allowed to go the way as revealed by trends already noticed and accepted, will push real investment lower still. If all does not go well, the economy will slip to its firm rate of saving and investment of about 8 per cent.

Secondly, a shift of inter-sectoral priorities from industries to agriculture and intra-sectoral priorities in the industrial sector from basic to consumer goods industries, coupled with a new consumption-oriented strategy instead of the old production-oriented planning, are calculated not only to ensure smaller planning activity and a low rate of growth but also to put more power in the hands of powerful economic groups and interests who will act as substitutes for governmental policy functions and dictate whatever is left of the latter in the hands of the State. The decline of political power of the State has its counterpart the decline in economic power of the State, both in a framework of depreciated national power, political and economic.

The only new prop that is being put up is a policy-framework for opening the country to large-scale foreign investment. If foreign investment comes in massive proportions, for which there is not much reason to hope, the crisis may be postponed. But if it only trickles in, following the dismantling of the planning structure, the crisis will overtake the economy in two to three years' time. The onset of an economic crisis, at a time when the strategic economic power has decisively moved out of the hands of the State and into the hands of the business classes, would demand a political change. A low rate of growth or economic stagnation can unleash the sort of violent populism which a weakened central authority may not be able to withstand. Those who are sitting pretty on a static power structure are likely to be washed away. It should be a good enough reason for Mrs. Gandhi to act much before the election towards dynamizing the economy as well as the polity.

It might be imagined that a decline in the bureaucratic semi-monopoly capitalism of the State would have reduced the power of the bureaucracy. On the contrary, its power has increased. For quite some years now bureaucrats and managers of public undertakings have been blamed, rightly or wrongly, for all the ills of the public sector. They have, however, not only fully survived these attacks but have strategically regrouped themselves as a collectively conscious power elite. It is on them that political leaders of today including the Prime Minister have come to depend almost totally for decision-making. At no time since Independence was any proper relationship established between the bureaucracy and the citizenry. Most officials perceived their departments and agencies as serving particular groups as opposed to the general public. The more frantic the attacks on bureaucrats, the more solidly they united; the more rapid the decline in the power of the political leaders, the more decisive became the voice and role of bureaucracy. This situation can be called one of the growth of pseudo-administration. Administration is pseudo when it grows in power, particularly autonomous power, at the cost of its proper functions. The origin of this pseudo-administration can be traced to the early days of Nehru. Interference from political leaders in norms and procedures of bureaucracy, not necessarily made to speed up decisions on implementation, produced a sort of bureaucrat who either became a willing ally or an accomplice of the politician or simply withdrew to the inviolability of his sanctuary of non-decision making. So long as there were powerful politicians at the top of the Government, some degree of functionalism was achieved. However, as soon as lesser men came to power, the bureaucracy developed its own initiative and power to thwart all the good and bad decisions of ministers. And as such bureaucracy developed into a full-fledged autonomous factor of power. In Mrs. Gandhi's strategy of acquiring power, bureaucrats play the most crucial role in more than one direction, particularly in gathering information on other leaders and finding out about the moves and countermoves of other groups, factions, and leaders. It should not surprise anyone if elements of the higher civil service emerge openly among the partisan forces led by leaders engaged in bitter in-fighting and torn by dissensions. There is no such thing as a faceless bureaucracy—its facelessness being the cover of its efficiency and dedication to its work. Our newspapers and parliamentarians have helped top bureaucrats to rush to mass media for projecting a proper image. The ICS corps, now fast dwindling, produced allies and accomplices in politicians. The new officer corps, despite its contamination by the ICS, is ruthless, tough, and has complete contempt for the politician. These are the people who are going to fill the vacuum created by the decline in economic and political power of the State. This new "caste" or "class" of people, conscious of their power and stakes, is the structural centre of the new power elite and political order in India. In contrast, the professional politician is the loser.

One of the most significant developments in recent years has been the growing divorce of Parliament, not only from its own functions of serious legislative deliberations, but also from the centres of power, even though its dominance on day-to-day politics may create an impression which is contrary to what it is. One indirect evidence of this contention is the total irrelevance of Parliament when it is not in session. Parliamentary debates reflect more of political alignments or loyalties between leaders and ideologies, both of which are becoming increasingly irrelevant, than any national policy considerations. There does not exist any committee system which in all other parliamentary systems is the centre of serious deliberations. Nor is there any alternative to that. Parliament may block decisions, put ministers in the dock, occasionally highlight some of the crucial national issues, but it does not affect the real centres of power. The only link between Parliament and the real centres of power are loosely knit lobbies which cut across all sorts of spectacular divisions and adapt or shape themselves to conflicts and balances outside the framework of Parliament. It is largely an illusion that in the present Parliament there is a Government party and there is an opposition, both evenly balanced, as given by the distribution of seats between two sides of the Lok Sabha. In fact, most of the opposition parties and groups are paired with different groups constituting the Congress Party. That is why the real strength of the Prime Minister must not be judged alone from the majority in the ruling party but from both sides of Parliament. Whereas in other democracies power and initiative have gradually shifted to the executive, in India the shift is away from the executive and Parliament, within the executive from political leaders to the bureaucracy or administration. A multi-party system is supposed to provide a check on the power of the bureaucracy. To some extent the post-Nehru party system has done so, as was reflected in the deflation of the Planning Commission and public sector bureaucracy. However, this check was not direct and came in the wake of the regional distribution of power through which the new party system worked systematically. Central bureaucracy has devolved powers to the States' bureaucracy and not to any one else outside itself. Whatever shift of power towards the political executive that took place in Nehru's time has now been all but dissipated.

Every polity rests or functions on some balance between a few major macro power variables. For example, in the U.S.A., the balance is between the Pentagon, the President, the Congress, big corporations, etc. In India no durable balance has yet emerged. During Nehru's rule, some sort of balance seemed to emerge under Nehru's charisma between the bureaucracy, political executive, business, and Left forces in general. Since his death the political

Strategy of Static Balance

executive has lost predominant power whereas the two remaining variables, the bureaucracy and the business, have emerged most powerful and lasting. The only new factor to emerge is the power of the States' political executive. The military bureaucracy has multiplied itself several fold but the degree of its politicization is very low yet. For quite some time the military as a factor of power will remain behind the wings unless some other force becomes rash enough to politicize it by invoking its support. Another new factor to emerge is the lobbies—both inside and outside the Parliament. Many of them cancel each other, but all of them put together seem to fill that danger zone existing between the Government and the ruling party. It seems that in the Centre, of all factors of power, the most powerful to emerge is the civil bureaucracy although its internal cohesion and self-awareness have not yet been fully realized.

One of the most stabilizing factors in the Indian polity today is the highly streamlined local power structure at the district and all other levels below it. In fact, by and large, the Congress Party at the local level is nothing but the local power structure itself as an aggregation of dominant castes, dominant economic groups, and other active elements in the society. The power structure runs parallel to the district administration as well as in partnership with it. Any military take-over in this country is rendered improbable in the face of this vastly expanded local power structure. But the civil bureaucracy will find it a most natural ally. A civilian dictatorship will not have to upset any part of the existing local structure in order to rule and get things done.

The only hurdle in the way of civilian dictatorship is the new power acquired by the States' political executives. If, however, the latter goes the way the central political executive has gone, and there is no guarantee that it would not, the process of political control passing on to the bureaucracy will be complete. The present political balance or imbalance between a weak Centre and strong States is unworkable and is increasingly becoming dysfunctional. It is only a matter of time before the States' bureaucracy emerges as the last and inevitable link in this chain of a new power system. A few more SVD-type Governments in the States will complete the chain. In such a situation it would not matter who remains the Prime Minister, Mrs. Gandhi or somebody else. The Prime Minister's position and authority will always remain precarious because there is no certainty about the existence of the power and effectiveness of any political institution, including Parliament.

The emergence of an overpowering, self-aggrandizing, and power-centred bureaucracy interfering and conducting the business of the nation does not appear to many as an inevitable finale to the internal dynamics of a static structure of power. The ruling bureaucracy in India is far from homogenous. Inter-bureaucratic conflicts are not unknown. The class, caste, and status differentiation and the inability to communicate or take responsibility at crucial moments go against its emergence into a supreme power. The very high social status the bureaucracy enjoys may be unlikely to persuade it to topple the system which bestows that status. The existence of a multi-party system is another barrier to its efforts to collect power over and above the heads of politicians. Even a bigger barrier than that is the decentralization of political power to States and from there right up to the Panchayat level. To some degree, policy-making and its administration are vitally separated. It is also a fact of life that the bureaucracy in India has developed the characteristics of reproducing within itself many of the basic political conflicts which characterize the contemporary political system in India. The efficiency of our bureaucracy is not a proven fact. On the contrary, it has not developed sufficiently any of the Webrian attributes such as responsibility, rationality, impartiality, achievement orientation, specialization, discipline, professionalization, hierarchy, etc., without which no bureaucracy can really become efficient. Although Indian bureaucrats are recruited on merit, they behave as if they are part of a spoil system. At every level where the bureaucracy has overriding power, its capacity to legitimize itself has not been a success story. As a modernizing force, it has also not revealed itself as of great relevance; at places, bureaucrats have been found to be as deeply steeped in obscure traditions as the worst of traditionalists. Last but not least, the emergence of a large middle class, the character and tradition of the Congress Party, the impact of the ICS, growth of strong local centres of power, particularly at the States level, etc., may all appear to provide checks on the power of bureaucracy.

Nonetheless, it is not realistic to stick to this Kafkaian image of bureaucrats and their cynicism. Despite the aforementioned barriers to its assuming dictatorial powers, the bureaucracy may be pushed into this role by the vacuum created by the political processes analyzed earlier. Our bureaucracy is getting increasingly involved in political processes at all levels, more effectively and brazenly in some. In fact, we never had at any stage a strictly neutral and instrumental bureaucracy. Its decisions always had large undertones of policy. These forces, resting on a static power structure and a low-level economic and political development which today effectively checks the power of the bureaucracy, may intervene decisively to get the society back on the path of political stability, for the country cannot live for long with the forces of economic and political decline. In the absence of any other political force performing this task of national regeneration, the burden will fall on the bureaucracy. As a powerful integrative factor, the bureaucracy will have to be increasingly relied upon to fight the divisive forces because the political processes as such have become divisive and disintegrating. The decline of the political executive's power will remove the major obstacle in the way of bureaucratic dictators. Political decentralization in India has been carried out without the corresponding decentralization of the bureaucracy and this gap will work against democratic forces and in favour of bureaucrats. Besides factions, groups and interests constituting the contemporary unlimited pluralism of India have more and more come to seek power and influence by clustering around the bureaucracy whose decisions have acquired significant political content and leverage in all major political developments. This is more true of business interests than others. The new consensus emerging between the Government and the business, as is seen in their common outlook on planning and other economic policies, is the handiwork of bureaucrats. Business has found perfect allies in new bureaucrats; so have almost all the major elements of the local power structure. The struggle between the Centre and the States and its resolution is carried on by the respective bureaucracies which have built up for their own safety some sort of a combination to defeat politicians at both levels. Without attributing to bureaucracy any of the desirable characteristics such as imagination, judgment, capacity for abstraction and generalization, good leadership, super-intelligence, etc., one can see clearly that, along with the military bureaucracy, it remains, of all others, the most coherent element in the national power structure. It is a massive and a compelling generalization, but nonetheless seems true.

It may appear that it is by default on the part of democratic political forces that the bureaucracy may seize power. But appearances in this case are not deceptive. Political leaders, parties, and groups have all but abdicated their functions and roles for carrying on the business of the nation above a certain critical minimum level. The growing contempt for politicians has created among millions the urge and desire for change towards either limited pluralism or authoritarianism. The former choice is still open to political forces, but it may not remain so far long. The rise of the bureaucracy to power will certainly destroy the sort of strategy Mrs. Gandhi has evolved for its obvious unoperational character. It can be argued that Mrs. Gandhi may change her own strategy when such a change is forced upon her. But then the bureaucracy may not need her as an ally.

Finally, let us turn to external factors. Irrespective of its other consequences, the policy of nonalignment or one of equidistance between the great powers insulated for a long time the ruling leadership of India from those pressures which the hostility of or alliance with one or the other power would have entailed. At times the balance tilted in one direction but only to be pulled back to the other. That insular position no longer exists. The Americans today have probably the lowest ever leverage in this country whereas the Russians have the maximum, so much so that it is no longer relevant to talk in terms of tilting the balance. The Russians have a much firmer grip on Indian politics via their controlling the terms of defence supplies. The Americans have, on the other hand, gradually allowed themselves to be nudged out, first because of their preference for Pakistan and subsequently because of their preoccupation with Vietnam and internal disorders. Today it has become impossible for Mrs. Gandhi, no matter how much she tries on her own, to extricate this country from the Russians. It is also unlikely that the Americans, with their international position retrieved and the renewed Nixonian confidence, will sit idle. They should be relied upon to tighten their hold and expand it, at least to match the Russians. It is not absolutely necessary for the two super-powers to come to a clash in their respective attempts to expand their influence or tutelage in India. They may carve out their respective areas of operation. Whatever they do, whether clash or cooperate, the position of the Prime Minister of a considerably weakened Centre will grow still further uncertain and weaker if not subservient. Mrs. Gandhi may, in the end, be the only Prime Minister acceptable to both the super-powers. But that would be so much the worse for her. One obvious conclusion is that the entire strategy of Mrs. Gandhi is inconsistent with remaining in power as an independent Prime Minister. It also precludes any hope that after she has firmly established herself in power by defeating her rivals she would return to national issues.

December 1968

PART TWO

7

CRACKS IN THE INDIAN PARTY STRUCTURE

IN THE INDIA of today, it seems impossible to escape hearing statements such as "the country is disintegrating" or "we have never had it so bad," although occasionally someone somewhere is found painting the brighter side of things, but with much the same effect. It should be the easiest and, therefore, also the laziest way out to believe that the truth lies somewhere in the middle. Statements of this kind are apt to mislead although they are trite and no more than commonplace. However wide the belief might be that despite all efforts all of India's problems survive, the very first step of identifying the problems remains untackled. One can put one's finger on innumerable individual or smaller problems, but not so easily on the larger or national problems of which the smaller problems are corollaries. The purpose of this chapter is to attempt to identify just one such problem, namely, the problem of the party political stability and balance.

The fourth general elections disclosed two significant trends. Firstly, a near balance emerged between the voting strength of political parties and their respective legislative representation. The excess weightage or over-representation of the Congress Party, reflected in its holding for fifteen years three-fourths of the seats in Parliament and two-thirds in the State assemblies on the strength of less than half the total votes polled was largely, though not completely, removed.[1] Political defections to some extent

[1] In the 1967 general elections the Congress Party polled 40.73 per cent votes and won 279 seats out of a total of 515 seats in the Lok Sabha (Parliament). For the State assemblies, the corresponding figures are 40 per cent and 1,661 seats out of a total of 3,453 seats. (*Report*, Election Commission, Government of India, New Delhi, 1968, pp. 5-11, 107-13.)

further redressed that imbalance. Secondly, almost for the first time the role of the opposition changed dramatically from simply exercising vigilance over the ruling party to exercising power in some States. Both these trends would have been welcome as the prerequisites for a stable democracy in India, but for the contrary results they produced. The first yielded a totally fragmented party structure and the second resulted in a series of unstable and patchwork coalitions. The consequences have been disastrous. A year's political experience has provided the final affirmation of the earlier weak and confused tendency of the shift in the entire political power structure from stability to multiple crises.

National politics revolves around three inter-related and interdependent concepts: ideology, power, and pattern of action. These concepts become operational through the medium of national political parties. Partyless politics is not known to the world of today and anything that depreciates the power and role of parties depreciates national power and purpose. There are several indicators rudely reminding all parties that they are being alienated from politics and power and at all levels.

The first and foremost aspect of this alienation is the emergence of the tremendous and continuous political agitation "on the street." Issues do not matter: any issue is good enough to bring thousands of people of all classes on to the street, all too often resulting in an outbreak of violence. One or the other political party always backs the agitation as a part of its political strategy, which is openly or implicitly directed against some other political party, generally, though not necessarily, the ruling party. Often in a State the ruling party has itself indulged in this activity, contrary to its responsibilities as the gaurdian of law and order. Agitations launched by the DMK in Madras on the language issue, by the SSP in Uttar Pradesh on the abolition of land rent, by the Communists in West Bengal on *Gherao*[2] and against the Centre's food policy in Kerala are a few examples of this. Voters are bound to get disillusioned with such activity, because basically it changes

[2]*Gherao* is the storming of the management by the workers and forcibly keeping the former indoors until such time as the workers' demands are accepted.

nothing; the *status quo* continues, except that parties depreciate in quality, stature, and strength. Strangely enough, some parties appear to enjoy enormously their own decay, if not their internal splits; for, the more these parties get alienated from the voters, the greater is their reliance on violent populist agitation.

Two other significant ways in which parties have declined as effective instruments of power are (*a*) the shift from the national to regional parties, and (*b*) a further downward movement from the combined strength of national and regional parties to communal, caste, rural, and other splinter groups and factions.

There are three categories of political parties: (*i*) national or inter-State parties, which are seven in number; (*ii*) regional or one-State parties, sixteen in all; and (*iii*) scores of local caste parties, groups, factions and independents who are generally held together by a powerful local personality. The Election Commissioner recognizes the first two categories but not the third. A fact of considerable importance, often ignored, is that during the last general elections, the second and third categories cut into the strength of the first, together gaining 50 per cent more seats in Parliament and 80 per cent more in the various State assemblies. The third group, which operates outside the recognized party system, also improved its position: the independents alone nearly doubled their strength in Parliament and showed a 50 per cent gain in the State assemblies.[3]

Regional and communal parties overlap and their improved strength, such as we have discovered it to be, can be apportioned almost equally to the rise of communalism and regionalism. The Muslim and Sikh vote, particularly, has gone overwhelmingly in favour of the candidates of their respective communitites, cutting across parties at all levels. The magnitude of the caste influence has not been quantified yet but every micro-analysis has revealed its overriding importance, the more so in the State and local elections.

[3]*Seminar* (Monthly), New Delhi, June 1967.
It is quite surprising that Professor Myron Weiner, writing as he does well after the last elections, should base his analysis on outdated facts. The results of those elections are at variance with his statement, "it would be accurate to say that personal leadership in India is being replaced by party leadership." (*State Politics in India*, Princeton, 1968, p. 40.)

Again, in almost every party, including the Communists, there is a growing divergence between the politically established top and the insecure and politically active base. Persons in the latter, for sheer survival, are inevitably driven to find their own pattern of action such as factionalism and deviant localism which are often subversive of the party pattern and discipline. As a result of this divergence, no relevant functional relation exists between political orientation and political behaviour.[4]

To all intents and purposes, the Indian party system functions today without any systematic set of policies, although, on the surface, a semblance of conflict between ideologies is artificially kept up. Parties which seem to be locked in ideological warfare are really engaged in shadow boxing rather than in serious argument of principle. Not only are the contradictions between the parties' respective principles and practices growing, but many parties can no longer be distinguished from each other by their professed ideologies. And yet, paradoxically, these days one hears a great deal about the need for like-minded parties coalescing, without anybody systematically identifying even two like-minded parties. It is quite significant that on the major issues which came up for debate in Parliament during the last two years, the Jana Sangh and the Swatantra—the two so-called most like-minded parties of the Right—were mostly at variance with each other. On the contrary, the Swatantra Party, while always demanding a ban on the Communists, found itself supporting them on issues in which, strangely enough, the ruling party had a large stake, such as the Presidential election, the position of the Prime Minister, Mrs. Indira Gandhi, Kashmir, Kutch, Nagaland, Fundamental Rights, and non-proliferation treaty. Parties are, by and large, either too doctrinaire or too opportunistic to leave much scope for ideological convergence, a necessary prerequisite for the growth of a healthy party system in a plural

---

[4]Down below at the State level, parties gradually cease to be of any continuous operational value; non-party politics so completely takes over as to make parties the object and not the instrument of activity. Also local groups which capture parties are largely unconcerned about what national or other policies parties profess. The more easily a party goes traditional, the more surely can it rely on local support. This phenomenon may be described as the fundamental recession of parties.

society of infinite complexity. It is not surprising, therefore, that the rapid politicization of the society, brought about essentially by political parties, has been accompanied by an equally rapid growth of a feeling of contempt for politics, so much so that the entire political activity appears more contingent than necessary. Parties are getting increasingly alienated from the masses, not so much for what they say or do but for the infuriating divergence between their professions and their deeds.

It may be an exaggeration to say that Indian democracy can be run only by supermen, but it is not incorrect to say that at the head of each party there must obtain a determined leadership to keep together the various pressure groups constituting the party. In India, the leadership represents the consensus in that party. The Nehruvian consensus, which broke down with Nehru's demise, had two qualities. It kept in check the fundamental ideological cleavages of our time; it also helped to force numerous competitive pressure groups in a party to converge. However, this consensus never took deep roots. After Nehru it was replaced by a general dissensus and politics of power without policies. This displacement was mostly responsible for the intensification of inter-party conflicts or party in-fighting.

The crisis of leadership and political defections, which is so much talked about, is a reflection of this dissensus. For two decades, the in-fighting of the Congress Party was conducted, part in name and part in substance, on alternative programmes of differing groups, factions, and leaders. Each opposition party in the country was paired with one or the other faction in the Congress. This situation no longer exists, indeed the situation has been reversed. Now, it is the turn of the Congress to look for allies in the opposition as a hedge against defections from its own ranks. In this state of affairs, the parties have come to lose their coherence and identity.

The crisis of leadership is also a reflection of the fact that political parties, particularly the Congress Party, lack organizational effectiveness. The parties neither have a properly organized hierarchical structure nor is their leadership controlled by their respective rank and file. In the latter sense, no party in India is truly democratic. A hierarchical structure, like the one Nehru had evolved, imparts immense prestige to the leadership, whereas the exercise of control by the lower ranks is likely to bring with it grass-root support for an accepted programme as well as an increased sense of responsibility and loyalty for furthering the party's goals. Unfortunately, Nehru acted more like the Grand Moghal than either as a political administrator or as an organization man. Although he gave a contrary impression, the model he actually chose was rather that of an historical bureaucratic empire than that of a modern efficient political organization. Between an alienated secular aristocracy and political priesthood he exhausted the type of leaders which he collected around himself. Like all such attempts before him, Nehru's patrimonial administration, personalized leadership, and political infeudation failed to take roots and the monopoly of power of the Congress Party gradually broke down and was followed by a near-collapse of the control mechanism within the party. Other parties' respective organizations were seriously affected by what happened in the Congress, so much so that the older structure of control in all parties became so amorphous that it no longer operated within their respective organizations. Today's political parties are generally not trusted because their leaders are not trusted, and this is not surprising when leaders leave their parties at the slightest provocation. Consequently, the party system has continued to depreciate and has become unstable and dysfunctional.

Party instability also arises from a major contradiction between the unitary character of the parties and the federal structure of the polity in which the parties seek to capture power. For 17 years, this contradiction was abridged, if not partially resolved, by a powerful national leadership and by the same party holding office simultaneously both at the Centre and in the States. Both these situations have now changed. The rise of regionalism and the consequent conflicts between the Centre and the States have profoundly disturbed the unity of every party, including monolithic parties like the Communist Party, and of the nation. The party most seriously affected, of course, is the Congress although all the seven national parties are more or less victims of this contradiction.

For example, some time or the other the Congress in Madras, Kerala, and West Bengal, the Swatantra in Gujarat and Bihar, the SSP almost anywhere and everywhere, and the Jana Sangh in all the Southern States have had to face this contradiction without any success. And whenever a party has tried to expand its influence and power in more States, as was recently attempted by the Jana Sangh, it has been obliged to lose its character, its face, and to jeopardize its programme. This is a cruel and double contradiction and yet it forms such an essential part of Indian political life that any attempt towards acquiring national status compels a party to become less programmatic and vice versa; in its attempt to unify itself, a national party runs the risk of being reduced to a regional party.

In the last elections the defeat of the Congress Party in some States was almost entirely due to its inability to allow the State Congress parties to deviate from such central policies as impinged largely on those very States. Had the Congress allowed freedom of action to its respective units in Madras on the language issue, in Kerala on economic reforms, in Punjab on State's reorganization, it is doubtful if the party would have had to face the debacle that it did. In not one of these States was the Congress vote much smaller than its national average. In general, therefore, the parties' inability to resolve the contradiction between their unitary structure and federal responsibilities has taken them one step further in their alienation from power.[5]

[5]Professor Myron Weiner barely mentions this problem and where he does, he argues to the contrary. He writes: "There are structural incompatibilities in having a centralized party structure function in a federal system with the result that over the years the State party units have become increasingly autonomous and the central units have become increasingly unable to control subordinate bodies." (*State Politics in India*, p. 20.) Without denying that the State party units keep struggling for autonomy, I find that practically no State unit of the Congress Party has been able to run counter to the Congress Party's centrally adopted policies. It is the lack of this autonomy in policies which has really made the State units suffer defeat. Of course, there is a large measure of autonomy exercised by the State units in many matters of importance. Weiner seems to confuse the growing autonomy of the State Governments, which is a fact, with that of the State parties, which is not yet so.

There is no particular virtue in having only one or two parties, although many a bipolarist would like to see only two parties in India, one completely Right-wing and the other Left-wing. Nowhere else has such bipolarity really worked; it is indeed an invitation to start a civil war in India. Besides, a multi-party system seems more appropriate for a large plural society. However, in two essential ways party fragmentation in India can be distinguished from a competitive, multi-party system. First, the number of Indian parties is becoming so large as to make the manning of Government increasingly difficult. Besides seven inter-State and sixteen one-State parties, there are several other local parties, largely illusory, shifting, and unidentifiable. Indeed, every independent candidate for Parliament constitutes a party because behind him or her stand a cluster of local caste, communal, linguistic, or other groups. Second, the more significant character of party fragmentation in our country today is that no party is able to improve its position in relation to others without increasing this fragmentation and, therefore, without diminishing the sum-total of the power of them all. This is a stark fact in the present political position which alienates parties not only from one another but also from the total national power.

In the last elections, the Congress Party failed to secure a majority in six States—West Bengal, Kerala, Madras, Punjab, Orissa, and Delhi. In the first two States, the Left parties and in the last two the Right parties defeated the Congress. In Madras and Punjab, the regional parties came out victorious. Subsequently, the three States of Uttar Pradesh, Madhya Pradesh, and Haryana were lost due to defections in the Congress ranks.[6] Excepting the DMK in Madras and the Jana Sangh in Delhi, no party was able to secure an absolute majority in the other States, and coalitions had to be formed of almost all the non-Congress parties, ranging from the Left Communists to Swatantra, on the basis of some quickly improvised common minimum programme. Except in Orissa and Kerala, the break-up of these coalitions, soon after their formation, showed that these were incoherent and hastily patched up, and,

[6]The Congress won back the State of Haryana in the mid-term poll held in May 1968.

properly speaking, not coalitions at all. These represented desperate attempts on the part of fragmented parties to capture the shadow—only the shadow—of power.

Any serious analysis of the structure of coalition parties in India today can be made only within the frame-work of the fragmentation of parties which is characterized by the following.

Firstly, the components of all State coalitions are only sectional or regional parties, lacking national perspective and strategy. Being sectional or regional parties, they look inward for support to narrow groups and are not subject to strong pressures for assimilation into the national political culture. Localism dominates their tactics so very much that it is difficult to find any consistent pattern of support to them from one State to another, from one class to another, from one caste to another.

Secondly, lack of consensus and ideological coherence is more pronounced in them than in the Congress, even though political differences between some of them are as little as between tweedledum and tweedledee. Separateness is more basic to them than relatedness.

Thirdly, most coalescing parties can be described as factional or personal political parties, i.e. they are less held together by any effective common programme and organizational norms than by the personality of a leader or the lure of office and the spoils of power. These parties cannot be said to have consistent and exclusive appeal to specific groups and classes because of the low level of integration of the general social structure and party system in the country.

Fourthly, these parties are not unified at any level of Government. Being in power at one place and in opposition at another, and without any of them having been called upon to bear national responsibility, they often take absurdly contradictory stands. By contrast, the Congress, despite being in office and in opposition, is generally more consistent except when faced by contradictions which arise as a byproduct of the in-fighting among its leaders.

Fifthly, the present coalitions do not provide an inclusive category in which relations between parts change for a better integration of interests and maximizing policy effectiveness. In fact, a host of primary groups, in one or the other party, have no fixed determinate loyalties. The same is true, though not to the same degree, of the Congress—hence, the defections.

Sixthly, largely because many of these parties came into existence in response to the arrogance and corruption in the Congress Party, but without definite alternative programmes or any decisive mandate from the electorate, they together with the Congress have reduced the effectiveness of our parliamentary and other institutions. The Indian Parliament remains a constitutional instrument, but no longer the real focal point of power; deadlock and non-decision making have increasingly become its characteristics.

These characteristics to a smaller or greater degree are common in all the opposition parties and add to a powerful force, making the structure of coalitions a byproduct as well as the mainstay of instability. This instability cuts across both the Right and the Left dominated coalitions. Each party attempts to improve its position at the cost of some other coalescing party, though not necessarily at the cost of the Congress, despite the fact that the prospects of defeating the Congress depend upon their working jointly and not severally. That is why the coalition Governments are plagued more by internal conflicts than by external subversion from the Congress. They can collapse under their own weight, as indeed some of them already have.

This particular dialectics of the inter-party struggle has created a peculiar psychosis. No political party today feels unconditionally viable in the sense that it cannot be destroyed as an independent decision-maker. This is a warning against putting too much faith in the coalitions of opposition parties. They inevitably belong to the politics of fragmentation in which fragments are caught in the dynamics of a life-and-death struggle and are largely impervious to the fate of the aggregate. These parties lack proper consensus, shared organizational norms, effective coordination, and concerted effort.

Nonetheless, despite their negative-oriented coalescing and defiance of every rule of political logic, it would be wrong to expect an early ending of coalition Governments. On the contrary, the 1967 elections in general undoubtedly ushered in an era of coalitions as a new factor or institution of power. Coalitions may be formed or broken but inevitably one set would be followed by another—with the occasional rule by a puppet party in the interregnum—given the present political spectrum. "Coalitionism" is the institutionalization of the fundamental drift from the concentration of power to its decentralization. The opposition parties' passion for a fixed enemy reveals their tortuous groping for new alignments and moves for a better place in politics.

There is one other crucial feature of the coalition parties which is often ignored but has the utmost relevance for future. Many of these parties are constantly drawn towards the gravitational pull of the Congress. In relation to one another and in relation to the Congress Party, they are being repelled or attracted, in ceaseless friction, by the Congress magnet. Thus, several parties or groups within the non-Congress coalition provide the second line of defence for the Congress, despite their overt violence and negativism against it. Indira Gandhi's gathering of strength and capacity to check possible revolt within the Congress Party against her rests largely on this second line of defence. This paradox constitutes the essence of contemporary Indian politics as well as a pointer to future. The other arm of this paradox is the inability of the Congress Party to resolve its own internal contradictions, to become more coherent and to act responsibly as a functioning party in the national interests. But a solid coherent Congress Party will lose its magnetic force.

However, as argued earlier, any relative shift of power between the non-Congress coalitions and the Congress, consequent upon the struggle for power between them, need not necessarily take place at the cost of each other but may be reacted at the cost of the national political power. In other words, a situation of growing power vacuum may develop, and it certainly has. There is large and unmistakable evidence of the fact that the unpopularity of coalition Governments is not accompanied by any increased popularity of the Congress Party. The logical outcome of this mutually frustrating struggle is a still further decline of the Congress in the next elections, without the gains of the opposition being disturbed in such a way as to result in more stable coalitions. The distribution is rather likely to favour the independents or small groups, which are grouped around caste clusters or areas of localized dominance.

It appears that the Congress Party, in its desperation to dissolve coalitions, is ceasing to be the real solvent of coalitions and is heading straight towards itself becoming a coalition Party. This may sound rather strange in view of the "quit notice" that it served on the opposition at the Hyderabad session.[7] But a moment's reflection can show that if the Congress Party breaks up coalitions and gets back to power with all the functionless old apparatus of its poor organization and hopelessly out-of-date policies—there is no indication that it is changing in these respects—nothing can stop its further decline. Even assuming that massive efforts will be made to regenerate the Congress, it does not require a shift away from the Congress of more than 3-4 per cent votes in the next election to reduce the party to a minority. Certainly, those opposition parties which largely eshewed electoral alliances during the last elections, but have also tasted blood since, are unlikely to make the same mistake again.

All trends point towards many more unstable coalitions emerging from the existing or new party fragmentations until such time as the Congress Party agrees upon entering into coalitions with other parties in the States in which it has not got the absolute majority. The Congress has so far avoided taking this step because, to be logical, it will have to reconcile itself to the idea of a similar coalition at the Centre—where it has got the majority—of parties with which it seeks to coalesce in the States. Such a decision cannot be easily arrived at, for the division of power in the Congress at the Centre is based on such a balance of weakness as would make any further division, through a coalition, unacceptable to the existing sharers of power.

There is also the other possibility. If the Jana Sangh, a Right-wing mass party, seriously moves and attempts to change itself from a regional to a national party, as it did at its last annual session at Calicut, we may get two large, essentially Centrist, coalitions facing each other, one slightly left of the centre around

[7]*Hindustan Times*, 8 January 1968.

the Congress and the other more or less to the right of the centre around the Jana Sangh. If there is any truth in the dictum that chaos creates its own order, then this is probably the most likely polarization one can anticipate in the midst of existing instability and fragmentation. In the absence of either of these possibilities materializing, cracks in the Indian party system will get larger and become more menacing.

December 1968

8

CENTRE-STATE RELATIONS

THESE DAYS it has become fashionable to demand the transfer of power from the Centre to the States. Once it was only the addicts to the concept of "freedom first" who had reviled the concentration of power in the hands of the State. Now the protagonists for decentralization are spread over a wide spectrum, from extreme Right to extreme Left, though it is seldom clearly specified which power is to be decentralized? Political, economic, or purely financial, or all of them! When the chips are down, all that the State Governments seem to demand is financial re-allocation of national revenues in their favour.

In a general way the argument *per se* for any radical financial devolution loses much of its weight when it is pointed out that between 1951-52 and 1966-67 the proportion of States' shared taxes and grants-in-aid to their total resources has increased from 22 per cent to 37 per cent and, in absolute terms, from Rs. 87 crores to Rs. 761 crores. If in these statistics we add central loans given to the States, the ratio increases from 29 per cent to 50 per cent and magnitudes from Rs. 160 crores to over Rs. 1,450 crores. The overall resources of the States increased five times and those of the Centre almost six times, whereas the central assistance to the States increased nine times. No one can say that this is a small measure of financial transfers to the States.

Today the combined resources of the States and the Centre are evenly balanced and it appears that if past trends of gradual transfer of resources from the Centre are maintained—there is no policy yet in sight that may reverse them, except the sheer lack of finance itself—in a decade or so the scale would decisively be tipped in favour of the States. For some years now, the Centre's own revenues and expenditures have become extremely inelastic and thus any re-classification of revenue heads on the principle of elasticity will be operatively meaningless. The central Government has been left with little manoeuvrability to re-allocate resources in any new direction because it just cannot augment resources any more until the growth rate picks up once again in the non-agricultural sector. Ironically, or not quite so, it is in such a static framework—and *static* is the word—that political pressures for re-allocation are mounted against the central Government which today has neither policy nor guts left to take decisions on any rational principles. With a continuing shift in the national income in favour of agriculture, it is the States' resources which should, presumably, acquire elasticity. The States, however, are unwilling to oblige the country for obvious political reasons.

There is no particular economic virtue in having one or the other ratio of the overall division of resources between the Centre and the States, unless it can be shown that such a ratio is justified on grounds of functional responsibility, efficiency, optimality, or any other criterion. These criteria are violated totally by the Centre as well as the State Governments. One could go a step further and say that whatever the ratio, the entire financial arrangement is archaic, incomprehensible, and damaging. Hence, the argument has to be carried to the field of politics and economics, particularly of economic planning. It cannot be gainsaid that the degree of economic mismanagement and political dysfunctionalism of the polity has reached frightening proportions. The State Governments as much as the central Government, the public sector as well as the private sector, are equally responsible for bringing about this sorry state of affairs.

Protagonists of States' power have appropriately drawn attention to the danger of the rise of private oligarchies. They, however, fail to show how the modification of the existing financial position will lead to their elimination. Nor do they care to juxtapose private oligarchies with their public counterparts. These are crucial questions because big business has not only ceased to be an engine of growth, but has become as powerful a determinant of the State politics as of politics at the Centre.

Anyone looking at the vast, sprawling, inefficient, and corrupt bureaucracy is bound to plump for decentralization as a way out.

But the problem of making institutions function effectively and honestly is different from dismantling them. Every modern State has a bureaucracy; we cannot possibly do without one. Also, no socialist with a conscience can support the sort of public sector that has come in the wake of the Five-Year Plans, notwithstanding bright patches here and there. And yet the public sector is a must. Besides its being inefficient, disorganized, and burdening the whole economy with inflationary costs, the public sector does not fulfil the important functions attributed to it.

First, it no longer reaches the commanding heights of the economy, if indeed it has not already slipped into a position at the rear. It does not generate the type and amount of surpluses which would have made it self-sustained. Second, contrary to expectation, it is not at all a bulwark against private oligarchies. In fact, private and public oligarchies, presided over by a powerful bureaucracy and dithering leadership of the Congress, have joined in a conspiracy to hold the nation to ransom. Every socialist should remember his first lesson on socialism: State capitalism is a doubled-edged weapon; it can clear the decks for a socialist transformation or degenerate into a position of total subversience to the private sector. It is a matter of politics, not of economics. What needs full emphasis here is that the public sector at the States' level is no better than that at the central level. Nobody can seriously argue in favour of the States' public sector as a countervailing force against private oligarchies.

The case for the public sector is one of utter economic necessity. Its problems are completely different from those emanating from any new scheme of re-allocation between the Centre and the States, namely, norms, efficiency, and autonomy in management. Any major shift in it towards the States, not necessitated by functional imperatives, will not only cause widespread dislocation but also put a premium on inefficiency and greater political interference. Only one set of private oligarchies will be substituted by another; probably it will be the same oligarchies changing patrons. On the side of the private sector, the Government having once created monopolies cannot make them behave like competitive firms; they have to be abolished. It is not clear how the State Governments are going to control or abolish monopolies. There is a greater possibility of the monopolies controlling the State Governments themselves instead of being controlled by the latter. To make a distinction between the national bourgeoisie and the State bourgeoisie is a pseudo-Marxist myth. Today, every State Government, whether of Left or Right persuasion, is more than anxious to invite the so-called national bourgeoisie to invest capital in that State. The real distinction is between big business, on the one hand, and medium and small business, on the other.

Therefore, if the problem is one of establishing economic and administrative norms, fulfilling functional responsibilities, and providing political determination to carry out these tasks, one must look a little deeper into the processes of political balance and imbalance in the polity—particularly between the Centre and the States—before any new division of powers is even suggested.

Division of political power in a society depends very little on its Constitution, though constitutional restraints are important. It depends upon the party system, pressure groups, political mobilization, economic strength, elite position, and a host of the other factors. The history of all modern societies may readily be understood as the history of the enlargement and concentration of the means of power in economic, military, and administrative institutions. The rise of the nation-State, industrialization, development of the means of production, and institutionalization of the means of coercion led to the centralization of power. In the West, this process was slow and was spread over for a long period. In the Soviet Union it was accelerated and encapsuled in a much shorter span of time. It is only now that these countries have begun to look into the need for decentralization and removal of regional disparities—the problems in which the Indian polity is prematurely caught.

The first decade of our Independence was characterized by a degree of concentration that was forced upon India by the exigencies of economic and political development. Then it came to a halt, and subsequently it was reversed much before the critical minimum of centralization had been achieved. To some extent this reversal was one of the factors that slowed down the rate of economic growth. And as the growth rate declined, the States' demand for political and economic power correspondingly increased. It was like a vicious circle. Often loud protestations are raised against the Centre's dictation of the States through its grants and loans policies. How is one to locate this dictation? In fact, the contrary is more true. The Centre today cannot impose a single piece of economic policy on any State, not to speak of forcing it on all States. It cannot but just acquiesce in the States' demands within the overall limits set by resource availability. Food policy is a case in point. No one would seriously believe Peter Pan version of the States bubbling with a desire to initiate economic development.

The trend towards the shift of power from the Centre to the States began during Nehru's lifetime. Nehru increasingly came to rely on the personal loyalty of strong Chief Ministers instead of institutionalizing the loyalty between the office of the Prime Minister and that of a Chief Minister. These State satraps, in turn, consolidated their power, by all legal and illegal means, virtually taking over the States' administration and the Congress Party organizations, ignoring the Centre's and the AICC's directives on policies which did not suit them and their supporters. Nehru later realized the danger but it was too much for him to reverse the process.

The shift in political power to the States was as much the cause as the product of the widening contradictions between the professed policies of the party, largely enunciated by Nehru, and the structure of the Congress Governments and parties in the States. Ultimately, these contradictions engulfed the Centre also, almost completely after Nehru's death. For example, the National Development Council became more decisive than the Planning Commission in the making of economic policies and programmes of the Centre and the States. Chief Ministers' conclaves became more important than the Central Cabinet. The Chief Ministers' power was never more decisively deployed than in the election of Mrs. Gandhi. The abdication of the Congress High Command in favour of its State committees for selecting candidates not only for the assemblies but also for Parliament further marked the rise to power of States' satraps at the level of party organization. Finally, at the Centre a bifactional or multifactional situation became more and more a reflection of opposing alignments in the States rather than of different ideological standpoints.

The internal power structure of the Congress was profoundly affected by these developments which now have emerged in the form of Centre-States imbalance. It is not true to say that the emergence of non-Congress Governments has created this imbalance and the conflict over the division of power between the Centre and the States. It is a legacy of the past. Today, it is the Congress-run State Governments which thwart any centralized policy on economic and financial matters. It seems that current pressures and strains on the financial strength of the Centre arise from the fact that while political power has shifted much, financial power has lagged behind. This contradiction can be resolved either by the Centre regaining its political power or by abdicating its financial responsibility still further. Professor Gadgil, Chairman of the Planning Commission, unfortunately, is plumping for the latter solution.

There is one other aspect of the shift of real political power from the Centre, namely, fragmentation of parties and their growing alienation. There are several aspects of this development. Only two of these, relevant to the power equation between the Centre and the States, are mentioned here.

Two significant ways in which parties have declined as effective instruments of power are (*a*) the shift from the national to regional parties, (*b*) a further downward movement from the combined strength of national and regional parties to communal, caste, rural, and other splinter-groups and factions.

The aforementioned analysis leads to the simple conclusion that any further devolution of economic and financial power from the Centre to the States will only crystallize the existing political imbalance and acclerate the depreciation of the national power in the country. In any large country, particularly in a federation, there is always a particular balance of forces on which the system rests for its stability and growth. The idea that a society is based on a balance of power requires us to assume that the units in balance are of equal power and that they are truly independent. We cite two examples. In the USA the balance exists between (*i*) the military, (*ii*) the business corporations, and (*iii*) the executive-legislative institutions. In the USSR the balance of power is maintained between (*i*) the party, (*ii*) the public sector bureaucracy, and (*iii*) the military. China is struggling yet to build a new type of balance in which it appears the army will become an irrevocable power factor. In India, the real balance never came to be established at any permanent level. Whatever balance, or semblance of it, existed during Nehru's era has disappeared. We cannot identify what units in the power balance will finally emerge. For the foreseeable future, if the present trends of a fast deteriorating political and economic situation continue, the only balance that can be stabilized at the Centre is between the inevitable military force of a million men and a politically powerful central Government.

Looking backward one cannot fail to notice that this was the sort of balance Nehru was anxious to avoid until such time as new forces developed through popular democracy. If the Centre becomes politically and economically a weaker force, there is nothing to stop the military from first becoming an autonomous factor of political power and then, probably, taking over in any situation of national emergency. The military will find in the bureaucracy, private and public oligarchies, willing allies or junior partners but certainly not the countervailing forces which could create a new balance of power. India must have strong, dynamic executive-legislative organs at the Centre to balance the growth of military power until such time as new functional units of power emerge. A period of twenty years is the minimum required for this balance between the two units to transform itself into any other balance. The States must realize that their asking for a weak Centre would amount to their committing political suicide. Economic and political power must be first functionally centralized in good measure and for quite some time before decentralization is taken up. A functionless division of power will be an exercise in futility.

It was argued in the preceding paragraph that the States can grow strong only when the Centre also is strong, and in a dynamic setting. In a static situation any positive shift in the relative strength and power of the States will take place only at the cost of the sum total of the power of both, that is by the depreciation of the total national power. Such depreciation will inevitably lead to a balance of weakness and power vacuum, which could be filled by military dictatorship or by some external force.

We return now to the economic and financial implications of decentralization. Here we are faced with not one but two sets of problems, namely, problems between the Centre and the States and those between one State and another in which the Centre is indirectly but inevitably concerned. Let us clear the second problem first.

It is often ignored that power weightage *between* States is an important determining factor of Centre-States relations. This factor has unfortunately been submerged in the more heady political tussle between the Centre and the non-Congress States. In a federal system with constituent units unevenly developed, large fiscal inequalities will appear so long as their fiscal capacities are not equal. The burden of taxes and standards of public services will differ from State to State. It is also natural that industrialization, specialization, and integration of economy on the principle of optimal utilization of resources should tend to concentrate high income groups in certain specific areas. Such developments took place in the West also but then their Governments stood largely outside the process. In India, Government at all levels are heavily involved in the problem of inter-regional and inter-personal disparities which impinge heavily on the division of political power. Without a high rate of economic growth and some common goals being highlighted, it would be impossible to modify this new political factor which is otherwise purely economic.

If redressing the imbalance between States is allotted a high priority, only a strong and not a weak Centre can carry out this task by re-allocation of resources. A weak Centre is tantamount to having no Centre and thus leaving the rich States grow richer and at a faster rate than the weak States, widening the regional and spatial disparties. The Centre must have enough political powers and economic and financial leverages in the States if it is to be an effective arbiter for eliminating spatial distortions.

Truly, the problem of spatial imbalances is not so much between one State and another as between different areas or sectors in the same State. For example, in Maharashtra, the districts of Bombay and Thana control about 80 per cent of the industrial income of the State. The rest of the State is as poor as any other. It has been rightly stressed by some that the Centre's efforts have so far been superficial in removing spatial distortions. Such efforts will become even more so if the Centre lacks the very power it needs to perform this function. For the present the question of redressing spatial distortions should be addressed to proper quarters, i.e. the States. However, within the limits of resource availability, the nation cannot afford to give a high priority to this problem. The tendency in the country to demand high priority for every problem lies at the root of the total distortion of priorities as originally adumberated in our plans for development.

One other problem can be cleared at this stage. If one of the objectives of decentralization is mass participation of ordinary people in the process of development, then the real problem is one of delegation of power and functions from the States to local bodies which have suffered neglect and brutal suppression at the hands of State bureaucracies and politicians. There are glaring cases of many local bodies which have had no elections for more than ten years.

Some States are so large and unwieldy that only a relationship of vassalage exists between State Governments and their respective local bodies. For example, instead of rationalizing and dynamizing their tax structure, the State Governments have been subjecting it to political expediency. Panchayats have been refused the transfer of land revenues to their jurisdiction. Some States have instead gone to the other extreme of abolishing this tax altogether. One crucial experience of decentralization has been its capacity to rake up all the social dirt in our rural areas, such as caste, communal, landlord oppression, etc. Social reforms must precede decentralization if the latter is to make some sense to the people.

Centralization of taxes and financial control are the inevitable results of federalization in growth, and not a function of a particular division of powers. In principle and constitutionally, the States in the American Federation had been given status and power unequalled anywhere else. Nonetheless nothing has been able to stop the centralization of economic and political power of the federal Government that resulted from industrialization, fiscal discipline, equity, and external exigencies.

It is often stated that the Indian Constitution divided the powers between the Centre and the States from a definite economic angle: it gave most sectors of flexible and growing revenues to the Centre, and sectors of rigid and low revenues to the States. There was once an element of truth in that assertion though today the boot is on the other foot. For example, in 1950-51 the share of three important taxes—customs, income tax, and corporation tax—constituted 73.4 per cent in total revenues of the Centre. That ratio drastically declined to 42 per cent in 1967-68. Only excise revenues have gone up and there is no particularly good economic reason why all the excises should remain with the Centre. However, it is no more than a big illusion to imagine that excises are an elastic tax revenue. The implications of these figures are: (i) the so-called flexibility of the Union Government's revenue heads is illusory in nature; (ii) heavy reliance on indirect rather than on direct taxes has led to reliance on inflationary methods of finance; (iii) and if now excises were to be transferred to the State list, without placing an overall limit on them as determined by consequential inflation, an anarchic situation would be created.

Ever since the emphasis shifted towards larger investments in agriculture, and relative shares of the national income moved in favour of agriculture, it is the States' revenue heads that have become more elastic with their tax base broadened. It is the States' refusal to mop up through taxation additional incomes from that growing base that has created a situation of perennial financial criess in the country. For lack of investment, the industrial growth has already slowed down to dangerously low levels. Besides, the States' tax heads related to areas where socio-economic reforms were most urgently needed. The States largely neglected this task. One cannot have it both ways: that States need resources for development at the grass-roots whereas necessary reforms at that level should be somebody else's responsibility.

During the years of a high rate of growth in India, the Centre was able to meet in good measure the economic demands of the States. Not unnaturally, perhaps, political pressures for the transfer of economic power from the Centre to the States coincided with the period of decline in economic growth. There is a strong correlation between the two. Once the economy is put back on the growth path and the Centre becomes politically strong, these pressures will get softened. In this respect there are three sets of problems which have bearing on the Centre-State relations.

(*i*) *Priorities and Policy-frame.* Federal planning requires of the Centre to make such macro decisions as would determine the priorities for the economy as a whole. At this stage planning decisions cannot be expected to take up the problem of spatial or interpersonal inequalities. Consumption-investment pattern, choice of techniques for all major projects, long-term and short-term growth path, allocation of investment funds between three or four major sectors, etc., are problems about which decisions can be taken only by an authority which is responsible for the country as a whole and not to any one or more States alone. The States cannot at all be made to sit in judgement on these decisions, though today it is the States which take these decisions through the National Development Council and also blame the Centre for taking wrong decisions. Once these priorities are determined, a policy-frame consistent with those priorities must be prepared and accepted. Once again a broad policy framework lies within the functional responsibility of the federal authority. Today, the States have become politically so powerful that they do not allow any systematic policy-frame to emerge and be effectively put through, because one or the other group of States do not find this policy politically popular. Not that the Centre has ever faithfully fulfilled its part of policy administration—both have been playing politics. Nevertheless, these contradictions between priorities and policies, if allowed to persist, will foredoom planning as sometimes they did in the past. How it will help to transfer more responsibilities to the States is not clear.

(*ii*) *Plan Implementation.* It is by and large true that the Centre proposes and State disposes. It is now commonly accepted that the Centre is so weak and dependent on the States for implementation that even nationally accepted policies can be easily sabotaged by the States. Administration of food distribution is the most glaring example of futility in plan implementation. The much dreaded "vertical federalism" in which, by controlling matching grants, the Centre was accused of dictating to the States has turned out to be a matter of lack of coordination of schemes at the appropriate level, a blackmail in reverse to extort grants from the Centre and a total distortion of priorities. Implementation is devoid altogether of any norms being fulfilled either by the Centre or by the States.

(*iii*) *Planning by Pressure Groups.* Apart from their mutual pressures on each other, the Centre and the States are respectively subjected to different types of pressures for making their plans for expenditure and resource mobilization. Partly the type of pressures exerted are built into the division of functions between the two. The functions of the State Governments are biased towards welfare activities much more than those of the Centre. Unfortunately, the new pressures and demands from the States on the Centre have an unduly large distributive bias to which the latter often yields. Consequently, the economy today has come to be pressurized by all sorts of distributive economic ideologies, leaving little scope for productive investment. The authorities at various levels seem to have lost nerve for planning investment and fulfilling productive obligations. For example, the new formulas for the distribution of central grants to States, evolved at the recent meeting of the National Development Council, only about 20 per cent is related to the productive or matching mobilizational performance of the States. The rest is based on no criteria of productivity at all. It seems that every new financial arrangement arrived at between the Centre and the States is politically oriented and anti-growth. Already, saving-investment levels have reached the lowest critical levels. Any further shift of resources towards the States under the existing political motivation holds gloomy prospects of growth potential. Such prospects will ultimately weaken the Centre as well as the States.

Invariably, the entire discussion or controversy on Centre-

State financial relations is restricted to revenues only; very little is ever said about the nature and pattern of expenditure. Every penny of the Centre and the States is today heavily, if not inviolably, committed to expenditures incurred in the past. A colossal amount of wasteful and dead-weight expenditure has been built into our fiscal structure, so much so that the non-development expenditure has come to acquire a momentum and a rate of growth of its own, which is much higher than that of development expenditure. The loss of fiscal manoeuvrability is attributable to the inability of governments, at all levels, to scrap, to re-allocate within a Government, or to transfer from one Government to another the expenditures already committed. There now exists a fundamental imbalance between the committed expenditures and the need for their rational re-allocation. This imbalance takes the form of crisis during periods of low growth and thus of inadequate resource mobilization.

The single most important factor responsible for this state of affairs has been the Planning Commission which encouraged vast extravagance in the name of grandiose plans or by giving financial teeth to statements of vague intentions, often outside its own priority system, whenever an extra bit of money was forthcoming. For example, one of the numerous damages that PL 480 imports have inflicted on the economy is the proliferation, through the use of counterpart funds, of economically irrelevant schemes, the deadweight of which will remain on the economy even after PL 480 imports cease. It is not at all a question of the Centre dictating to the States but one of stopping itself from pandering to their consumption-oriented demands as well as the demands of its own pressure groups. It is a question of adhering to predetermined priorities which now have become victim of *ad hocism* masquerading under the garb of planning. While it is right to suggest that the schemes the States are to implement should be based on independent resources and not be subject to the Centre's financial blackmail or bribery, it is more important that the control on actual plans and schemes must be as vigorous as demanded by the consistency and limitations set by the overall plan. To achieve this a strong and responsible Centre is needed, not a weak and dithering one.

It needs stressing again and again that the main task is one of determining the right kind of expenditure and not one of resources. Resources and their allocations are the camp-followers of the pattern and level of expenditures.

I suggest the following guiding principles for any future arrangement for Centre-State economic and financial relations.

First, a clear-cut statement of central and States' projects and schemes, within the strict limits of overall priorities, must be prepared by the Planning Commission on a functional bases. Any other expenditure—except that on defence—must be confined to an overall fixed limit or carried at the cost of some other non-development expenditure incurred in the past. An unambiguous distinction between development and non-development expenditures for all layers of Government must be agreed upon.

Secondly, after having functionally determined this, the States must be assured of financial autonomy to the full measure of their obligations. The present-day financial dualism must be scrapped because it is a source of conflict and suspicion between the Centre and the States. It is not the business of the Planning Commission to carry on an annual exercise in horse-trading with States for determining the States' financial plans. Its function is to lay down laws of performance and see to it that they are not violated. The Centre, on the other hand, must be adequately empowered to stop any State from diverting its finances to channels other than those laid down by the priority system. There is no exaggeration in the charge that the States have often deviated from a proper course of action for reasons of political expediency. The Centre, however, can perform all these functions only if it disciplines itself on the same lines. A Centre that can be easily subjugated by numerous pressure groups is a poor instrument for high level economic management.

Thirdly, the State financial resources and autonomy must be made a function of their fiscal mobilization, otherwise autonomy will have no meaning and become a gigantic dole from the Centre.

Fourthly, before the States are guaranteed financial autonomy, the division of functions, obligations, and resources between a

State and its local bodies must be firmly built into the overall scheme of economic and financial allocation. This may be done either through constitutional amendments or by conventions.

Can all these objectives be achieved by a weak Centre?

September 1968

9

PARTIES, POWER, AND PELF

COMPANY DONATIONS are largely a problem of the Congress Party. Being the biggest beneficiary of such donations, the Congress Party finds itself sharply divided on the issue. The opponents and protagonists of such donations to political parties are, however, caught up in some sort of shadow boxing. The disputants have very curious logic. Company donations, some argue, should not be banned because such a ban would put black money into political circulation, as if politics today is not vastly fed on black money, as if also the two types of funds, white and black, are quite distinct. It is further argued that as some parties are financed from foreign funds, a ban on company donations will put a premium on these parties against others which depend entirely on internal finance, as if the foreign element is not already involved in the donations that come from companies which have foreign collaboration, as if also the ruling party has not used foreign aid for its own perpetuation. It never occurs to these people that they are moving in a vicious circle. White money and black money are products of a single process. Foreign powers use money only in different forms for the same objective, namely, creating their lobbies and leverages in this country. If a vicious circle has to be broken, it can be done only at a carefully chosen point because it cannot be broken at all its points, or else it will not be a circle. What can be very strongly argued for —and this is also the argument of this chapter—is that a ban on company donations is not the appropriate point of attack, for the rot in election politics has gone too deep. However, there are other powerful arguments which fall more in the category of hows rather than whys of the donations. For example, the vast body of shareholders have no say in the matter, companies giving donations are generally those large ones which are financed from official agencies, donations are given to individuals rather than to parties, etc. These objectives can be met by making proper legal arrangements.

On the other hand, the supporters of the ban are equally illogical in linking this question to such extraneous considerations as socialism and morals. If we were a socialist society, there would be no big business existing as such. The image of a political man in India is unfortunately confined to the extremes of either a saint or a thug. A saint never touches money and a thug never does anything else except somehow get it. It is utterly fruitless to recall nostalgically the socialist or Gandhian professions of the old Congress of the days of our struggle for freedom. In the game of the politics of power, which the entire Congress Party is inevitably caught us in, money is a crucial instrument. The Congress is neither a party of socialism nor a crusador of Ghandhism. The sooner this is realized the better it would be.

It is, therefore, a matter of some urgency to focus attention on the role and functions of money in acquiring and sustaining political power by a group or a party. It is no secret, though facts are not yet quantified, that Indian democracy, particularly its electoral system, is becoming most expensive and spendthrift. If something is not done quickly to lighten this burden on a young democracy and to control the influence of money in politics, the entire polity will run the risk of becoming dysfunctional and being caught up in the rat race of politics chasing money and money chasing politics.

It is worrying enough for a poor country like India, which has chosen a full-throated democratic way of life, that its electoral processes continue to be ever more costly. Without a deep commitment, no one dare ask voters for their votes as well as their money. Money for politics must in the nature of things come from those who can afford to part with it. What is disturbing is that money is coming from those, and in ways, that subvert party politics. Against this background, the question of company donations of less than Rs. 2 crores annually seems almost peripheral.

A cursory look at two other democracies, one in which company donations are banned, i.e. the USA, and the other which does not impose any such ban, i.e. the UK, many give us some insight into the nature of the relationship between money and politics. In the USA money is called the mother's milk of politics. In a year of presidential elections, the total expenditure on elections at all levels is estimated at about $ 200 million or about Rs. 150 crores. The occult art of raising money is practised with aggressive perfection by tough money raisers in view of the ban on company donations.

Jo Kane, J.F. Kennedy's uncle, who was drafted to educate his nephew in political craft, is reported to have told his pupil in the very first lesson that "it takes three things to win: the first is money, the second is money, and the third is money." J.F. Kennedy spent, as also his brother after him, about a million dollars a year for several years on preliminaries before he came to fight actually for the American presidency. "Kennedy bought the elections" was a phrase which appeared in every book or article written upon that great eventful election of 1960. Kennedy would never have won but for the millions of dollars his billionaire family put at his disposal. The vicious role of money was sharply brought out during the primaries in which the Kennedy group successfully threatened, blackmailed, and finally succeeded in dissuading Hubert Humphrey's supporters from giving him money and virtually starved the man out of the primaries.

In the USA in view of the ban on company donations or for that matter on any individual donation over $ 5000, it is either millionaires or racist demagogues who can ever hope to get elected to higher office, the more so to the highest. It is said, and there is the irony, that in the USA private big money alone can yield saner politics. It is millionaires like Kennedy and Rockefeller who are liberals, while the not so rich ones, like Goldwater, Wallace, and Nixon, are demagogues and chauvinists. For, a party having a broader financial base does not imply necessarily that the choice has fallen on a more liberal-democratic candidate. For example, 650,000 individuals sent their campaign money of $ 100 or less each to Goldwater who proved to be the best money raiser as well as a disaster for the Republican Party. He collected about $ 18 million of which about one-half came from small donations. As mass support for a candidate, small donations pouring in for Wallace are likely to exceed anything known before. The so-called broadening of the base for financial support may act inversely to progressive democratic politics. It is said that an American takes his politics seriously and one result is that he frequently gets mad. When his blood pressure rises he may react by reaching for his cheque book, if not his gun. The so-called participation of the people in politics is not always intelligent and for social good; it is often a vicious backlash.

Although company donations are banned and there is a limit on individual contributions, money is collected through political committees constituted of rich people. It is through these committees that big business and others create their leverage with candidates on a strict basis of money given for some promise of benefit. This method is highly corrupting. Thus, in the USA three types of people are able to manipulate politics, in the absence of company donations, (*i*) millionaires as candidates for higher offices, (*ii*) chauvinists and racists appealing to the atavistic instincts of ordinary citizens, and (*iii*) businessmen who give money in return for the promise of a specific advantage. It is also well known that laws are evaded where election expenses are concerned and the Government is defrauded by uncountable millions this way. Tax evasion has become so ubiquitous a technique that, as pointed out by one analyst, "if it was exposed and pursued across the board, the jails would be full and legislative halls empty, while the political business of a great nation would grind to a standstill."

How are the two major British parties, Labour and Conservative, financed? There is no ban on company donations to political parties, nor is there any limit on individual contributions. Trade unions and cooperatives provide the bulk of the finance for the central Labour Party, and have directly or indirectly anything up to one hundred and twenty-five candidates of their own on the election list of the Labour Party. Since this party is organized electorally, i.e. constituency-wise, the constituency parties make their own financial arrangement for their activities including election campaigns, although some help is always forthcoming from the central Labour Party. The Conservative Party does not spend more than the Labour Party does because of the formidable income of the trade unions. Trade and industry provide funds

Parties, Power, and Pelf

for the Conservative Party through the Federation of British Industries. Only a few hundred people provide these funds. It would appear that funds are available to British parties on the basis of sharply defined class interests, who also spend money independently of parties for thep ropagation of their own policies. For example, the Federation of British Industries spends about a million pounds a year on propaganda. Over the last decade, as the differences between the two parties narrowed down, even the Conservatives have seen the wisdom of organizing themselves and their finances on a constituency or electoral basis. In the UK the role of money in politics is not as important as in the USA, despite the fact that there is no ban on company donations. Politics is usually free from its perversion by money bags.

In India, political parties are financed in several ways. First, there is the membership fee which is kept at a very low level. Therefore, parties cannot hope to collect more than a few lakh rupees each from this source, for there is no system of effective mass membership. Secondly, money is donated by companies, but only two parties, the Congress and the Swatantra, are its sole beneficiaries, the Congress getting about three-fourths. The total from this head is on an average of Rs. 1.6 crores a year. Thirdly, and probably the most important, source is collections, in black or white money, made by party bosses and individuals who do not generally deposit their collections with their respective parties but keep it with themselves to help their own retainers, workers, and legislative supporters. Lastly, foreign money which is transmitted in many open or secret channels. The most open channel is the transmission from international trade unions to their respective communist and anti-communist members; or the free despatch of books and other literature, the collections from the sale of which are used for party funds. There are known and unknown ways in which foreign money is illegally given to political parties, such as the use of PL 480 funds, rupee trade funds arising from trade with Eastern Europe, Chinese gold, etc. It would appear that two most vital sources of party finance are collections made by bosses within the country and transmissions from abroad.

Some idea about the magnitudes of these two sources can be had from a rough estimate of the election expenses incurred. The Election law imposes a limit on expenditure of Rs. 25,000 and Rs. 10,000 each for parliamentary and assembly candidates respectively. Not one of these elected members can claim, with a clear conscience, to have spent within that limit. In fact, a number of elected members openly admitted, although after the date of filing objections, to having spent ten to fifteen times the prescribed limits. In the fourth general elections there were 2,369 candidates for the Lok Sabha and 16,503 for the State assemblies. On an average a candidate spends about one to one and a half lakh rupees on parliamentary elections. If a candidate spends Rs. 100,000 in a constituency of 500,000 voters, the expenses per voter come to 20 paise per voter, that is equal to the cost of two post-cards or one small handbill per voter. Allowing downward adjustments for several ineffective candidates, if one assumes an expenditure of Rs. 100,000 per parliamentary constituency, and Rs. 25,000 per assembly constituency and Rs. 200 per candidate for several lakhs of candidates for local bodies, the total election expenses may go up to over Rs. 100 crores. This estimate does not include expenditures on midterm polls. This order of expenditure makes India the costliest democracy in the world in relation to its GNP, total or per capita. Unless something is done quickly to check this unnecessary burden, democracy may go bankrupt and collapse under its own weight.

Therefore, whether or not there is to be a ban on company donations is itself not a matter of great consequence. If at all, the case is much stronger for retaining such donations than banning them. What is of great consequence is the way politics is organized and conducted, namely, party structures, norms of political behaviour, political mobilization, and interest articulation, to which fund raising activity, including company donations, is inevitably appended. In a fragmented party structure, like ours, these aspects of functional politics as well as their norms are bound to get distorted. To acquire money by all legal and illegal methods and, in turn, to help those who put up this money become the primary and autonomous functions of numerous parties and leaders in a fragmented structure. Interest articulation is rendered difficult because every group has simultaneously to keep pace with or keep a hold on numerous fragments in the structure. The number of candidates for each seat is so inordinately large, including those who are put up as dummies to split the rival's vote, that election expenses per seat are artificially multiplied. Money is available to candidates who openly jump into the election frays with clear prsopects for defeat on the ground that these candidates, even when defeated, have leverges with the administration, ministers, or the power structure at some critical level.

Political parties' professions regarding the purity and inviolability of their respective ideologies stand in sharp contrast to the interests of the pressure groups constituting each party; in many cases the two are patently inconsistent. Insistence on ideological purity excludes by definition, in most cases, collection of money from sources and interest groups from whom alone money is available. It is so because the mass of voters is too poor and the middle class too alienated from politics to give any perceptible financial support to political parties. Every political party is an aggregation of interest groups and yet it expresses contempt for such interests in order to keep up a facade of ideological purity and is, therefore, driven to look for money from dubious sources. The Congress Party has always been financed by business houses. This was so in the period before 1947 as it is today. Nehru's Congress was no exception to this rule. However, it is only recently that the dangers of total reliance on big business money have come to be appreciated, partly because all the political and administrative institutions, policies, and programmes, and their human instrumentalities have revealed themselves to be directed towards helping one and only one class, and partly because the proliferation of welfare activities under pressures from the local power structure has thrown the economy into a perpetual crisis. Thus it is clear now that the ills of our political and economic life, including the perverting role of money in politics, can be traced to the non-specificity of functions and non-observance of norms by institutions and elite as well as to the lack of differentiation between the two.

There are two basically different patterns of political culture—elite and institutional. Although all modern political cultures are mixed, they are dominantly either of one or the other ideal-type. The avowed decisions of the founding fathers of the Indian Constitution and other political leaders were in favour of an institutional system and to that purpose a vast proliferation of institutions, at all levels, was undertaken. Every conceivable and possibly transplantable institution has been set up in India, most of them borrowed from abroad. In practice, however, right from the beginning practical politics tended towards an elite culture. Nehru, who was responsible for formally institutionalizing politics, was really responsible for institutions becoming dysfunctional and held in contempt because he allowed his charisma, and his psychophants, to so dominate and violate institutions as to almost destroy their total functions and norms. It is characteristic of an elite culture that institutions are only of symbolic importance and downgraded. Their functions, anatomy, norms, and procedures are at the mercy of the elite. Corrupt and second-rate elite could easily destroy these aspects of institutions; only elite of political stature and strong commitment can establish dynamic relations between the two. Over a decade or so almost every institution in India has come to be so downgraded at the hands of highly acquisitive and unscrupulous elite as to deprive it of its functions and norms. So much so that even political parties, as institutions, have been reduced to becoming instruments of elite struggle only, in which the effort is directed always at maintaining a reductive *status quo*. Change takes place only within the elite instead of a change of elite and their functions. The more the elite came to dominate institutions or let itself be formed extra-institutionally, the more its power rested on making institutions normless and dysfunctional and also the greater was its reliance for money on individuals and extra-institutional sources. The elite's *modus operandi* shifted from maximally norm-oriented politics to a non-operational *pseudo* global value system. The political input was money and the output also was money; politics was left with no other real purpose. The elite easily threw the responsibility of political deterioration at the door of institutions. Consequently, the transfer of resources from interest-group institutions to political institutions, i.e. from one smaller collectivity to another larger one, was replaced by money flowing from companies and individuals to bandicoots or their retainers only.

A commentator once remarked: "The growth of political corruption in India is a testament to the success of parliamentary democracy. Ministers and members of legislative bodies are men of influence; they can get things done. This is the way it should be." The statement is an expression of utter cynicism, and if it is not so, then it reflects the fact of Indian politics being totally a politics of the elite, and rather a corrupt elite.

In this situation of elite monopoly and downgrading of institutions it became inevitable that parties should remain at the mercy of the competing elite for financial support. Elections have become so expensive and for so many that almost everybody gets caught in the vortex of money; money-spinning has become a whole-time political job for a host of operators. Institutions cannot collect money because they are sufficiently discredited. Membership of political parties consists of those who have to be supported and fed by the party leaders for being retained as members. People of some genuine commitment find this power game too dirty and too expensive and hence opt out of politics. The remaining political elite must, for sheer survival, remain as appendages of the money bags, no matter whether the money is white or black; mostly it is black. Whether or not to impose a ban on company donations is utterly irrelevant to this situation. However, if donations from companies, as collectivities, are made straight to political parties, as collectivities, and not to individuals, the situation could improve vastly.

The party machine is the pivot of a political party, taken as a collectivity. A political machine is a dirty word, although parties cannot do without it. Politics is the pursuit of power and the political machine is its medium. For the citizens, it performs articulating, arbitrating, and aggregating functions, the fulfilment of which is the expression of the effectiveness of political parties. Wherever there is a political machine there is also a political boss at the head of that machine, who is responsible for its organization, centralization, and maintenance in working conditions. The boss is an essential catalyst between the artificial idealist paper-system and the crass realities of political life. As a man of drive, ingenuity, and guile, even though living on graft, he must remain behind the scenes and spurn public office. However, bossism is a distortion of the real role of the boss; it is equal to a boss plus his holding crucial public office. Bossism reduces the credibility of political parties, and, as a force, proves in the end totally destructive of the programmatic and mobilizing functions of the party and its political machine.

When a boss aligns himself closely with the bureaucrat on the one hand and the money bags on the other and thus becomes the only link between the two, he oversteps his role and overrules that function of the machine by which it aggregates and balances various interest groups. The other side of the picture is the boss's pressure on the bureaucrat through bribery, blackmail, or jobbery. The Sanathan Committee sharply stated that "the tendency to subvert integrity in public services instead of being isolated or aberrative is growing into an organized, well-planned racket." The boss thus has ceased to be an integral part of the machine, instead he has come to pocket it. By his holding illegitimate and disproportionate power, by the use of graft, corruption, and violation of laws, etc., he has corroded the very bases of democratic functioning of every political party and the norms of the Government. Bossism implies laying emphasis entirely on money and power as attributes to the political machine's providing channels of mobilization. He collects money by all sorts of methods. No wonder that the money bags have started complaining of money being extorted from them by pressure and blackmail, as one often hears these days.

However, at the local power structure, the boss of the Congress Party machine still performs, along with fund-raising, other aggregating and distributing functions and thereby enables himself to keep the structure fairly streamlined and articulated and thereby also maintains and strengthens himself. The real strength of the Congress Party lies in its local power structure which no opposition party has yet been able to break decisively. But as one goes at the higher, State and Central, levels of power structure, bossism of the worst type is practised. At these levels the loss is more responsible than anybody else for breaking the laws of the band, perverting norms of every institution, and thus bringing into contempt politics and parties by turning himself from a boss to a politician. He ends up by seeking power for power's sake and as a means of plunder. He makes the life of proper politicians insecure and uncertain. His money raising activity becomes his personal affair, whether collected from companies or individuals. Politics moves a step further downward, from interest groups to individuals, and from lobbies to personal politics, threatening the entire party structure. Truly it is bossism and not money that lies at the root of political corruption, though both feed on each other. All this is as true of the opposition parties as of the Congress. The Sanathan Committee brought out the fact that the opposition plays the same game, otherwise many of the parties would be out of business because they have no prospects of ever getting to power. K. D. Malaviya is of the opinion that "while the Congress Government was very strong and its leadership influential all round, the opposition parties did not show much concern about the way funds were made available to the Congress organization, either for its day-to-day activities or for its general elections. They tried to copy the Congress methods wherever they could. Methods of collecting funds were, therefore, more or less the same in all parties but as the problems of administration grew in complexity and the perpetuation of the same political party became oppressive, the attention of the political parties was drawn to the methods of collection of funds."

The hold of bosses and the practice of bossism have gone too deep into the Congress Party structure. The Congress President and the Prime Minister have to depend on, as well as to contend with, these forces. It is well known that the conclave of the Chief Ministers, several of whom were party machine bosses turned into politicians, and members of the Syndicate, who are bosses-cum-politicians par excellence, were responsible for the election of Mrs. Gandhi as Prime Minister. Otherwise, she was not in the picture at all. Ever since her election she has been able to hold the balance of forces precariously within the party because of inherent contradictions between bossism and a functioning party Government. Bosses have proved too powerful to allow Mrs. Gandhi to function as an effective Prime Minister, as well they might, because, to be an effective leader, a Prime Minister must reduce to proper limits the role of bosses as catalysts between the Government and the groups within and outside the party. Since the bosses in the Congress Party are also politicians, they naturally prefer the Prime Minister to be their puppet. This unresolved conflict and continued crisis of leadership in the Congress Party has brought the Government and the Congress Party to a grinding halt as well as weakened the position of the Prime Minister.

Because the bosses collect funds, it was considered in Mrs. Gandhi's camp that their financial wings should be clipped. To that end it was suggested that company donations should be banned, as if the bosses depend on that source alone for their financial power. Naturally the bosses reacted adversely. If the bill ever comes to be passed, it is unlikely that the power of the bosses would be measurably reduced. But they would, on the other hand, rely more on individual finance for which they would not only be not accountable but also which they could use as they please.

The problem of political corruption through money, as discussed earlier, is a function of the party structure, party machine, and party bosses. It is impossible to do away with this corruption without properly delimiting the functions of each one of these components of power. And this is no easy task; nor is there any straight forward answer to it. The first and foremost condition for change is that a proper functional delimitation must be made between the institution of the Prime Minister and the head of the party in power, at present the Congress President. The relations between these have never been institutionalized and the existence of harmony or disharmony between the two has been tied to the existence of personal equation or non-equation between the two. This is the worst way to approach the task of rationalziing the party structure. The Congress party is likely to get deeper and deeper into the political quagmire.

However, if the problem of financial allocation to parties has to be tackled independently in the short period, it could be done in two ways. First, all contributions, whether from companies or individuals, should go straight to party organizations and never to any individual, be it the boss, the Chief Minister, the Prime Minister, the Congress President, or any other person. Secondly, every party must be forced by law to publish its accounts and be held accountable for all expenditure incurred by it or on its behalf. If these two methods were adopted, bosses would still remain bosses, but their capacity for mischief, such as encouraging groupism, and maintaining a large body of toughs and cookies blackmailing Government leaders, would be considerably reduced. Controversy over company donations, it would appear, amounts to no more than shadow boxing at present.

August 1968

10

ANATOMY OF POLITICAL DEFECTIONS

THE PHENOMENON OF political defections has entered its second stage. At the first stage, defections were unidirectional, i.e. from the Congress to the opposition. Now the process has gone into sharp reversal, although the defectors from the opposition do not always join the Congress. Puppet Governments backed by the Congress mark the interregnum. It is not surprising that the opposition parties, which once hailed defections from the Congress as one more blow to it, quickly agreed with the Congress, on a resolution by Venkatasubhia, to the appointment of a high-level committee to stop the rot.

Nonetheless, it has not been sufficiently realized that political defections, except those arising from the defectors' imperative ideological affinity with the other side, are a symptom or a by-product of our polity's two pervasive defects, namely, a fragmented political party structure and pseudo contemporary politics. A simple count of national, State, and local political parties, many of which have programmatic differences as between tweedledum and a tweedledee, give their number over two scores. Defections highlight the disintegrating effects of party fragmentation, and its corollary, the continuous politics of winning friends and splitting enemies. Psuedo-politics is distinguished from rational political activity by the type of motivation or purpose, and the alleviation of neurosis for the promotion of private good against an improved satisfaction of human needs according to professed national or party objectives. Pseudo-politics also considers the *status quo* as best and resists change while noisy professions are made for the fundamental transformation of the society.

Attempts to stop defections by legal methods or by some simple agreement among parties without tackling the two aforementioned basic problems are most likely to founder. A moment's reflection on some of the suggested, but ill-fated, remedies should reveal the ticklishness and intractability of the problem.

Suppose political parties are agreed upon checking defections by way of imposing on the defectors the desirable penalty of their seeking re-election. How, then, are the floating votes of a large number of Independents going to be controlled? No law or agreement can stop them from joining, and also probably leaving, a party if the latter does not mind such shifts. The emergence of new party political alignments is inevitable in a fragmented party structure and, therefore, the larger the floating votes of Independents, the more potent is their role in encouraging defections or realignments.

Coalition Governments are the order of the day. But most of them are unstable coalitions. Many more are likely to follow the disintegration of the old ones. It is as impossible to stop the formation of coalition Governments, as it is to stop them from disintegrating by some constituent party simply withdrawing its support. Individual defections from a party may be barred and that is largely the problem of the Congress Party, but the defection of a party from a coalition or a cluster of parties—which is largely the problem of the opposition—can in no legal way be put to a stop. Making or breaking of coalitions today is nothing but a *tour de force* on the part of political defectors.

The communist claim that their party is free from defections is hollow because every political crisis in the country throws them into a deeper crisis and splits them vertically down to the lowest level. The necessity for a new political alignment encourages defections in one case and splits in another, and both are equal in their net effect on political instability.

A group of potential defectors from a party can make nonsense of any law against defections by paralyzing the party through simply defying the whip. They do not have to defect. They can wait until they are thrown out, and that is nothing but a most perverse way of allowing defections. The withdrawal of a whip from a member in the Western democracies amounts to that member's political extinction. Here it may put a premium on his vote.

It is sometimes suggested that a system of recall is the best and most democratic sanction against defections. An elected member can be recalled only if more than half the constituents sign a demand for such a recall. But if the number of voters in a constituency were as large as over 700,000, such a petition would never come to be signed in view of the harrowing experience of the legislators with regard to the cost and effort required in doing no more than contacting voters during the general elections. The Election Commission is not at all equipped to go into the details of testing the veracity of signatures on the proposed petitions for recall. Recall remains no more than a futile text-book solution.

It is also argued that repeated mid-term polls will eliminate defections by inflicting heavy losses on defectors. But such losses will have to be borne, equally and gratuitously, by loyal members as well. Besides, continuous election politics, or the fear of it, will paralyze governmental functioning. An occasional mid-term poll is not ruled out, but if the timing of polls becomes irrelevant in general, then, apart from legal complications, politics will never get stabilized at any functional level. The remedy of repeated mid-term polls is worse than the disease.

If a limit were to be put upon the number of ministers a government can appoint it is claimed that political defectors would be effectively deterred. This suggestion is practicable and easier to find acceptance by major political parties. But it is of very limited value. So long as other avenues of profit are open, and there are quite a few, such as licences, permits, and contracts, defectors are unlikely to be seriously deterred. Besdies, defections do not take place for profit or spoils alone; there is also the motive of sheer survival for a group or faction whose existence is threatened by other groups in the parent party.

Finally, it will be almost impossible to get a consensus among parties or make them accept a self-denying ordinance not to admit defectors. If ever a large party is faced with a clear choice of remaining in perpetual opposition or sharing a Government on the support of defectors from elsewhere, it will be tempted to flout the agreement at the first available opportunity. If one party or group flouts an agreement, no one remains bound to adhere to it. Therefore, neither laws nor conventions against defections can directly weed out the poison of defection. What then are the other practical methods available to us?

History has yet to pronounce its final judgement on whether democracy can survive under one-party dominance in an underdeveloped country. The experience of the last 20 years in several countries is contradictory. However, in a country beset with several political parties, democracy can function only if alternative Governments manned by different political parties are a feasible proposiposition. Otherwise, opposition parties will become thoroughly irresponsible and reckless and, in turn, the country will get the sort of Government which its opposition deserves. Generally, the people who talk of bipolarization have in mind the classical distinction between Right and Left, although they forget that our society is not divided on a natural class basis which would give us bipolarized parties. Hence what they ask for is moonshine. But some degree of polarization can take place on the basis of a cluster or group of parties facing one or more such groups. For this to happen two preconditions must be satisfied. First, there must be a reasonable balance between the parties' legislative strength and their respective support among the voters. This balance was to a large extent created by the last general elections. Secondly, there must be a built-in mechanism that forces like-minded parties to coalesce. Parties in India, in general, are not homogenous; they are amalgams of incompatible groups. It is quite common that a groups within one party may find greater affinity with some faction in another party than with the groups within its own party. Hence, defections are not looked upon by them as something contrary to the standards of intra-party struggle. Once a concrete, coalescing mechanism starts working new political alignments will find their direction and purpose in distinction to the makeshift alignments or coalitions of today which break up as soon as they are formed. That is precisely why, in the present system, parties which seek political alignments within the present functionless party structure for their narrow immediate gains are unlikely to stand by any agreed solution against defectors.

However pre-eminently desirable in itself, no solution of the present impasse is worth considering if it does not lie within the realm of practical politics, in particular a solution, such as the introduction of a presidential system, which requires a radical modification of the Constitution. If the Indian people were given a chance once again to prepare and set up an institutional system which suits their genius, one can say with reasonable certainty that the job would be much better done. But this chance is not available even as a theoretical possibility and hence any consideration of it is irrelevant.

The only solution which would require the least legal and constitutional change, be acceptable to major political parties, and have far-reaching effects in forcing parties to cloalesce lies in changing the existing electoral law. If the law were only to lay down that (*a*) every candidate seeking election must come through a political party and (*b*) any political party which does not secure a certain minimum percentages of the total votes polled would be denied representation, in one stroke we would get two far-reaching results. The number of parties would be drastically reduced and like-minded parties would be forced to coalesce. A large number of Independents who take away about 20 per cent of the votes but get only less than 5 per cent of the seats would be weeded out, and the party system in turn would be strengthened and streamlined.

April 1968

11

DEMOCRACY TO POPULISM

THERE IS a tendency to discuss the role and composition of the political power structure in India either in terms of class-based categories, like Right and Left, or of the political parlour game of personalities and pseudo-events. There is danger in such an approach, to say the least, of reading too much or too little in a situation of unexpected change or crisis without showing clarity of purpose or direction for the polity as well as for the Government. Of course, the contemporary Indian political situation is highly amorphous, tentative, and confused. But there is no point in adding insult to it by pushing in preconceived theories and superficial hunches and prejudices. To avoid falling into these and other pitfalls one must clearly state the breakdown of the forces constituting the power structure, their characteristics and motivations, alternative courses of action and their possible results.

One other fact needs some stress. Among the journals and newspapers of Left persuasion one finds an almost in-built innocence, if not dogmatism, for asking only the dialectical questions while in their counterparts only the pragmatic questions. If the actual situation had corresponded to this twofold categorization, we would have had by now a clear identification of structural and functional parameters of the polity and economy. No such system or subsystem of power structure and functions is obtained in any major work. We cannot ask either structural or functional questions all the time: they are the two ends of the scale and must be properly balanced.

Let us give an example. Everybody is asking for bringing down prices—obviously, a functional question. Nobody seems bothered to realize that prices cannot be brought down, or even kept stable, so long as the present structure of production, income distribution, and expenditure remains unchanged — patently a structural question.

A warning is needed here. In pursuit of developing a system analysis, some West-oriented intellectuals have been importing prefabricated American theories and attempting to transplant them on a completely different soil. For example, for quite some time now, these analysts have been repeatedly putting forward the theory that the basic, almost permanent, factor of power in India is the dominant party, the dominant caste, or any other dominant group. The elections of 1967, the collapse of several Governments of a dominant party, and the furious pace of political change have made a short shrift of this theory. It is not that caste and community have not played their vital role; in fact they have. It is the principle of "dominance" which stands shattered.

The same also applies to the theory of the dominant class. It is not a helpful assumption for the study of the power structure in India to accept that society is stratified on the basis of class divisions found in the developed Western countries. Although class conflict cannot be ignored, what needs understanding is that *it is a constant and not a variable* in the dynamics of the present political power situation. It may become an important variable but not until it reaches a critical quantitative level and the dominance of the contemporary polities of populism is broken.

In one definite sense, the recent elections have proved most disruptive not only of the *status quo*, as was desired by most people, but also of actual and potential stable majorities in the legislatures. Although the era of rubber-stamp legislatures is over, a new and potentially dangerous situation of precarious majorities and minorities has been created. In other stable democracies, Governments have run through the full period of the life of their parliaments with as dangerously low a majority as anything from one to five. In India, even a majority of fifty is exceptionally unsafe. Disequilibrium is desirable only if it leads to a new and a higher level of equilibrium, otherwise it is likely to lead to anarchy, perpetual crises, and dysfunctionalism.

The electoral system in India has built into our party political structure a diverse and significant number of "loose fish" of Independents and small splinter parties which take away anything up to 20 per cent of votes with less than about 5 per cent of seats. There are also other parties with the percentage of votes polled being nearly twice that of the seats won by them.

Among the factors which have stood in the way of the growth of the opposition, not necessarily as a bulk opposition for the sake of opposition but as a potentially alternative Government, the most important has been the party political fragmentation which the electoral system has largely helped to bring about. There is no proper balance between the votes cast for a party and the seats won by it. Any party with about 35 to 40 per cent votes polled can either have a landslide or a comfortable majority or be completely eliminated. Kerala and Madras are the examples for the latter, and generally the States where the Congress has secured a majority belong to the former. The Congress Party which benefited from the electoral system so far and sat pretty safe on it now finds the tables turned against it by the same system.

It is pointless to talk about bipolarization in this "fish market." We have got the most disruptive electoral system with all the aura of legitimacy behind it. The present party position in India is something comparable to that of pre-Hitler Germany with too many political parties. It may also be mentioned that the stability and streamlining of the party structure in postwar Germany largely rests on the electoral law which makes it impossible for Independents and small parties, however popular, vocal, determined, and well-organized, to exist.

If, for example, we had made two simple changes in our electoral law, namely, that every candidate must be a party candidate and every party which got less than, say, 4 per cent of votes polled would be deprived of its seats in the legislatures, we would have now been left with only half a dozen stable parties and by the next election with probably three or four. Parties of the same political persuasion or ideology would have been forced to coalesce and every party would have been obliged to remain faithful to its declared programmes and policies. Instead, we have got a crazy patch-work quilt of parties and parties within parties. Besides, the present electoral system will never be able to throw up a party system that will make it possible to have party identification on the bases of social or class stratification and, therefore, it will reduce to nonsense the corresponding theories based on such an identification.

The only logical conclusion is that we are stuck in a dead centre of acute party political instability and fragmentation. All that is being said, therefore, by way of pretensions and self-congratulations about the success and resilience of Indian democracy is nothing more than optimistic sentimentalism. Incidentally, this instability is likely to help the ruling party if it cares to cash in on the weakness of other parties in order to remain in power for a full five years. But the same could also prove its fatal undoing if the opposition, in turn, resorts to the same tactics. Nevertheless, the relative balance could remain on the side of the Congress Party.

It can be argued that it is not the fault of the electoral law; it is the voters who are to blame. While the voters voted against the Congress, they never voted for a national alternative. Hence, they must be spanked. But, the cruel fact is that there was no national alternative before the voters and there is no likelihood of one emerging under the present electoral system. All parties other than the Congress are essentially regional parties, their strength ranging from one to three States. The absence of the emergence of a national alternative will lead to further political instability and party fragmentation despite short-term honeymooning between parties which are mutually exclusive on grounds of ideologies and political substance.

In another, and equally definite sense, 1967 elections have brought the party political structure in consonance with the actual political reality. So far, political power was monopolized by the superstructure of the Congress Party, a situation which was a clear distortion of the underlying reality. In true sense the Congress did not enjoy the monopoly because it could not use it for good or ill. The elections have structurally struck the balance between the Congress Party and its real strength. The same applies in some measure to the opposition. What was a political fact of the structure, for quite some time before the elections, has now been crystallized in a new position of the parties.

This fact of the power having partly but decisively moved out of the radius of the Congress Party raises two questions, one of identification and the other of strategies, functions, and purposes. (*i*) What are, in India, the centres and constituents of power as well as their functions and end products? (*ii*) In what way has the structure of power within the Congress Party been modified and what is the capacity of the new structure to cope with functional problems of political, social, and economic development? Such questions exclude a sophomorphic view of elections or an excessive reliance on individual and local fortunes or nasty misfortunes. *Indian polity has reached a point where its success or failure no longer depends on this or that party or leader but it depends upon the great imponderables that lie behind them.*

In tackling the first part of the first question we have to find the kind of politics which the instability of the party structure, based on balance or parallelism between the Congress and the non-Congress parties, will throw up. A logical answer would be in favour of the politics of instability and devitalization, despite the euphoria created by non-Congress coalitions. Before accepting or rejecting such an answer one must clearly state its rationale and mechanism. It is neither possible nor necessary to go into the detailed workings of each party separately. We shall concentrate on their common contribution to the nature of political activity, though there would always remain some characteristics and strategies peculiar only to individual parties.

To some extent, we have had a taste of the politics of the future in the pre-election, extra-constitutional, extra-legal, and street politics of mass agitation, conducted not by way of a classical revolutionary movement but as a violent popular movement. This movement capitalized on the growing mass discontent, the increasing dysfunctionalism and internal weakness of the Congress Party as well as on the image of the party being led by a divided leadership and a weak and ineffective Prime Minister. It was in the streets that the Congress was first defeated before it could be defeated through the ballot-box.

Almost all the oppositon parties in India are essentially populist rather than doctrinal parties. Of course, doctrinal professions are profusely used but only as aspects of party strategy, useful in the battle for power, not necessarily as policy guides for voters and members or for implementation if returned to power. Otherwise, how can one explain a ministerial coalition of dozens of parties which were a little while ago engaged in a mutual war of attrition for their respective ideologies. The argument that the people forced them to coalesce precisely reveals their populist character. Otherwise, how can the Swatantra Party be believed honestly to profess sophisticated modern conservatism and sell it to its vast majority of tribal and most backward supporters? How come that the ultra-Leftists have joined forces with the Jana Sangh? And so on. Populism absorbs traditional parties and modern reform or revolutionary parties as well as their ideologies and uses the latter as an instrument of mass manipulation. In essence, populist parties are anti-ideological parties despite the great fanfare and flourish of ideologies.

Let me briefly state the characteristics of populist parties. (*a*) Their leadership, despite considerable variations, comes from the middle and uppper middle classes. (*b*) These parties have always some popular mass base, however restricted or shifting. (*c*) They are anti-*status quo* parties whatever the *status quo* happens to be. (*d*) They are extremist and rely on extra-legal mass agitation techniques of political activity. Agitation is confined mostly to urban areas; it is carried on in such a way as to involve all the major, though diverse, sections of the urban population. The agitational technique often degenerates into violence bringing in its wake the hatred of the law-enforcing police and administration. (*e*) They may use the language of socialism or freedom, communism or fascism, regional or narrow chauvinism, nationalism or internationalism, but these slogans are meant only to capitalize on the discontent of the people. (*f*) For fear of being liquidated they openly or secretly seek foreign patronage. (*g*) They are ready to coalesce with their opponents to increase their own strength and bring down the established power. (*h*) One of their major activities is to bring into disrepute the democratic institutions and destroy their initiative and authority.

In the entire spectrum of opposition parties, there is not one party which would fall outside this aforementioned characteristic framework, though some sections of this or that party may be opposed to it. The very logic and force of the politics of deadlock, inaction, dysfunctionalism and official corruption forces even non-populist parties to turn populist to survive. For example, the Masani group in the Swatantra and some sections of the communists may not be populist, but that would make no difference to the total situation. In the final analysis, even these sections will be swallowed by vast, galloping populism.

The growth of populism within the opposition was largely a reaction to the politics of the Congress Party, which could also be described as populism applied in reverse to the opposition. In the early years of its rule, the Congress Party not only did not reciprocate the tolerance and moderation of opposition parties, it simply treated them with contempt. The Congress Party identified itself with the State; it misused the official machinery against its opponents; it exploited and capitalized more than any other party on caste, communal, and narrow group feelings and interests; it subverted the opposition by constantly bribing one or the other party or faction back into the Congress; and finally it, more than any other section, observed the laws of the land in their breach and contempt.

Its most notorious populist political activity was its successful attempt through mass agitation to overthrow the first communist Government in Kerala at a time when the Congress was at the height of its power in the Centre. The chickens of the Congress have come home to roost. Yet, the Congress remains the only party capable of checking this decline towards populism, if only its leadership realized their heavy responsibility and also that this is probably their last chance to survive.

To some extent populism was the product of the Gandhian techniques of disobedience which gave the post-Independence mass agitations and political fasts an aura of legitimacy in the name of Gandhi. But Gandhi, a superb realist, knew the dangers of his technique also, and thus provided the necessary safety valves like constructive work, village uplift, strict personal and party discipline. These safety valves or loopholes do not exist any more. We are today left with naked populism of the Congress and non-Congress parties. Once again, the logical conclusion which follows from the aforementioned facts of politics points towards increasing instability and fragmentation of the party political structure with programmes of national reconstruction thrown into the background.

I also hazard to predict that if a situation of 15 to 20 per cent annual rise in prices continues to take place during the next few years, we will land ourselves in a full-fledged populism of the Latin American type. It must be strongly emphasized that populism is not inconsistent with the formal democratic structure but it totally destroys the essence and ethos of the latter and ushers in the politics of total dysfunctionalism and economic immobilism.

Two elements which so far remained outside these populist movements were the oligarchic princes and the men of the armed forces. The last election saw a major intervention from the princes in the Congress and non-Congress parties and they are now handsomely sprinkled in many parties as well as in the Cabinet. It would not be improbable, if, in the next phase, the armed forces decisively attempt to partake in the national political scene, not necessarily in the form of a military dictatorship but in the form of a partnership with the civilians. Another likely development is that the process of "opposition conversions" will no longer remain unidirectional, i.e. from the non-Congress to the Congress parties. Haryana and U.P. mark the fact that it is going to be a two-way political traffic with its characteristic unprincipled brutalism, thus adding another factor in party instability.

The fact of the power having partly moved out of the Congress Party to the populist opposition has been accompanied by an even more dangerous shift of power from this country to the hands of the big powers. Not only do the questions of war and peace on India's border lie outside the power of India, her internal freedom of action is vastly reduced. The scandals of CIA activities pale into insignificance compared to the reported massive influx of money from various centres of world power during the recent elections. There is no sense in closing one's eyes to this new factor of power within the country. The corruption and large measure of interference in internal affairs, which adroitly and silently worked behind

Democracy to Populism

the legitimacy of foreign aid, have now been brought naked to the surface.

Today, the Congress Party, or for that matter any other party, cannot be relied upon to defend India's independence. This process started in the declining phase of Nehru. Like the distortion of the nominal and actual strength of the Congress Party within the country, as mentioned earlier, there exists a large measure of unreality about our nominal and actual freedom of action. The growing weakness of the Indian economy has gradually created a power vacuum, which the new structure and forces of world balance of power inevitably are coming in to fill.

Populism can be simultaneously xenophobic and subservient to foreign power. The Congress Party had increasingly come to rely upon foreign support to perpetuate itself in power and the opposition is only fighting the Congress at its own game. The real danger is that we may not be allowed to have national solutions to national problems. No party stability is possible if the parties are so structured as constantly to balance the internal struggle for power and external pressures. We have already lost the momentum in foreign policy.

In conclusion, the headstart of Indian democracy and its traditional patterns have yielded to widespread populism. Populism can be described as a dysfunctioning democracy in which every party tries to outbid the other in first creating and then exploiting the resentment of the masses. When in power the populist parties will act as "distributing" rather than as "producing" parties. Parties of opposing ideologies and economic programmes will join together precisely to achieve that goal. In the name of providing cheap food and ameliorating the misery of the people, unproductive expenditures will be unleashed without slashing the wasteful and non-productive and politically oriented expenditures which have already taken hold of the economy.

Populism means a combined pressure of all the text-book or operating distributive ideologies. Thanks to Nehru, who laid the firm foundations for "a revolution of distribution" through his ritualistic socialism, and to populist parties riding on that bandwagon, India has reached the point of the lowest rate of economic growth in the world. And there is an irony in it: every attempt to redistribute income or expenditure only brings back the old pattern of distribution with a vengeance through inflation. Morarji's daring self-denying ordinance not to permit deficit financing in the Centre or the States is going to be the subject of the biggest and most violent attack because such a step, if successful, would break up the *leit-matif* of populist parties, although in itself this step will seriously retard production. Most probably, Morarji will also opt for some controlled deficit financing.

Such is the nature and consequence of the division of power between the Congress and the non-Congress parties. This structure of power is most likely to become, in the coming months, increasingly dysfunctional, unproductive, anarchic, and violent. Above all, it will make our Constitution an unworkable document, because a Constitution like ours cannot stand the stresses and pressures of pseudo, inconsequential politics and violent populism and still function purposefully. India has reached the critical stage of a somber and inexorably vicious cycle of political overdevelopment and economic backwardness. The Nehruvian myth of inevitability of gradual progress stands exposed; in fact, there is no cushion of time for India to allow things to drift.

In such a situation a weak leadership will become increasingly irrelevant and a weak Prime Minister, like Indira Gandhi, will be incapable of unfreezing the politics of populist dysfunctionalism. India has thus entered a new phase of rapidly changing Governments, unstable coalitions, political violence, distributive pressures, increasing foreign intervention, and finally the most critical stage of her survival as a nation-State.

June 1967

12

BACK TO NATIONALISM: CONSENSUS AND DEMOCRACY

FROM DISENCHANTMENT to weariness, and from indignation to helplessness is the current national mood. There is a nasty stench in the air and everyone, except those who sit on the rot, knows where it comes from. The nation is decomposing at its vitals. With two decades of bigotry, arrogance, and corruption of political monopoly behind it and in its moments of utter degeneration and possible suicide, the ruling party is pushing India towards some dark, unknown abyss.

Over the last twenty years we tried almost everything conceivable, at least, in theory. We experimented with a variety of institutions, with the subtlest of ideologies, with the theory of the economic big push, with democracy carried to the lowliest man, with socialism crying itself hoarse from multi-storeyed house tops, with new methods and procedures about methods and procedures, etc. And yet, despite all solutions, our problems survive and with utmost vengeance and ferocity. We are apparently stuck with the age-old solution to all problems, "solving problems by failure." How can this course of national suicide be reversed?

One essential step is to throw overboard the dead-weight of, what Kenyes called, the older parrots. There are too many blows given to the nation in the name of Nehruism and I do not know how many times Nehru will have to die before his ghost is finally laid to rest and the nation allowed to find a new faith in her destiny.

Nehruism slowly emerged as a national consensus about a decade ago, but today it is a chilling strategy of weakness abroad and short-term cheap tricks at home to bypass crucial national issues. Its sphinx-like demise marks the double tragedy of a great nation and of the historical opportunity that came to its leaders after almost a thousand years to grasp the nation's destiny and clear the garbage and shame of history. Nehru cannot be judged as an ordinary ruler of a big country; his balance-sheet would always demand his juxtaposition to this historical moment and the *carte blanche* the nation gave him.

What was the Nehruvian consensus? Whatever else it was, however abstract, it was certainly not an ideology nor could it be subjected to "system analysis" as commonly understood in political science theory. And yet it was unmistakably some sort of a national consensus.

As a positive-cum-normative statement of it, the Nehruvian consensus meant four things. (*a*) Nonalignment which, implicitly though not explicitly, called for non-interference of the great powers in India. There is no systematic explanatory statement on record, as is sometimes asserted, to imply an independent nationalist foreign policy for making friends and foes on that basis. (*b*) A federal democratic constitution entirely Western in form and content, which completely bypassed the enormous complex social structure and its behaviour pattern in the hope that this political modernization imposed from above would short-circuit the process of social change via political participation, economic progress, and welfarism. (*c*) Planned economic growth through a set of policies and objectives which themselves were to emerge either from compulsions of growth or some undefined consensus of sub-nationalism, ideological convergence, and a host of other conflicting forces. (*d*) Secularism, democracy, social stratification, democratic decentralization, and educational expansion would take care of other social and political tensions in the community.

Nehruvian consensus has now completely broken down. Never before has India's dependence on foreign powers been so abject as it is today. Never before have the questions of India's security and war and peace been so completely out of India's reach as they are today. A formal democratic super-structure is intact but it has become utterly non-functional and is treated with total contempt. Not only has economic growth ground to a halt but at no other time and under no other system could big business enrich itself as it has done under the banner of Nehruvian socialism. The nation's integrity is threatened by such divisive forces as linguism, communalism, regionalism, casteism, and what not! Above all, instead of a confidence of national resurgence there is a climate of unpunished and unchecked intellectual treason. This climate is comparable to that of Britain in the thirties when the leaders and intellectuals were divided in their loyalties between Hitler and Stalin and thereby brought ruin on the nation.

There must be hundred and one causes, general and specific, that failed the Nehruvian consensus. Unfortunately, they cannot be allowed to crowd here. Nevertheless, the assumptions, processes, and approaches which went into the formation of that consensus deeply disturb and concern us.

A consensus has to be national *per se*. In a nation which has emerged from a long period of subjugation and which also contained within its bounds a multiplicity of new and old conflicting forces, an overpowering and crusading sense of unification and oneness must accompany any workable consensus, because in such a society, the weakness or strength of a consensus directly emanates from its basic foundation, i.e. national or collective conscience.

In recent years there has occurred a profound decline in the collective conscience in India, partly because the Nehruvian consensus was never nationalistic enough in tone and emphasis. Nehru's attitudes towards nationalism in the post-independent era remained ambivalent. In 1950 he said at Lucknow that nationalism as a war cry warms the heart of every Indian and that "any other force, any other activity that may seek to function, must define itself in terms of nationalism." Not much later he also said that "nationalism is essentially an anti-feeling and it feeds and fattens on hatred and anger against other nations."

This ambivalence needs little excursion into history. To Oxbridge and other British historians, for whom "the world" began with industrialization in the West, Indian nationalism was the product of British imperialism and its history, culture, tradition, and religion had no or little part in it. To them India was only a geographical expression, not a nation, just as to many pseudo-Leftists and Westernizing "modernists," it is not a nation even today.

Whereas the first crusaders of Indian nationalism in the 19th century looked upon political progress or freedom to result from such reforms in Indian society as were to bring out the superiority or at least non-inferiority of the Indian civilization, the later brand of nationalists, though rightly insisting on freedom first, were so deeply convinced of the superiority of the British institutions and culture that they came to rely heavily on supra-national principles in their struggle for freedom. Whereas the former imbibed and spread the spirit of the Renaissance, the latter developed and spread Faustian contradictions.

The colonial rulers came to use not more but less and less force because they had many other cultural and political weapons and immense technical superiority, a much more convincing and effective set of tools. Gandhi tried to combine the passion for freedom with a sense of Indianness, but since he essentially did not want to disturb the *status quo* of the Hindu society, the combination wore very thin. Had our national movement been revolutionary in the true sense which it was not, this combination would have been inevitably more profound and lasting. It would have proved a dynamic force of gigantic magnitude in radicalizing the freedom movement as well as cleansing and preserving what later Ramsay Macdonald came to accept as the "beautiful soul" of India as expressed in her nationalism.

The founding fathers of the Constitution and the intellectuals behind the Nehruvian consensus were even more impressed by the superiority of the British political institutions and culture or their variants elsewhere. Indian tradition was described as the enemy of "modernization," Indian social values as inimical to individual freedom and progress, its social system or structure as incompatible with democracy, etc. The Nehru era was a period of the grand exercise in national intellectual masochism. Of course, the Indian society, probably more than any other society, needed a big clean-up and ruthless extermination of accumulated inequities, rigidities, and the fossils of centuries. But what the new consensus attempted to do was simply to throw away the baby with the bath water. Ironically, all the social dirt and the garbage has come to stay with a vengeance through the same Western system which replaced Indian nationalism.

In brief, not being nationalistic enough or having the right spirit of national renaissance, the Nehruvian consensus became largely a decorated superstructure without solid foundations. It could not but collapse.

A national consensus is vaguely about the sort of society we want to live in and therefore must equally emphasize rights as well as the duties of citizens. The Constitution and the political system of the Nehruvian consensus was a romantic and distorted projection of Western liberalism which evolved over years in Europe a set of fundamental rights and stressed the spirit of individualism. The Indian Constitution and laws put an exaggerated emphasis on individual rights but ignored totally the duties of citizens and revealed the intellectual adolescence of their authors.

The liberal spirit of the West stimulated a great deal the movement for self-determination in the colonial era. But what was lacking in the post-Independence consensus in India was operational policies to keep check on hot-house ideas and theories imported from the West. Besides, on a false and irrelevant premise that the old Hindu society stressed more the obligations than the rights, the most ruthless individualism and groupism were released without realizing that the old attitude was a remnant of an era of religious and political persecution and did not belong to any permanent social tradition of India. The casualty was both a sense of obligation and the traditional principle of brotherhood and national unity.

Today we have been left with the loud and shrill cries of rights including the right of blackmail, treason, corruption, breach of law as well the right to get away with it. No consensus can have any meaning in this situation, particularly if law and order has broken down. Almost all the contemporary ideologies, pressures, and institutions constituting the Nehruvian consensus add up to a structure of unlimited pluralism and distributive pressures on the economic system. The federal political structure, democratic decentralization, welfare State, socialism, land distribution, theory of balance among group interests, educational expansion, etc., are all distributive ideologies without necessarily requiring any emphasis on productivity and efficiency. Only when the national cake, i.e. national income, came to grow slowly was their squeeze felt terribly on the economy.

Nevertheless, thanks to that consensus, there is yet no realization about the fatal pressure of these distributive ideologies. Nehru had a great sense of history but no sense of time. For example, socialism is an historical inevitability but how can one forget that it took the greatest socialist country forty years of productive effort before anything worthwhile could be distributed to the Soviet citizens. The Nehruvian socialism, on the other hand, began with production and distribution alike.

An important characteristic of a workable consensus is that its general pattern should be able to determine the relative role and function and degree of competitiveness of its component parts as well as hold them together in a consistent fashion. In other words, social progress cannot be had only at either of the two extremes of the scales, namely, functionalism and dialectics; the two must exist and reinforce each other in right proportion.

The Nehruvian consensus was essentially functional in approach and completely discarded the dialectical part, with the result that it ceased to be functional in the end. It never tackled the basic problem of arriving at a theory of society that could achieve an adequate balance between stability and change, between equilibrium and disequilibrium, and even between consensus and conflict. If it ever was one, Nehruism as a political system, following David Apter's threefold classification, was reconciling and not, or at least not enough, mobilizing and modernizing. The former has the characteristics of pyramidal authority, multiple loyalties, built-in compromise, pluralism, and ideological diffusion. The last two have tactical and strategic flexibility, unitarism, exclusivism, ideological specialization, neo-traditionalism, and modernizing nationalism.

But the worse part of Nehruism was that, while it accepted one system in principle, it tried to behave differently. In this contradiction lies the emerging frigidity of the Indian system about which Professor A.H. Hanson has remarked that "many of the difficulties which Indian planners have encountered spring from the fact that they are constantly attempting to transcend the limitations of the reconciliation system within which they have to operate and the tendency to assume the existence of attitudes and the viabilities of techniques which are meaningful only within the framework of a mobilizing system."

What were the means, techniques, and choices open to the Nehruvian consensus or used by it? It is not possible to enumerate all of them or analyze fully the most important ones. Nevertheless, something must be said about their failure story.

(*i*) A democratic consensus is bound to fail without a dominant two-party system. For twenty years, instead of a two-party system, we had more or less an effective one-party rule through a curious mixture of scores of fragmented parties, groups, and factions.

(*ii*) A consensus must be arrived at through some recognizable process. It may appear strange but it remains a fact that the Nehruvian consensus was never subjected to a full-scale national debate. It was never even questioned until the Swatantra Party came into existence. Lack of debate was more pronounced in issues of foreign policy.

(*iii*) A consensus is either participant or non-participant. All sorts of institutions were set up for people's and elite's participation and they did participate, but unfortunately the character and functioning of these institutions was such that what emerged out of the participation was not a consensus but a series of violent conflicts, and ironically the functionlessness of the entire system.

(*iv*) Every consensus, and more so a democratic one, needs a proper structure of leadership at all levels. What Gandhi gave India was not really a synthesis between traditionalism and modernism as is often assumed, but a novel and working synthesis between the elite and the masses as an instrument of political action. On the other hand, over the last twenty years, not only has the gap between the elite and the masses widened politically but also the cultural gap has sharply cut the society vertically. At higher levels Nehru, unlike Gandhi, employed a personal vassalage relationship to remain in power. The result, as Bagehot would say, is the legacy of tenth-rate leaders desperately and perpetually trying to become ninth rate.

(*v*) The choice and use by a consensus of some militant organization depends upon the degree and intensity of inequities, exploitation, and irrationalism in the society. There was a formidable accumulation over centuries of these ugly forces which needed a quick sweeping away. Every decision could not be left to natural compromise. The Nehruvian consensus was totally unmilitant. No wonder that the forces of communalism, caste, and faction have been let loose on the country in their most vicious form.

(*vi*) Politics is all about power and a political consensus is a balance of power between numerous components of the power structure. Unless there is an effective and operational agreement among the components about some minimum code of conduct and respect for the law, no consensus can succeed. It is wrong to create a model of a politician being either a saint or a crook; it must be of persons working with outer as well as self-imposed limitations. When adult franchise was introduced in Europe, the laws of the land were tightened and were made to be respected. In India we have neither the respect and the effectiveness of the law nor a consensus about the code of conduct. In fact, political fragmentation and animosities have become so deep as to exclude any agreement on political rules of the game among the major competitors for power. It is a situtation of one irresponsibility counterpointing another.

Consensus or no consensus, a nation must develop a critical minimum power to defend against other nations. If there is also a consensus and it is held as a value system, the minimum critical level of that power has to be raised to meet physical and ideological onslaughts from other competitive systems. It may not be true or relevant for a small country, but for a large and potentially strong one there is no choice but to compete for power simply because every other comparable political entity is doing so.

We are living in an age of a one-parametric world in which power is the final determinant of a nation's place in the international hierarchy of power. In other words, today one is either a spider or a fly and at best what a small country can do is to avoid being a fly. But the choice for a big country is unique as it is likely to be broken into pieces so as to be reduced to the level of a fly. It is humiliating for India to compete for power with Pakistan in terms of the simple dimension of her potentialities.

Power also determines material goals (including that elusive and most general of all the generalities, i.e. world peace) and the international freedom of action a nation enjoys. "Usually the assertion that a nation's goal is the welfare of humanity is not an outright lie but a half-truth." And it turns into a nightmare for a country with little power to back such goals. The weaker a nation at any time, the narrower and more specific must be its goals to protect itself from being dragged into world-wide conflicts because global goals are a function of power and the amount of sacrifice a nation is prepared to put in.

If a nation without enough power builds into her national consensus universal goals, it invites the charge of hypocrisy and possible humiliation when asked to defend those goals. It may or may not be true that power corrupts or lacks principles, the absence of power certainly corrupts. Today it is the weak rather than the strong powers which are corrupt and unprincipled. A powerful nation has a much greater sense of responsibility today because there is too much at stake for her. Finally, power like national consensus is not static but a dynamic and subtle concept or force. A large country in its transition to growth and power must develop first negative power to prevent others from doing harm to its interests. Positive power comes later. Nehru left India without negative or positive power, for war or peace on her borders today is at the mercy of other powers.

The Nehruvian consensus deliberately underplayed the goals and determinants of power. Nonalignment was too broad, too general, and too much directed to a distant horizon and thus defied all the requirements of power and, therefore, came to a sorry end. This consensus had very little indigenous quality; it was the projection of an external rather than an internal reality. By denying itself the virtue of being specific and more narrowly defined, it undermined the national unity in favour of abstract universal principles. The more India lost face and prestige abroad, the more loud was the cry of nonalignment and the greater became her dependence on others for succour and security. Nehru turned himself into a professional neutralist after one or two conspicuous achievements. His Miltonic passion for resounding titles led him to stick to the most defiant artificiality. He never understood the reality of the potential power in India which gave him an early success.

Here is the comment of A. F. K. Organski: "The expectation of true power may also be traded upon, and a nation expected to be great tomorrow may find its present power position improved for that reason. India is a good example. Part of India's present ability to influence other nations rests upon the peculiar moral position that her leaders, Gandhi and Nehru, came to occupy, but another part of her present power is due to more material considerations. India, with her gigantic population, possesses one of the important prerequisites for being a great power. If she ever modernizes and mobilizes that population, she will indeed be a nation to be contended with. It is with one eye on the future that East and West are vying for the friendship of India."

The old national consensus is shattered completely now; in fact it was hardly a consesus in the sense of having been nationally arrived at. It revealed itself as an amalgam of Nehru's private myths. A new consensus, therefore, must be created. It cannot be created as an academic exercise but only through the concerted efforts of the most conscious segments of the political elite while taking into account the forces, alignments, power structure, and the socio-economic realities, all of which also have to be modified through the working of the same consensus.

The purpose here is to point only to the single most solid foundation of a new consensus, namely, nationalism. By now every other power has revealed the all-pervasive force of its nationalism. By contrast, the Nehruvian consensus amounts to national self-abdication. Nationalism has to be regenerated in all its healthy aspects, i.e. as a component of the structure of policies, a dynamic path, even as an ideology, an inescapable instrument, and as a frame of reference. Nehru said in 1960: "How superficial is the covering of what we like to call nationalism which bursts open at the slightest irritation." He looked upon nationalism as a covering and not as a foundation for the progress of the society.

What is nationalism? This word has been a subject of interminable discussion and it is not my purpose to disentangle the historical, philosophic, psychological attributes from the political meaning of the word. Nationalism can be classified into two categories: domestic and foreign. The former, as a unifying force, is concerned with internal social and economic arrangement, change, struggle, and power structure; it is locked in essential conflict with particularism such as subnationalism, regionalism, communalism, and castes. The latter, as defined by Rupert Emerson, is that "reduced to its bare bones, nationalism is no more than the assertion that this particular community is araranged against the rest of mankind" in the present of the world divided into nation-States.

The second approach does not permit this term to have a pure theoretical construction, in the sense of having logical rigour and perfect internal consistency. We are not living in the 18th and 19th centuries of which nationalism was the product. In the second half of the 20th century, when national self-determination is no longer an issue, the term "nationalism" has to be used contextually as Ernst B. Hall, the famous author of *Beyond the Nation State*, has suggested. That is "an approach that tries to bridge the epistomological chasm between those who want to derive general deductive laws on the one hand and those who prefer to concentrate on painstaking narration of discreet, if related, events on the other. Contextual analysis is more ambitious than historical narration and more modest than the effort at deductive science. It sees the phenomenon under investigation as a part of a 'whole' but defines the 'whole' in relatively modest and easily observable terms."

Therefore, whether nationalism is good or bad or will prove a curse or a blessing is not a matter of definition. The fact remains that it is not on the wane "in the countries of its origin." It remains a great historic process and the paradox is that nowhere is the emphasis on it so great as in a communist society or in the centre of free nations, i.e. the United States.

Let us anticipate the Marxists' objection to nationalism. Lenin wrote in 1913: "Marxism is irreconcilable with nationalism even the justest, purest, most refined and civilized." After three decades, the most sympathetic historian of the Soviet Union, E.H. Carr, summed up that "the socialization of the nation had its natural corollary in the nationalization of socialism." What has happened since then is a gruesome story of naked nationalism first revealed in the ruthless exploitation by the Soviet Union of other communist countries and then in the irretrievable clash of national interests between the Soviet Union and Communist China. The greater the global involvement of big powers, the greater has been the rise of nationalist tendencies in the world.

In the historical growth of communism, nationalism was once an enemy but today it is, to use the language of strategy, the highest common denominator in global power competition. Yet Karunakar Gupta, presumably a Marxist, writes, while approving Nehru's foreign policy, that "under the circumstances, the defence of national interest in Indian foreign policy would mean safeguarding primarily the interests of the propertied classes."

I have no doubt in my mind that if communists were in power in India they would defend every inch of territorry against the Chinese more jealously and nationalistically than anybody else as, for example, the Russians and Chinese are doing against each other. And they would give the higest priority to make India a great power. But a weak communist country denounces nationalism and can also commit acts of treason. What comrade Mao is doing today is not applying Marxism to Chinese conditions—that he did long ago —but imposing Chinese nationalism on Marxism; it is the latter which has to adjust to the former. No communist movement can succeed today if it goes against the stream of nationalism. Nationalism remains the dominant cultural complex of politically divided nation-States.

Nobody can speak better for the United States than Hans J. Morgenthau. "Throughout its history the United States has pursued a consistent foreign policy. Beneath the clamour of contending philosophies, the controversies of factions, the contradictions and reversals of individual moves on the international scene, the foreign policy of the United States presents a simple coherent pattern—to preserve its unique position as the predominant unrivalled power in the Western hemisphere" and now to maintain in Asia "the permanent power of the United States."

Until recently, nationalism was considered dead in Europe as if the mature nations were moving towards some permanent union as a part of historical belief in the inevitability of that development. De Gaulle has clearly given the call for the end of what he called the two hegemonies in Europe and this brought into focus the neo-nationalism of the industrialized middle powers. In Latin America and Africa the struggle for survival is the struggle of nationalism.

A general principle is that whenever international relations or pacts of interdependence threaten the prosperity and security of a nation, a nationalist outlook develops among its citizens, whether democratic or communist. The paradox of this age is that it marks the high tide of nationalism and defence of national interests while in theory—but only in theory as any assessment of the United Nations will show—it also points towards the possibility of the end of nationalism as embodied in the principles of world government, technological imperatives, growth of communication, etc. Yet, what Gandhiji said remains true: "Internationalism is possible only when nationalism is a fact."

The paradox is due to the uneven distribution of military and economic power in the world. For smaller countries the problem is not acute. For large countries like India the problem of lack of power is pressing on each one of their internal and external policies. Nationalism without power is a cry of corruption and brutalization. The philosophy of history as the march of ideas of freedom and progress is really not inconsistent with nationalism; only it has come to depend upon the latter and the power wielded by it. Power gives a country a choice, the lack of it does not.

India's foreign policy lacked power, rejected nationalism, left national interest undefined, and proclaimed abstract principles. The supreme principle of foreign policy is that national interests are supreme and that Indian civilization is in fierce competition with other civilizations. The Indian State is in perpetual struggle with other States, and India as a power centre is bound to clash with other power centres. Nehru wanted to buy political idealism and millennium at a cheap price. The price has turned out to be very high—the demise of nationalism. If the term "nation" had not always been able to explain the conduct of communist powers, it was because the element of power in their theoretical calculus was neglected. Now the naked truth is that the nation-State and its nationals are the only entities which work through power within the contemporary world. It does not mean that a nation-State is an end itself. It is the defence of the instrument that is relevant. Nationalism is the most unifying force for weaker countries like India in defence of their integrity and interests.

Is nationalism inconsistent with socialism? We have shown above that it is not so externally. What about inside a country? Like nationalism, socialism is also a slippery concept. Today anything from a simple welfare State to a complete communist society can be called socialism. Socialism is a great dream of humanity and an historical inevitability whether realized gradually or otherwise. It is also a matter of degree, means, and speed because all over the world the people are building their societies on the socialist, humanist principles of equality, despite occasional and short-term aberrations.

In the modern world, a welfare State is nationalist in the sense that its psychological foundations lie in people's valuations and expectations. Myrdal has painstakingly tried to show that a growing identification with the nation-State and with all the people within its boundaries is a natural result of the development of the democratic welfare State—a State which is "protective and nationalist." Even so great a critic of nationalism, Elie Kedorrie, makes nationalism, "the cohesion of the State, loyalty to it depends on its capacity to ensure welfare of the individual, and in him, love of the fatherland as a function of benefits received." It is true that in Europe nationalism matured under national bourgeoisie. It is the experience of the last twenty years that this is no longer enough. A part of the national bourgeoisie can be anti-nationalist and subserve the interest of neo-colonialists.

It is wrong to call pragmatism the philosophy of nationalism, because raised to the level of a philosophy and its logical extremes, pragmatism produces scepticism, nihilism and ultimately despair.

Pragmatism in the garb of Nehruvian ideology has led to the growth of reactionary and particularistic forces in India. Indian socialism came to a sorry state due largely to the rise of particularism of all sorts—caste, communailsm, regionalism, and religious fanaticism. Only the integrating force of nationalism could remove these barriers to a socialist society, as well as produce, if necessary, the right type of dialectical conflict. Above all, socialism as well as nationalism would insist on rapid industrialization and economic growth and put the burden on shoulders on which it should really rest.

It is often feared that a return to nationalism could lead to the revival of Hinduism and its reaction, the minority communalism. Irrespective of any logical or historical relationship between religion and nationalism, the politics of the last few years in India has unmistakably revealed that it is the low level of nationalism which has made people return to religion and virulent communalism, whether of the majority or minority. Besides, Hinduism as a religion and as a social tradition or system is not coterminus with nationalism. Whatever is best or relevant in that tradition has to be fully utilized and even carried forward if vast masses have to have faith in themselves, discover their identity, and discriminate between national and other narrow loyalties.

The absence of a nationalist outlook has led the whole class of our Western educated intellectuals, strangely both of Right and Left persuasion, to resort to wholesale denunciation of Indian nationalism and Indian values. Having been uprooted from these traditions by their education and class distinctions, they divide their loyalty between their subcaste or region and the cosmos. They do not see anything but weakness and rot in the Indian society and it would come as the greatest shock to them if India ever were able to emerge as a strong nation. They do not realize, for example, that Mao has always used the traditional idiom as the medium of communication between the elite and the masses and also between himself and the elite. Nationalism as well as the Hindu way of life are not deterministic laws but only ways of acting and thinking.

The real problem is to separate the wheat from the chaff by

consciousness and skill of the leaders who set and control the pattern of behaviour and know the goals of the society, because Hinduism by itself is not necessarily nationalistic.

Professor Vikas Misra, in his study of Hinduism and economic development, remarks that "nationalism is by no means an essential attribute of Hinduism, indeed, the history of India often shows the contrary, the predominance of group interests over national interests. The Hindu social structure also strengthens group loyalty." In other words, nationalism is, to say the least, going to offend some part of Hinduism though not reject what is vital in it. Hinduism as a religious-cum-political technique as used by Gandhi has probably outlived its utility. But the spirit behind what he said is worth noting: "My Hinduism is not sectarian. It includes all that I know to be best in Islam, Christianity, Buddhism, and Zorastrianism."

Early Muslim nationalists like Sir Sayyid Ahmed Khan likened the Indian nation to a blonde and her two eyes were the Hindus and Muslims. Indian nationalism was dealt a heavy blow by the division of India on religious lines. Only the revival of nationalism can reduce the sectarian force of religion as well as salvage that part of the Indian nationalist tradition, which, in the words of Annie Besant, is "not a plant of mushroom growth but a giant of the forest, with millennia behind it." The cry of the wolf of Hindu revivalism is utter defeatism and lack of self-confidence.

How is nationalism related to modernization and change? Two words coined by Indian sociologists "Sanskritization" and "Westernization" have done immense harm to the conceptualization of change in Indian society. The former, despite all attempts at its sophistication, has not meant anything more than the creation of new permutations and the internal convolutions within a social system, i.e. it referred only to "static change." The latter, though wrongly equated with modernization, referred to the absorption of some institutions and certain behaviour patterns from the West. It has been cruelly disproved by the Indian experience that Westernization necessarily implies either industrialization or modernization in the sense of a high rate of investment and savings or a pervasive technological and scientific bias.

Thus, not very surprisingly, the concepts of Sanskritization and Westernization have not only utterly failed to explain the internal dynamics of the change in India on the national scale, they have, as descriptive parameters of small group behaviour, also set up false and misleading indices of change.

Nowhere in our plans, institutions, and behaviour does the relation between modernization and nationalism appear in any positive form. Modernization without the sanction of nationalism behind it has led, on the one hand, to the development of the "fascination effect" and apish mentality for an indiscriminate import of bogus cultural values and commodities from the West and, on the other hand, to a yawning technological gap between the unchanging primitive *charkha* and a few imported islands of technical excellence, thus further aggravating the dual economic culture from which we began. India has not understood the concept of "national" or, what D.R. Gadgil calls, intermediate technology and has created an unbalanced structure all along the line.

The so-called modernization in political and cultural life has also created a new and more pernicious dualism between the elite and the masses, the privileged few and the poor humanity. The sociologists keep unduly stressing the importance of group mobility, cultural transmission, diversification, phenomenon of dominance and resistance, intensity of interest-group activity—all as symptoms of political and social progress. There is no other more pernicious nonsense that has been kicked about for so long. By their standards, the DMK is very national, the Arya Samaj progressive, caste healthy, religion forward-looking, and what not? What is needed is a strong dose of nationalism to root out these poisonous weeds of divisive and corroding particularism, and a unifying force which forces through these groups and their narrow loyalties certain behavioural and institutional compulsions towards efficiency, rational allocations, and satisfying national priorities.

A feature of the Indian nationalism of the freedom movement was its identification with true modernization despite a temporary backsliding by Gandhi. The reports of the National

Planning Committee of the Indian National Congress bear testimony to that assumption. No price was too high for the nationalists' commitment to modernizing the society and destroying the *status quo*. Nationalism would have certainly proved the strongest force in this transition and transformation.

Somehow, political modernization was understood by later-day Indian leaders to be least concerned with nationalism. In the words of Rupert Emerson, they ignored "the proposition that the rise of nationalism is normally associated with deep-running solid ferment and change which disrupt the old order of society and bring about a rise in social consciousness and awareness of ever-widening segments and classes of the people at large. On this basis nationalism is seen as one of the major manifestations of what Karl Mannheim has spoken of as the fundamental democratization of society."

Indian democracy has reached a point where unless it is given a new outfit, a new functionalism, and a new faith, it is in danger of being liquidated. Democracy in the West slowly evolved, first to arbitrate over a small number of issues and later to expand so much as to manage and settle a whole range of social, economic, and political problems. In India, democracy was intended to perform the latter function right from the beginning and quite obviously it could not succeed in its allotted tasks. And yet the spirit of democracy has seeped quite deep into the Indian mind, reinforced by the traditional behaviour of tolerance and let-live.

In Europe, in the early days of the rise of democracy, conservatives came to look upon nationalism as an antidote to democracy and a means to check the latter. How sadly it dawned on them that nationalism could be equally anti-conservative and revolutionary in character. In the last few decades, democracy has fought all its *successful* battles under the banner of nationalism that "is peculiarly a product of a response to the distinctive forces which have gone into the shaping of the modern world. These forces are inherently and inevitably democratic in the sense that they mobilize submerged elements and classes of society into a new social role, eat away at traditional attachments and relationships, and work towards the building of a new great society into which, in principle, all men are actively drawn; the general conception, derived from the changing social scene ... [is] that the people, the mass of ordinary humans, are of consequence, that they are achieving a sense both of their own worth and of their right and ability to do something about it, that leaders must speak in their name. The national era came to be the era of mass communications and mass production, the State could no longer be seen as made up of the ruler and those who happened to be its subjects, but became in principle the nation and instrument of the nation."

Political activity, like other activities, has its own goals and objectives. In developed societies, democracy has travelled a long way and has made political activity also a rational end in itself. However, if objectives become blurred and mutually irreconcilable, lack minimum consensus and impart intellectual cynicism and escapism, the autonomous political activity degenerates into pseudo-politics. This phenomenon is quite common in underdeveloped and unstable societies. India today faces this problem as one of the most serious challenges. One other feature of this pseudo-politics is that it considers the existing politico-economic system as best and resists change, while noisy professions on grim problems and big change and fundamental transformation are constantly voiced for public consumption.

The India of today is a grim example of a growing gulf between profession and practice all over the political field. While politics is fast becoming an end in itself, there is also taking place a general deterioration in ordinary political norms and disregard of the determinants, implications, and consequences of this type of political activity. Most of our political leaders talk all the time in terms of total normative dimensions lent in practice often indulge in vulgar and corrupt pragmatism.

It is a sign of the same pseudo-politics that political activity in India is massively encumbered by clashes of mutually hating, pseudo-ideologies, despite the long and bitter experience that such ideological-dominated thinking and activity has had little relevance to the actually controlling factors of the contemporary social structure, politics and change.

It is amazing how the ideology of equality and socialism has degenerated into non-discrimination against stupidity and incompetence, and the ideology of liberalism has become a tool for the maintenance of the illiberal *status quo* and the exploitation of the weakest section of the society. It is my contention that existing forms of political activity and the consensus on which they are based cannot save democracy from its pseudo aspects. Nationalism alone can pull out the weeds of pseudo-politics as well as give faith to the masses to work for a new consensus.

There is no guarantee that nationalism will always lead to democracy. But democracy without nationalism cannot survive. If nationalism ever goes against democracy in newly independent countries, it will simply be a short-term tactical retreat because all over the world democracy and nationalism as political phenomena have closely coincided. One World Government is a distant dream.

Probably the most crucial role of nationalism in India today rests in our accepting it as an approach to the defence of national interests, as an ideology of unity, and as a self-respecting attitude to action for self-reliance. As a complex of nationality, nation-State and national patriotism, it is the most significant sanction behind some minimum unity of thought and action. Whereas the nationalism of the super powers carries the danger of leading them straight to imperialism, nationalism of potentially strong countries like India emerges as the bastion of anti-imperialism by putting premium on unity, defence preparedness, and self-reliance. In face of the internal fragmentation of politics and disunity as well as external weakness, the ideological force of nationalism must, of necessity, be fully integrated in India's national and international politics.

Ideological nationalism is revolutionary while pragmatic nationalism moves slowly. Time is running out against India and going back to nationalism as a sober calculation and not as psychotic emotionalism is the inescapable path to survival and rapid change. Today it remains probably the only reliable means of interpreting the ills, problems, and frustrations as well as the goals of our society. It is also the only means left for creating a new healthy psychological environment out of the chaos of ideologies, non-decision making, and politics of dysfunctionalism.

Nationalism does not mean the rejection of other ideologies or the creation of an ideology-free society because nationalism in itself is not a coherent and systematic body of doctrines and beliefs, but is a means to get at the best workable ideology or ideologies. In short, nationalism alone can create an ideological consensus in the dynamic sense, make the beginnings of a new consensus in place of the old and now defunct Nehruvian consensus. There are enough and lasting shared experiences and political values in India to sustain nationalism and the nation-State as the impersonal and ultimate arbiter of India's destiny.

It is particularly so today because the current ideologies propagated in India have very little intellectual content as they are divorced from the Indian ethos. There are all sorts of nationalist movements in the world and around India's borders that are going in search of an ideology. Since the Nehruvian search for an ideology has not been nationalistic, it has lost its acquired ideology and nationalism bequeathed to it by Gandhi. The size of Nehru's bite was big and puffy but the quality of his chewing was utterly hopeless.

The preceding discussion has yielded at least two important conclusions, both of which are important in creating a new national consensus in place of the Nehruvian consensus. First, nationalism is not inconsistent with the value-system on which the Indian people have been brought up either by Nehru or the national freedom movement. In fact, it was the lack of nationalism which corrupted if not destroyed that value system. Nor is it inconsistent with internationalism except that so long as wide disparities of political and military power, industrialization, standard of living remain, we shall have to contend with divergent and not convergent nationalisms. High correlation between nationalism and underdevelopment is a sign and urge for creating a more solid and surer internationalism. It is the global involvement of super powers which is hindering rather than helping internationalism. The policy of the new but weak nation-States is not to remain alone in the world if they do not want to be submerged.

The second conclusion, and more satisfying to high-minded sceptics, is that nationalism is a powerful revolutionary instrument, but nevertheless an instrument. Since it is the principal instrument of world powers, we cannot afford to reject it unless we find a better one to replace it. As Ernest Baker has pointed out in this connection, "we can judge tools by the efficacy with which they fulfil the purposes for which they are used." Our rejection of nationalism so far has created for us numerous humiliating positions, and we must grasp it now and fully use it before we discard it again. I doubt if any other nation is going to discard it during the next half century, which is most likely to be a century of national development, opportunities, and crises.

Nationalism is not a set of principles which tell us how to organize our society. But looking around at a spectrum of nationalism, whether of Right or Left, traditional or revolutionary, democratic or otherwise, it remains the most powerful force for social development. Even Marxism today exists only in some form of national socialism. For India the doctrine of nationalism as a substitute for the fading collective conscience and pseudo-politics is a must for rallying the people in defence of unity, to give them an identity and sense of belonging and civilized optimism, to create a passion for national reconstruction through self-reliance, for socialism and democracy, i.e. for a cohesive and refreshing new national consensus.

February 1967

13

BACK TO NATIONALISM: QUASI-INDIAN POWER ELITE

THE NATIONAL MOTTO of the Indian intellectuals today is "betray." It does not matter whether they are liberals, Marxists, or pragmatists or something above all these. It also does not matter whether they are engaged in scientific, speculative, theoretical, philosophical, or practical work. They are undoubtedly one of the strategic sections of the national power elite, although their honeymoon with the rest of the power elite was nasty, brutish, and short; in their mutual alienation the two run now almost parallel to each other. Their betrayal does not lie in any flight from the corridors of power and escape to intellectual autonomy, because no such withdrawals have taken place. Their betrayal originated first in their taking for granted the cultural superiority of the white man and then in their willing acceptance of intellectual or academic colonialism as a political creed or a value system. A whole generation of those quasi-Indians has grown up who consciously go to the limits of refusing to accept India as a nation and that also at a time when the nation-State is the primary source of power and well-being of a people. Nehru was the patriarch of this un-Indian intellectual brood and his ambivalent philosophy and super-elite politics has survived long enough for them to remain in power and status.

Since intellectuals do not appear on the surface as organized groups in social and political stratification, their betrayal appears less pronounced than that of the politicians. Yet, in contrast to the politicians, the intellectual ruling elites are organized, perhaps unconsciously, in some sort of a closed society whose secret rules of functioning are difficult to unravel. Maybe, the curious social system and power strucutre of India make it inevitable for borrowed minds to behave as they do, as if they live all the time on enemy territory.

Very broadly defined, an intellectual is a person who pursues knowledge, gathers ideas which he wants translated into action. He teaches in the universities, writes books and articles in magazines and newspapers, produces works of art, makes laws and sometimes administers them, advises parties, evolves strategy to win or lose a war, etc., and thereby assumes leadership in different fields. To be educated is not sufficient to lay claim to being an intellectual, and certainly not an intellectual elite. Only those who play with ideas, form opinion and are either themselves policy-makers or close to other policy-makers are the relevant power elite. In countries like India, which are not only poor but also reveal a vast gulf between the two extremes of society, the elite and the masses, the former and its powers are identifiable. In the developed world, social mobility keeps the dividing line opaque and blurred.

Once again, for a country which is passing through a period of painful transition, its intellectuals also have historical and moral dimesnions as guardians of national heritage and creators of new values and norms—dimensions which more firmly demand of intellectuals their functional roles. Therefore, the vital question is why the intellectuals have instead reduced themselves to morally impotent and willing tools of foreign culture. If such a class really betrays, the betrayal must be multi-dimensional and all-pervasive. If one were a classical Marxist, one could dismiss this whole class of the intellectual elite as petty bourgeoise whose betrayal of the masses is historically inevitable. But in India, a vast body of intellectual elite themselves are Marxists of one or the other variety. This fact adds despondency to the situation.

From the high tide of national resurgence in the 1940s, there clearly has taken place a precipitous decline in national or collective conscience, accompanied by the growth of numerous divisive forces. It is the intellectuals today who take Indian collectivity no longer for granted; they have a national genius for worshipping other nations. As Marxists and devotees of Leninism, they denounce national consciousness as something opposed to class conflict and international proletarianism. As liberals and purveyors of Western democracy, they denounce all values and institutions in India as something opposed to modernization and individual freedom. The spiritual obeisance of the former to Russia and now to China made them so blind to the national chauvinism of a big communist country that they blamed and denounced India when she was attacked by China. The recent performance of the pro-Soviet intellectuals revealed how deeply enmeshed they were in subservience.

The liberals, on the other hand, are spiritually immersed in modern Western society. They refuse to see the penetration and domination of our social and economic system, not necessarily by Western value-system, but by Western imperialism. Imperialism in its new phase is no longer the primitive one which Lenin formulated but much more subtle, affecting the minds as much as the bellies of men. Under the camouflage of modernization and developing a comprehensive world outlook, both sets of intellectuals are consciously selling India and its self-realization down the drain. The CIA and KGB do not require any elaborate spying system in India, although they always need and keep some of it in operation, because there is very little which they require by way of information for strategic purposes. Their real *modus operandi* is the cultural and intellectual domination which would destroy the chances for this country regenerating itself.

Recent revelations about heavy recruitment by the CIA of American intellectuals, who are sent abroad ostensibly to conduct depth research, are pointers towards a new style of brain-washing through intellctual colonialism. People generally aware of all this are no less the victims of Western "snake-charmers." A man like Nirad C. Chaudhuri, whose mind is heavy with Westernism, denounces nationalism from house-tops as something harmful to our intellectual life. Marxists also do not realize that if India goes communist, the most disappointed will be the Russians and the Chinese, because they will then have to contend with the national communism of India, as they are mutually contending each other's. Unfortunately, every new Marxist thesis in India, following ever new splits in their ranks, is more heavily caught up in the Sino-Soviet dispute than with any serious quantitative analysis and its application to this country.

It is true of both Marxists and liberals that the development of historical consciousness about India seems alien to them. Liberals do not lay any special claims on history but Marxists who swear by it have no business to engage themselves in a systematic identity-dismantling of the Indian nation. By denying themselves the role of creating a dialectical synthesis between national and international interests and obligations, they have remorselessly been taking positions and attitudes which border on treason. By refusing to see the vital qualitative shift between a communist movement and its capturing power in a particular geographical area, they have failed to distinguish between the national interests of one nation and another, as well as to understand their respective attempts at founding new empires. It does not occur to both sets of intellectuals that the major developments and problems of India cannot be understood, much less tackled, in terms of Marxist or liberal interpretations alone.

For example, while fearing rightly the dangerous emergence of Hindu obscurantism, they seek refuge in obeisance to pseudo-internationalism instead of developing and supporting radical nationalism which alone can counter that false and divisive nationalism of the Jana Sangh or the RSS which could split the country both vertically and horizontally. Instead, they end up by denouncing nationalism and betraying their own nation in every possible way. There is no real conflict between tradition and modernity in the scientific sense; the two are historical phases in the same process, as Gandhi practised them. It is the conflict between traditional obscurantism and pseudo-modernism, the one without future and the other without roots, that lies at the root of the intellectuals' alienation and surrender.

Ever since the general elections of the 1967 in which the Congress Party lost several States to the Opposition, whether of the Right or Left, intellectuals of both variety have supported rampant federalism. The arguments marshalled for a weak Centre and strong States are based either on the nationality principle of Stalin or on decentralization of power as preached by Western democracies, forgetting that the former accompanied while the latter came after a prolonged phase of centralization. Besides, on the already proved inconsistent strategy of planning and low rate of growth are being imposed the demands of regionalism. These demands are only the counterpart of the decline of the conciousness of nationhood. There is not one Marxist or liberal intellectual today who seems worried about the internal and external consequences of a weak Centre.

The most disastrous consequence of this shift has been the curious convergence of Marxists and liberals on their plumping for a 3 per cent growth instead of 5—the critical minimum. Both have developed a tremendous stake in the continued weakness and *status quo* by which they can avoid or delay the shake-up at high places. The Planning Commission is fast becoming the refuge of intellectual functionaries of different ideologies.

More than ever before, the decline in national consciousness has been very rapid in the recent years of political and economic recession. The "other-directed" intellectuals were on the defensive in the early years of our independence which threw up several real challenges. Now they are on the offensive in the face of weak challenges and in search of soft options which are produced by a fragmented politics. There has taken place a tremendous spurt in foreign, overlapping lobbies, all of whom are meticulously sustained at the ideological level with the help of intellectuals. These lobbies, in turn, sustain the position, status, and material benefits of their respective intellectuals.

To support a particular ideological movement is one thing; to support a lobby with an ideological covering is another. The former demands commitments and sacrifices from the intellectuals, the latter showers benefits on them. The entire top professional establishment at the universities is nothing but a conglomeration of lobbies and nationally alienated people, bent on improving their material and status benefits. Their perennial philosophy is nothing but perennial hypocrisy.

The vast proliferation of higher institutions, consequent upon the education explosion, has provided festering places for the operation of foreign agents and those Indians who are ready to borrow along with technology the cultural and ideological patterns which are inconsistent with our own. Gradually they get alienated not only from the rest of the educational system but also from the entire dynamics of social and political change in India.

This alienation of the intellectuals is not really in the ultra-liberal or Marxist sense, although it appears as part of the fashionable despair now overtaking intellectuals the world over. It is an alienation born out of a superiority complex, allegiance to instead of a withdrawal from the prevailing power structure, a cultivated sense of despair and of intellectual authoritarianism against participation in contemporary movements. Since this alienation is fully compensated by intellectual servility to foreign cultures, no one truly feels either a complete outsider or a complete insider. A Dom Moraes or a Ved Mehta may go away but the rest of the brood are right here playing their own power game, and running parallel to the rest of the power structure. The University Grants Commission's scheme of opening advanced centre at several universities has served nothing but the interests of the twice born, who not only have one foot here and one abroad but also have split loyalties. Between this professorial establishment at the top and the educational gutter at the bottom is divided our new intellectual caste system, for which the UGC is entirely to blame.

Intellectual integrity can be defined within the limits of one's definition of the contemporary problems. If these problems are defined in the international context and completely divorced from the Indian situation, the intellectual is bound to end up as irrelevant, if not a sickly sentimentalist. Those who write guides on the models of Oxbridge and Harvard to economic and political utopias only end up in being primarily self-interested. Their quest for knowledge and academic freedom are no more than efforts to improve their own selves at the cost of the nation's resources.

The power and influence of intellectuals should not be underestimated, even if they are numerically small. They are an independent variable in the power system and seriously affect the impressionable minds of the younger generation and hence of the future elite. For example, when university intellectuals foreclose their identities by adopting intellectually supra-national but mercenary roles—a sign of moral and national decay—their postures leave a profound impression to the new generation.

This new generation reveals itself in its individual ruthlessness, in its denial of a value system except psychedelic modernism and a total ignorance of and contempt for the country. They view their own Indian languages with disdain. If there is any single major cause of the language muddle in this country, it is the vested interests of the English-educated intelligentsia. Several professors of Delhi University who come from non-Hindi speaking areas boast about their not having learnt more than a dozen sentences of Hindi in their two dozen years of stay in the capital.

Intellectuals by and large are responsible for the tremendous growth of the English language press through which, in turn, they affect opinions and policies towards directions which are their own handiwork. Nothing stands between their personal or parochial loyalties and their international loyalties. India seems to have disappeared somewhere between these loyalties at two extremes. Intellectuals are also attached to political lobbies inside and outside the Parliament, and provide powerful support against any climate being created for the need of national solutions to national problems.

In the arts, too, one finds the total impress of foreign, particularly Western, modes. Go to a theatre in Delhi or Bombay, and you find four out of every five plays are foreign-oriented. There is a rage for plays of the absurd which are completely irrelevant to our contemporary situation. The Oxonian accent which is now berated in England is the current fashion in India and it is artistically infuriating to watch this and our own public school accent being imposed on American or Yorkshire slang. It is worth noting that the impact of foreign plays or films is, if anything, negative on their Indian counterparts.

Regarding paintings, the situation is even worse. The invasion of foreigners who are comfortably settling down in our cities is having the effect of a perverse revolution of rising expectations. An intellectual today is incomplete without nine-tenths of his personal belongings, including books, having been produced abroad. There are well-known social groups run in the capital by foreigners to ensnare young intellectuals and to keep hold on older converts. The impact on all other classes is disastrous.

Our intellectuals have passed the stage of keeping up with the Joneses; they are Joneses themselves whom other people have to keek up with. Every other journalist is, ideologically, either a vocal leftist or ultra liberal. In practice, he is the most active stooge of tycoons and foreign missions. Journalists along with some university intellectuals and Government bureaucrats form what are called the Right or Left cocktail circuits. They are all engaged in a single game of denigrating India before every foreigner who comes to this country. The public power of this private corruption is a matter of great concern. Some distinction is always there between bureaucrats and intellectuals. What is common between them is more important. Their specialized pattern of recruitment, careers, and social-clubbing together is the same as was during the days of our old colonial masters.

Foreign aid has become, directly and indirectly, the principal instrument of colonialism, all the more so during the phase of the decline in this aid. Only a determined nationalist elite could have absorbed the necessary aid and then gradually dismantled it. The real essence of foreign aid is twofold: (*i*) that it has been used not as a supplement to internal resource mobilization efforts but as a substitute for the latter; and (*ii*) a large part of the aid has been directed towards establishing non-productive, politically-oriented institutions which employ a large number of the intellectual elite. So long as the rate of aid utilization was increasing, every vocal group was appropriately bribed. Once the aid started declining, and it continued to do so, the real imbalances and contradictions in the economy came to the surface in the form of recurring crises.

Threatened with their built-in security, the elite, liberal as well as Marxist, have become nearly hysterical in accusing each other's real masters, the USA and the USSR. It is not surprising that Left intellectuals, in the same breath in which they call for an end to India depending on American aid, also go panicky in their denunciation of America for reducing her aid to India. Both the Left intellectuals, who have been the direct beneficiaries of the aid coming from imperialist countries, and the liberals, who have not directly benefited from the Soviet aid, are now simultaneously plumping for the theory of India being an area of agreement, where the two powers can happily converge, and thus make a case for fresh efforts to get aid, private as well as public. Their democratic or communist susceptibilities are no longer injured in face of the joint Soviet-American pressures.

The real betrayal of both groups lies in their joint acquiescence not only in smaller aid from super powers, because they just cannot help it, but also in providing systematic models against India shaking herself for a big internal effort for a higher growth rate. For example, the nutshell of the recent discussion of "Namboodiri Marxists," at Kerala, has been the Left mandarins' acceptance of Professor B.R. Shenoy's thesis of no more than a 3 per cent growth rate. Didn't Marx say that history comes first as a tragedy and second time as a farce. Liberals, of course, never wanted anything more than that because they and their version of doddering democracy would just not survive at any higher rate of growth.

The method and type of aid utilization, the businessmen's general preference to get rich quick while the going is good, and the subservience of intellectuals and politicians to their foreign counterparts have brought technological colonialism right in the centre of our economy. The continuous import of the same old technology, its heavy consumers' bias, and the stifling conditions of collaboration agreements are crippling our industry.

The only effective defence against technological colonialism, namely, the development of our own science and scientists, technology and technologists, has become a victim of this colonialism. A scientist gets recognition in his own land only after he has been given recognition abroad. The entire atmosphere and organization of research in India is designed to dovetail it to scientific developments elsewhere and has little relevance to the development of those technologies, and such adaptation of imported ones, as would be commensurate with our own factor proportions as well as change those proportions in the desired directions.

Technology may be said to recognize no national boundaries. But there is as yet no such thing as its international application except nominally. Each nation alone uses and develops technology by its own conscious deliberate action. Technical change is one thing but a choice of a particular technique is quite another. Ideas are free but their economic application is a costly affair, which people only as a nation can undertake. The case for economic nationalism refers to determining investment and technological priorities and having, by a deliberate, conscious choice, a spectrum of techniques from the best downward. There can never be complete self-sufficiency in technology, although all major technical requirements have to be met internally. There is, therefore, a lot to be said for borrowing available technology, but for it to suit our needs it will require continuous growth of adaptive innovations which will have to be our own.

There are obvious and serious limits to the import of technology in this regard, for no foreign company can be expected to allocate funds for science or carry out research on Indian materials for adaptive purposes. Foreigners have a natural resistance to touch material which they are not familiar with. It is also in their long-term interest to make us dependent on their technological excellence. The import of technology without adaptation is technological colonialism. Besides, any further progress will largely depend upon the growth of science, because science and technology are interdependent in a circular casual sense.

In the words of J.B.S. Haldane, a scientist in India has a loyalty to science as well as to his country. Probably, the most significant aspect of economic nationalism is the growth of consciousness to make India technologically a first-rate power. Every nation has used and is using its political system, whatever it happens to be, in the direction of these collective decisions. One has only to look at the USA and the USSR to realize the truth of this assertion. Meeting the requirements of our defence are an essential part of this scheme of things.

Those mediocre scientists and technologists who have taken over the management of our science and technology are the worst instruments of intellectual colonialism because they are all genuflexions before foreigners while suppressing the potentialities of Indian scientists. Nowhere has this betrayal been more pervasive than in the corridors of the CSIR. Intellectual heirarchies and bureaucracies are more authoritarian, stifling, and persecuting than any other. This fraternity is as utterly cruel to its own subordinates as it is servile to its external and internal masters. In Delhi University, the Marxist professors persecute their non-Marxist colleagues and *vice versa*. Of course, they are fed by the same hand, the foreign foundations, their local agents, international agencies, etc.

One form or cause of this alienation is the conflict between the philistine bourgeoisie and the intellectuals. The bourgeoisie and its politicians seek to devalue the social personality of the intellectual, partly because the politician got himself emancipated from education long ago, and partly because the intellectual has grown into a socially irrelevant group in the very processes of political and economic development. This trend towards anti-intellectualism reinforces the self-imposed limits on the intellectuals of evolving national solutions. He recedes further into utopian internationalism which has only a thin dividing line with national betrayal.

Despite their double loyalties and self-imposed alienation, along with increased autonomous power, the Indian intellectuals do not feel secure or confident. This contradiction reveals their moral dilemma, schizophrenia, and ebbing integrity. Every jolt that the Indian society gets sends them into open support of the establishment, only to retrace quickly from there in defence of their own ivory towers. They can be as much Left of Marx as Right of Macaulay at the same time to have the best of both worlds. In the same breath in which they denounce foreign agencies as instruments of imperialism, they also manoeuvre to get lucrative jobs in imperialist countries. They denounce PL 480 and yet would make the first claim on its counterpart funds for their own "academic" institutions.

Many fads sweeping the Indian intellectual scene are born out of this insecurity and wielding of functionless power. By their withdrawal from the mainstream of political development, they have widened the cultural gap between the imperatives of development and its social prerequisites. This fraternity of pessimists exudes an artificial, tragic view of political and personal life. Much of this pessimism is borrowed from their Western counterparts who were the products of war, Stalinism, and deep American penetration in Europe. This fashionable despair is a calculated attempt on the part of our intellectuals to minimize their insecurity and maximize their power and pay-offs.

Caught between the closed, charmed, and exclusive circle of these sleepwalkers of our society on the one hand, and hostile, corrupt, external environment on the other, the new generation of sensitive intellectuals are fast developing totally nihilistic tendencies. For the new generation to play their part in society today greater commitment and sacrifice are called for. But the strong sense of nihilism with which they, so to say, are born prevents them from appreciating their own role. Instead, they fall an easy prey to ultra-ideological or corrupt pragmatist attitudes of the intellectual elites. The task of the re-integration of the intellectuals with society becomes increasingly difficult and remote, just it becomes of supreme importance.

December 1968

14

POLITICAL CHANGE AND DEMOCRATIC ALTERNATIVE

THE PREVALENT political mood in the country is one of bewildering gloom and despair. An attitude of impatient helplessness has seized even those who still carry on the political dialogue. A little more than a shadow remains of all the cherished goals which were set before the nation nearly two decades ago. Although the country is still one, its existence as a unified nation is seriously threatened, not the least by a big shift of political power from the Centre to the States and the growing tension between the two. India is setting a poor example for history as being the only country in whose case serious and prolonged external threats have not imparted an enduring sense of unity and strength to the nation.

Although the formal democratic, political structure is intact, a growing disgust is spreading with the way in which democratic institutions work, so much so that one often hears an angry demand for the "democrats" to lay off the backs of the people. One cannot imagine a more frustrating spectacle of hysterical and irresponsible legislatures. Planning and anarchy have become indistinguishable; for there are no norms of efficiency and honesty which have not been seriously breached by corruption, graft, and the lack of effective decision-making, while intermittent, short-run crisis cause tremendous hardship to millions. No wonder, some groups are desperately and even hopefully looking for authoritarian political alternatives, and others, while realizing that an authoritarian alternative is neither an imperative necessity nor a desirable vehicle of political change imagine, nevertheless, that such a foul atmosphere cannot be cleared without a storm.

However, there does not exist, and is unlikely to emerge in the near future, any nation-wide strong and disciplined force which could instal an authoritarian regime. It may appear to be a simple and cruel irony that, while no force is strong enough to topple the democratic structure, democracy itself is decomposing and rotting. Unless this drift is checked, the danger of Balkanization of the country cannot be minimized. Therefore, between the necessity of a major surgical operation and the impossibility of having one in the near future, there must be found some viable and new set of policies which can stem the rot and create essential conditions for a fundamental political change.

Indian polity suffers from many ills. It is not possible, nor even necessary, to delve into all of them. Serious attention should be paid to the most urgent, crucial, and fundamental problems of organic character dealing with the process of political change. Political change is defined as the acquisition by a political system of new capabilities to meet old and new challenges. The acquisition of these capabilities is inextricably tied up with the active instruments of the change, namely, political parties; there must be a smooth transfer through a popular vote of the Government from one party to another whenever so necessitated for a political change.

The purpose of this chapter is (*a*) to show why, in the face of a demonstrably urgent and crying need for change, there is a complete absence of a democratic alternative to the party in power, which has not only for so long retained power on a minority vote but has also become incapable of meeting serious internal and external challenges to the society; (*b*) to analyze known factors and instruments of political change and their effectiveness or lack of it in the contemporary situation of India; and (*c*) to suggest that changes in the electoral law can initiate new political forces and processes in the society.

The process of political change is a function of several factors. The important ones are: ideological struggle, character and functioning of political institutions and parties, practices and modes of operation of parties and other movements, distribution of political power, economic relations, calibre, and quality, and influence of leadership. In a dynamically stable society, these factors converge on a particular balance between political parties which in number may be effectively only two as in the UK, the USA, and West Germany, or more than two as in many European countries. This balance (or balances) must provide, in a democracy, the corrective to democracy's own excesses, generate forces and reaction against supine *status quo*, harness national and group energies, and avoid large-scale political frustration.

Among the factors mentioned above, some are unlikely to undergo radical change in any important dimension in the near future so as to make political change imperative. For example, there is no major change conceivable in the institutional structure of Indian democracy; almost all the necessary institutions exist and are functioning, although with diminishing returns. It is unlikely to expect any big shift in economic relations determined by the largely accepted but vague concepts of mixed economy, socialist pattern or State capitalism, and that extremely complex and cumbersome structure of economy which has resulted from the application or misapplication of these concepts. It is also fruitless to imagine a sudden emergence of new, dynamic, alternative, national leadership at various levels in the absence of a new political movement on a nation-wide scale. Therefore, the emergence of a democratic alternative should be estimated through the practical possibilities of the existing situation and not in abstractions.

Nevertheless, the problem of urgent political change, namely, that of providing a democratic alternative to the Congress, can be narrowed down to the analysis of one or more of the following four factors: (*a*) changes in the electoral law, (*b*) conflict of ideas, (*c*) party political organization, and (*d*) political practice. The Congress Party in its present mood may not like to consider the need for an alternative Government and relinquish power but, in the long run, in the absence of a serious challenge to it, this party, as it is at present constituted and functions, will decay with the decay of the society or would be wiped out, bringing in its wake anarchy or dismemberment of the country. The more sobre and less ambitious elements in the Congress are seriously concerned with this problem.

The electoral system determines to a large extent the character and strength of political parties. Only those features of the system will be referred to here as are relevant. Indian experience might go down in history as unique in the sense of her electoral system defeating its own objective. It is common experience in many countries that elections by simple majority through single ballot and those by proportional representation (PR) yield drastically different strengths of the contesting parties. Even different forms of the PR system seriously affect party positions as is evidenced by the results of recent changes in the French electoral law under de Gaulle. It was claimed and also corroborated by the European experience that election by simple majority or highest vote in single-member constituencies would eliminate smaller parties and ultimately result in a two-party system.

This claim has seen its total refutation in India. A simple majority or highest vote system has, on the one hand, yielded a party situation which in numbers more than approximates to what would have resulted from PR and, on the other and in effect, has established a one-party Government. This is the most significant feature of the fragmentation of Indian politics. Apart from the fact that the election commissioner recognizes as many as about 21 parties at national or State level, the number of parties actually participating in elections is about three times the officially recognized number. And then there are factions within parties, each faction being as good as a separate party. And, of course, there are factions within a faction!

Although the Congress Party has generally held about three-fourths of the total seats in Parliament and two-thirds of the total seats in the State legislatures, it has always been elected on a minority vote, with the additional feature that the gulf between the percentage seats held by it and the percentage votes polled for it is sometimes as much as 30 per cent. It is seldom mentioned that about half the voters in India do not vote; and if the Congress gets elected with a little less than half the votes actually polled, the basis of its legitimacy to power should be in serious doubt. Above everything else, the party position and competition is seriously threatened by the most anarchic intervention of Independent candidates which alone number about three times the total seats in contest. Two-fifths of the Independent candidates forfeit their deposits.

It is a great irony that thousands of candidates, independent or otherwise, stand for election with the clear knowledge and intention of losing; and this fact causes not only the fragmentation of party politics but also brings out the marginality and superficiality of the opposition by reducing its base in the legislature. For comparison, it must be mentioned that, to avoid this type of bizarre situation, several European countries restrict the election to only party candidates. It is not difficult to see that the present Indian electoral system, despite its great democratic content, is utterly unsuitable for creating a democratic alternative through a balanced party system; in fact, the electoral system has added new problems of its own to an otherwise difficult and complex situation.

The system certainly does not encourage voters to vote where their votes count. It is absurd as well as amazing that citizens should vote for a party they dislike and hate most of the time. The present system, thus, has not only outlived its utility but is also a positive and major hindrance to political progress. The suggested reforms will appear in the last section of this chapter. Let us look at some of the other factors for the possibility of their being used as instruments for political change.

The lack of political balance between political parties in India is often attributed to the absence of polarization of parties on ideological grounds. It becomes a matter of great despair for intellectuals who, in search for simple solutions, do not find political parties as primarily doctrinal bodies polarized between the classical Right and Left or some new version of that division. It is true, though, that Western political institutions were the result of a long history of struggle of polarized opposition, often irreconcilable between social groups and classes, but we in India today are no longer working with the institutions of the 18th and 19th centuries. In fact, we have telescoped in time the major Western constitutional developments of centuries and set up at once all the contemporary institutions as found in the developed world.

However, ideology as a weapon in the hands of parties and other institutions has its role and this cannot be dismissed by wishing for an ideology-free two-party system. Democracy assumes the existence in the community of substantial difference of political opinions. The clarity of fundamental ideas is essential in imparting clarity to party programmes as well as for providing a certain continuity in practice to party leadership. A consistent and clear programme in full view of the declared objectives is most likely to create confidence between the politically established top and the politically active bottom in the party, for it is not possible for the rank and file to translate by itself the great issues of ideology into practical issues. Politics is healtheir when it is policy-oriented than when it becomes a matter of expediency. Ideological struggle, if not mutually destructive, also attracts many dormant and sceptic elements of the society, particularly the intellectuals.

Nevertheless, a classical approach to ideological conflict not only represents a gross over-simplification of a complex phenomenon, but it is also erroneous in ignoring the experience of the last hundred years in the West that the classical Right and Left of extremes cannot coexist today, for they would not, one or both, accept the rules of the game of parliamentary democracy and be generally unwilling to compromise. The greatest danger of politics riven by paranoiac ideologies of the extreme Right and extreme Left would be either a civil war or the rise of authoritarianism. Therefore, for a modern democracy to survive, it is essential that the battle of ideas must emanate from a broad consensus on certain fundamentals. In fact, the advantages of political polarization can be had only within the limits of this consensus; political cleavages and political convergence must remain in dynamic equilibrium in a progressive society.

Independent India at its very inception was caught between conflicting world ideologies, which then appeared to be locked in a deadly struggle. The danger of Indian politics also getting sharply divided on the same lines was very real. It was, therefore, quite right for the Indian leaders to perceive this danger as well as the broad irrelevance of the ideological conflict for the major problems of the reconstruction of Indian polity and economy. Non-alignment was initially a declaration of non-participation in that war and conflict and an assertion of unity, independence, and Indian nationalism. Its later degeneration into a simple cliche or its impotence against aggression is a different matter.

The great prestige, tradition, and strength, of the national leaders and the Congress Party, which had always remained ideologically centrist ever since Gandhi took over the reins, militated against the possibility of any big ideological cleavage, despite the breakaway from the Congress of the parties of the Left. The natural or forced disappearance of some of the stalwarts of the Right in the Congress also helped in keeping the balance. However, the Congress in the years of its rule of compromise, accommodation, gloss, and patronage as well as absorption of various protest movements has been reduced to a cumbersome amalgam of almost all conceivable conflicting interests and ideologies without any genuine convergence on fundamental policies or consensus.

It is debatable whether, in the event of such a convergence, the trend would have been towards the establishment of a one-party Government or towards the growth of a democratic alternative to Congress. But the net situation obtained today is one of shocking absurdity and futility. There are today nearly as many political parties in the opposition as there are factions inside the Congress; nearly each factions pairs with an opposition party for supporting or not supporting a particular ideology, policy, or programme. The opposition parties do not oppose or support the Congress as a whole but its different factions. Although there exists a party spectrum which conforms to the classical and the modern distribution of parties, this particular juxtaposition of factions in the Congress and the parties in opposition has not only added an element of unreality to Indian politics, but has also caused fragmentation of politics.

Paradoxically enough, whereas on the one hand ideology has been reduced to a second or third order of motivation in politics, on the other hand the growing weakness and frustration of political parties has superficially ignited ideological conflict and created venom and distrust to fantastic limits. For example, the election manifestos of a dozen parties are indistinguishable, one from the other, and yet these very parties would bitterly and violently oppose one another with nothing but ideological sticks. The parties treat each other as blackly black and whitely white. The theoretical politics of the last two decades converged on the broad acceptance of such objectives as socialism, democracy, planning, and modernization. Yet, the ruling party which symbolized all these objectives represents today not their highest but their lowest common denominator.

Formally, there are rampant in India all sorts of ideologies and ideological groups and parties—in fact several parties ostensibly sharing the same ideology—as well as a broad confluence or convergence of fundamentals, and yet there is in sight neither a democratic alternative to the Congress nor any other method for bringing about desirable political change. There would have been a great pressure on opposition parties of nearly the same political persuasion to come together only if the electoral law was such that it did not encourage party political fragmentation. The same pressure would have also made the Congress more cohesive.

It may be considered that if the Congress develops cohesiveness under the pressure of bitter internal strains and tensions, it is likely to set up for all practical purposes a one-party State, particularly under the present electoral law. But it must also be considered that if this cohesiveness comes under the pressure of a more sensible party position in the opposition, brought about by a new electoral law, India may be on the road to having a stable democracy with modern ideologies playing their useful role. In case neither of these situations emerges, the Congress and the country may together disintegrate in each other's lap.

In several Western democratic countries, although ideologies remain at low key, political change and democratic alternatives are provided and assured by the growth of strong and popular parties, powerful organizational set-up, and well-knit units at various levels. The US is the classical example. Parties build up their own hierarchies, leadership, organizational patterns, party-machine cadre, research units, individual and mass membership, etc. Germany, which had been riven by ideologies for decades, has in the post-war years, developed an efficient party system with ideologies drastically trimmed to sustain their democratic structure. In India, 18 years of hectic political activity in the most open system, with an elaborate institutional structure and with scores of parties in the field, has not brought about an organizational take-off. Political parties appear loose-knit, sick or juvenile and their balance-sheet in terms of their programmes, discipline, cohesiveness, stability, and overall performance is not creditable.

Pluralism is the essence of democracy, but to avoid its being unwieldy and fragmentary, it is generally accepted that a few political parties should between them represent the vast multiplicity of conflicting interests, groups, and classes, though not as passive reflectors but as active organs for the meeting, compromising, and resolving of these interests. In short, parties must function as instruments of political change through the accomodation of conflicting interests. Indian political parties do perform this function but in a very perverse and self-defeating manner. For example, it is their common feature that one interest is represented through factions in several political parties. There is no opposition from these interests to factions and their leaders changing political parties overnight and sometimes even returning to the original fold without any embarrassment. Many parties have a floating leadership. Although organized parties are not allowed within a given party, factions within a party function like organized and mutually hostile parties. Traditional interests like those of the trade unions, peasant organizations, cooperatives, intellectuals, which are well-known parts of the democratic parties in the West, have, it is odd to observe, very little say in party policies and organizations in India.

Partly, this unhealthy and perverse situation was the product of the establishment, in one stroke rather than in stages of all the conceivable democratic institutions and their super-structures, and their imposition on a situation in which a debris of centuries had accumulated and needed to be cleared in one great sweep. It was not realized that some social and economic reforms were the absolute minimum preconditions for and not mere accompaniments of an efficient democratic super-structure. Such a cumbersome institutional system, if expected to work smoothly, required a large, complex, efficient, and shock-absorbing infrastructure. And this was an immense and a tough job which could be done quickly either by an authoritarian or a charismatic leadership.

India had the "benefit" of the second category, but the job was badly done through patching, grafting, clipping, and papering every crucial problem or fission. The political structure became more and more diffused and less and less functional in the sense that its most active political manipulation yielded very poor results. Largely, the situation, as portrayed earlier, was the result of the fragmentation of Indian politics and a great muddle of political parties and factions, the latter substituting for the infrastructure.

Consequently, not only had parties come to be burdened with floating leadership, fratricidal factions, and lack of policies but they also lacked effective organization and stability needed for their growth. Scores of small unstable political parties have spread all over the States in India, which do not have the education, experience, knowledge, and resources to cope with complex and technical State problems. At the lower level, political activity is almost totally factional. In every party there has developed at the top a wilful control of the caucus which is authoritarian and itself factional and thus a source of encouraging indiscipline and defiance.

The arbitrary way in which the Congress bosses dispose of, and quite unsuccessfully, factional disputes shows both strength of the caucus and its fundamental weakness. The Congress leadership bears in its impotence the unmistakable impress of the warring factions which constitute it. In the West, in the early years of mass democracy, it was the opposition to caucus control which led to the parties becoming the chief representatives of politics.

Resistance to caucus has not been effective in Indian parties. And the way out evolved of this difficulty has produced even more damaging effects. Too many parties and too many factions and the gift of producing another tiny party as if out of a hat, when someone's leadership is threatened, have stood in the way of stable and well-knit party organizations in India. The sociologists keep repeating to us the success story of group behaviour, organization, and membership participation. And here in this country we have witnessed the biggest failure story and yet no sociologist seems to be losing his sleep over it.

There is some sense in recognizing the danger of making a fetish of the interest group theory as the focal point of political organization. In the West this group politics has been raised to the level of a scientific, political theory and perhaps there is some justification for that. But, in India, the parochialism of group politics, its clash with national interests, and the way it has impaired and undermined the personal and tactical continuity of party leadership and organization point towards the dangers of this theory. Failure to distinguish between pressure group politics and political fragmentation can lead to absurd conclusions.

For example, to say, as many sociologists do, that recent politicization of castes in India is no more than the emergence of pressure groups at the lower levels is to distort the reality and to fall victim to "scientific" euphoria. The real question to be answered is whether, with the introduction of democratic decentralization and the rise of politically oriented castes, social tensions are resolved, economic exploitation is reduced and better trends are established towards the growth of a more integrated society, larger democratic political participation, welfare distribution, and the involvement of competent and well-informed leadership which can inspire confidence? The answer is not in the affirmative so far as the evidence goes.

The most serious danger arises from the fact that if groups and interests, as distinguished from factions, cannot be absorbed in a proper balance within a party, they exert undue and corrupting pressure on the governmental administration and bureaucracy to get their demand satisfied. Galloping corruption in the administration through pressures from innumerable political factions has not only resulted in the loss of confidence in the administration but has also seriously undermined its operational efficiency. Failure of group politics has also brought back with vengeance a pseudo-ideological conflict between parties and factions, and among top echelons, as a result of the interaction of a high level of political consciousness and a low level of organization. Group politics can serve a useful political purpose only if the number of parties, having a non-coincidence of the main cleavages of opinions, is small and also if there is such a balance between parties as to yield a democratic alternative for a desired political change.

Unfortunately, there is no motivation or force at present in India which could exert its influence towards interparty or intraparty integration. A faction or party, however small and ineffective, is the only instrument left for retaining one's political personality. There does not seem, therefore, any great possibility of a democratic alternative emerging out of any big effort to improve party organization in face of the growing fragmentation of politics, although the need for attention in this direction cannot be minimized. If parties tighten their discipline, set up units throughout the country and work through them, have research staff and trusted political cadre, and improve the functioning of the party machine, something substantial would have been achieved.

The character and functioning of the political system of any modern State are substantially dictated by political practices and modes of operation of political movements. In the first instance, every democracy in the world faces the perpetual dilemma of allowing or disallowing the existence of those parties or groups which neither believe in democracy nor conform to democratic political practice. This dilemma sometimes makes democracy, particularly if it is weak, in its struggle with authoritarianism, adopt the methods of the latter. A strong democracy, on the other hand, keeps anti-democratic forces in check by its own dynamics and without the use of illegitimate methods. Though we do not have any large-scale threat from authoritarianism, yet a sick democracy could invite it on herself through violent political practices. The nature of mass political activity outside the institutional system is such that it always runs into violent anti-democratic streams, particularly, if institutions do not work efficiently or are not held in respect.

The failure of democratic institutions and the weakness of democracy can largely be attributed to their failure to provide a smooth and peaceful change of Government when the change is urgently required. The way parliamentary institutions function reflects broadly the conduct of politics, and together they depend upon the parties having the prospects of being voted into power alternately. Those political parties which do not see any chance of replacing a Government successively elected with a minority vote also do not feel obliged to give regard to the rules of the game and, in turn, the party in power increasingly functions without a proper sense of responsibility and caution. Political practice ends up in perpetual pandemonium, walk-outs, and abuse of parliamentary privileges.

To the common man in India, parliamentary institutions appear as a fraud or a failure and, to those who demand either a one-party State or party-less democracy, a ghastly mistake. When the division of politics is carried to the point of general disgust and institutions are held in contempt, masses of voters are also treated by politicians as a necessary evil to be pandered to once in five years and ignored otherwise. The function of Government is to govern and that of the opposition to oppose, but if the Government misuses its power and the opposition is perpetually frustrated and led to total opposition, political practice is debased and corrupted to limits where institutions become non-functional.

Political practice and conduct are also determined by the position, behaviour, authority, and security of leadership. Floating and insecure leadership, being at the mercy of factions whose attitude is unpredictable, cannot be expected to observe the rules of the game. In a socially backward milieu there is absence, generally, of any stable, close relationship between modernist leadership at the top and traditionalist elite at the lower levels. Feelings of caste, communal group, and factions do not produce homogenous leadership within a party. Therefore, a great gulf grows between the practices of the leaders and their supporters, e.g. whereas the top leadership may like to organize popular political support for great issues of national and State importance, the followers may consider it a waste of time and energy. Lack of integrity and dishonest political practices have made politicians so disreputable in the eyes of the public that while recognizing that the game of politics is about power, the leadership openly denies having any such intentions.

It is the political parties which first break laws, rules, and procedures and adopt corrupt practices and then the rest of the community follows. It is not enough to have institutions and law-making bodies unless they are respected through a strict code of conduct and openly recognizable practices. In Europe, anti-corruption laws were tightened before the introduction of adult suffrage and mass parties. No such attempt was made in India and the supreme emphasis Gandhi put on a proper code of conduct was the one true message from him which the Congressmen have abysmally ignored. There is a lot that can be done towards improving the machinery of the law, setting up of conventions, norms and their stabilization, and tightening party discipline, but so long as political fragmentation with innumerable but ineffective parties remains the most dominant feature of Indian democracy, only a small improvement can be expected.

If the Indian people are given a chance once again to prepare and set up an institutional system which suits their genius, one can be sure that the job would be done much better. But this chance is not even a theoretical possibility and hence great and high-sounding manifestos on partyless democracy or basic democracy or any other form of institutional set-up, radically different from the present one, are all irrelevant. India has formally established almost every conceivable democratic institution found elsewhere in the world, and though marginal trimmings can be done here and there, the setting up of any big new institution is hardly on the agenda. There is, therefore, no point in wasting one's energies in looking for utopias. Consequently, desired political change can be conceived only within the existing system and with other methods.

The analysis of the issues given in the preceding pages could certainly have been more exhaustive and better evidenced, but a detailed study would need volumes. The general picture of political situation today and the functioning of the instruments of political change broadly suggest that the possibility of a democratic alternative emerging in the near future from independent improvements in ideological, institutional, and organizational aspects of politics is extremely small. In fact, the trend is towards further fragmentation, uncertainty, and lack of decision and confidence. Therefore, if anarchy or violent upheavals are to be avoided some minimum changes in the electoral law, on which there are unlikely to arise any big irreconcilable differences, must be introduced, at least to stop further fragmentation of politics, if not to achieve its integration.

There are three important functions of an efficient, democratic electoral system. The first and its primary function is to create truly representative bodies which are either constitutionally provided or established by custom. The second function is to provide a representative Government whose job is not only to represent but also to govern and govern effectively and responsibly. Third, with the growth of mass democracy and a multiplicity of interests and groups, the electoral system must be so devised as to give the ordinary voter clear-cut and fair choices to let him make a sensible decision. The lower the level of education and political consciousness among voters, the more simplified should be the choices and the procedures.

The way an electoral system performs these functions largely determines whether one representative Government can be replaced by another within the same law, and whether the Government's strength lies essentially in mass democratic support. It is argued here that the present electoral law in India is unsuitable to achieve any of the these objectives and, in fact, is undermining the whole process of building a stable democracy.

Certain important developments which have taken place over years in mature democracies of the West in making the electoral law a serviceable tool for a democratic system must be understood both in their form and spirit to see the defects in our electoral system, if only because we are working and experimenting with Western institutions.

First, in the West there is a clear and perceptible drift from parliament to the governing party bodies which organize the electorate politically.

Secondly, nomination of the candidates is by and large and

in some cases entirely through the parties only. The role of Independents is completely eliminated. This has been achieved either by specific provisions in the electoral laws as in some West European and Scandinavian countries, or by practice, custom, and party ascendency as in the UK. Individual candidates and their qualifications were important factors in the days of restricted franchise. With universal suffrage, the Independent candidate has become redundant. Political interests are represented no longer individually but through groups and parties.

Thirdly, voters are also becoming by pressure and by volition a part of the political group and not as independent entities; a distinct proportion of voters feels heavily committed politically to parties.

Fourthly, there is a trend towards the growth of bigger and bigger parties, and reduction in the number of smaller parties. In fact, the trend of power concentration became so strong that, in some smaller European countries, it was felt that two big parties would neglect several smaller interests or would lead to one-party rule and, therefore, these countries deliberately created smaller parties through proportional representation. The idea behind proportional representation was to preserve in the higest possible degree the strength of a few parties as against total polarization and futile intervention by large number of Independents and splinter groups as well as to balance the Government and the opposition through coalitions on either side of parliament. However, the trend towards greater interest participation in political life in these countries came after a prolonged dose of political stability and the establishment of a process of smooth political change.

Fifthly, very small deviation exists between the political divisions of the electorate and the composition of their respective seats in parliament.

Sixthly, electoral processes, procedures, and practices are divorced from any type of Government patronage or fear.

Seventhly, high percentage of voters participate in the elections.

Eightly, there is need for tightening of electoral laws against corruption from all sources.

India has acquired and capsuled the Western democratic institutions but has paid little attention to the aforementioned develpments to strengthen democracy. The framers of the Indian Constitution, in fear of being accused of paying insufficient attention to institutions needed for a new democracy, almost looked too exclusively and excessively to formal structure. They did not pay enough attention to the realities and the nature of political practices and methods which were to emerge from traditionalism, social and economic backwardness and exploitation, all of which were built into the Indian system. The electoral law was correspondingly framed to suit the formal political structure rather than to these realities of the situation and the possible psychological reactions and habits of the voters.

In the West, special stress is constantly laid and corresponding measures taken for making the electoral systems, through suitable changes, conform to the particular social structure and habits of each society, make the composition of parliament and party position conform to the division of the public opinion, guide the electorate to make intelligent decisions, simplify or complicate the election procedure as dictated by the educational and political standards of the voters, increase the power and prestige of parties against individuals and any tendency in the Government to steamroller legislatures through brute majorities, and finally work towards "excellence in the substantial activity of the electorate as a creative organ intended for the production of an effective parliament, and indirectly of an effective cabinet."

In India, on the other hand, there had been almost the complete absence of any debate on the merits and demerits of the existing system, the lessons of electoral experience since Independence, and the need for reform in the electoral system. It may be mentioned here that even the framers of the Indian Constitution did not show any profound interest in, and spent a relatively less time in dilating upon the suitability of, the then proposed electoral system except for providing a number of "don'ts" for the elected and the electorate in anticipation of the dangers of political corruption. However, whereas corruption has seeped into almost every aspect of Indian society, it can be said with some justification that we have witnessed, over the last three elections, negligible corrupt practices in the electoral process itself.

It would be of little use to discuss the merits of any particular Western electoral system, methods, or principles in abstract or out of the context of the needs of Indian democracy. No electoral system by itself can create a political heaven. There are three important considerations which must dictate the reforms in the present electoral system. (*a*) The system must be able to rationalize in a reasonable time the present irrational and anarchic party situation and to reduce the number of parties to a level which guarantees a proper balance between them as well as assures a smooth change of Government when needed. (*b*) The system must remain very simple for ordinary and uneducated voters to comprehend its meaning and make their choice without difficulty. The present system of voting as such is quite simple, though the voter is often confused with the multiplicity of parties, candidates, and their respective policies. (*c*) Simplicity need be accompanied by effectiveness. The system should guide the electorate in making an intelligent exercise of his or her voting right. Millions voting indifferently or cynically do not speak very well of the system.

The experience of the last three open and largely fair elections through a single ballot has not produced either a two-party system or a system with more than two parties but properly balanced. The charge against the single ballot system that it fosters inequalities of individual voters and seats has been established. The existence of some double-member constituencies has not introduced any serious modification of, or complication in, the system because the number of voters per constituency runs into several hundred thousands.

The opposition parties which are nationally recognized suffer the most from the single ballot system and naturally demand proportional representation (PR). It is possible that PR may produce better results for these parties, although it is not very certain because other smaller parties may make a dent in their votes. But the most serious objection to PR being introduced now is that it will freeze and sustain the existing irrationally large number of parties and that there would be no chance of integrating either politics or parties and hence there would be no urge and motivation towards stability.

One cannot foretell what may happen to the Congress under PR, but even if it is ousted, the coalition replacing it will be no better as it will also be like the Congress made up of several parties and factions, between whom there would be little else common except the desire to cling to power—the smaller a party the nearer it is to a faction in its character and functioning. PR and multi-seat constituencies will complicate the system and, in the midst of great ignorance, illiteracy, and the low level of political consciousness of the vast mass of the voters, will confuse instead of enlighten the voters.

It is often suggested that India should adopt the most popular European electoral system which is known as d'Hordt rule or quota system. By this system, the total polled votes for each party in each constituency are respectively divided in turn by some prefixed devisors. Of course, there is a difference between voting procedures and counting procedures and the d'Hordt system is more concerned with the latter. But the system is too complicated even for counting purposes and most unlikely to be accepted; it will certainly not remove the threat of independent candidates and too many parties.

It is also suggested that an electoral candidate must first get the signatures of a few hundred voters before he or she can be declared a candidate. This suggestion may reduce drastically the number of Independents if the number of signatures required is large, but will certainly not change the present party position. Moreover, this will encourage large-scale corruption and vote-selling. Besides, this suggestion is practicable or useful only in a constituency with a few thousand electors but not in the one with several hundred thousand electors.

Another step suggested is to ban the change-over of an elected candidate from one party to another. Obviously, this step, if taken, will help but only marginally and with great strain on the elected members' conscience and sense of responsibility. There is also a general support to the idea that more strict laws should be introduced for checking election expenditure and contribution of vested interests to parties. This step should be taken in any case whatever the electoral system. In fact, this and several other suggestions could be adopted to improve the present or any alternative electoral system. Even then, with all these suggestions implemented, the most important problem of fragmentation of politics will solidly remain through the existence of innumerable parties and Independents in the political field.

The aforementioned suggestions emanate from the contemporary European practices in one country or another. The general trend in Europe is to complicate the system because the simple two-party or PR system cannot translate the ethos of a highly educated and politically enlightened community, reflect total climate of opinion, and integrate specialized interests and different sets of values. The adoption of a complex system does not worry an ordinary voter in Europe because he is educated and politically conscious enough to make an intelligent and a discriminating choice.

The introduction of preferential voting or alternative voting, the development of a list system, and an elaborate ballot paper which provides useful and necessary information on candidates did stimulate, indeed, the interest of the voters and democratize further the European parliamentary institutions. These policies did not result in political fragmentation because (*a*) they came only as marginal modifications to a system which had remained stable and democratic for a long time; (*b*) Western societies had homogenous political, cultural, and econcmic structures; and (*c*) the overall system remained highly streamlined and simplified so far as party balance was concerned. These new features of the European electoral system, if introduced in India, will not improve the situation. Some of the features will unnecessarily create complications and confusion. We must look for something simpler but which also produces the desired results in the shortest possible time and without political breast-beating.

Examples can be multiplied, but we shall concentrate on the experience of West Germany during the pre-war and post-war decades. In the pre-war decades, the alternation between political fragmentation brought about by several mutually hostile parties and the rise of authoritarianism, as a consequence of that fragmentation, were the dominant features of the German polity.

Instability led to dictatorship and the latter led to war; the ugly history of the two world wars does not need any restatement. However, after the coming into existence of West Germany as a *de facto* independent State, an era of remarkable political stability and strength as well as of balanced party position began and continues despite the extremely difficult situation created by the partition of the country, the pressure of chauvinistic groups, and above all the threat from the East.

One of the most important factors contributing towards the stability and balanced party position is the Basic Law of the Federal Republic of Germany, 1949. Unlike other countries in Europe, the German law allows political parties, by the authority of the constitution in clear recognition that, to participate in the forming of the political will of the people, but with the express condition that their respective internal organizations must conform to a democratic process. This feature is not of a mere formal nature, it has the intent and content of giving prestige to the recognized parties. Candidates are nominated by parties "who are thus the creators and upholders of the political will of the people." (The pre-war attitudes of parties has undergone a fundamental change.)

The voters in West Germany no longer look upon their Government as something separate and a nuisance rather than as a necessity. The traditional mistrust of politics which undermined democracy has disappeared. A still more important feature is the imposition of two types of restrictions: (*i*) restrictions on parties which do not continuously have at least five members in the Federal or Land Parliament; and (*ii*) restrictions on the secondary distribution of seats through an alternative vote to only those parties which have obtained at least 5 per cent of all the valid votes polled. The results have been startlingly beneficial for a country which did not experience stability and democracy together for a long time. Parliamentary life became considerably simple and extremely effective in eradicating the entire basis of political fragmentation.

The voters offered their support mainly to three parties—the Christian Democrats (CDU/CSU), the Social Democrats (SPD), and the Free Democrats (FDP). In the four legislative elections of 1949, 1953, 1957, and 1961, the three parties polled together 72.1 per cent, 83.5 per cent, 89.7, and 94.1 per cent respectively of the total votes. It may be mentioned that, between 1946 and 1956, as many as 74 parties or electoral communities put up candidates at the Federal and State levels, but as a result of the electoral law, all but five were eliminated in the course of time.

The German electoral law provides for proportional, personalized representation and is quite complicated in voting and distribution of seats in parliament. But, as stated earlier, the trend towards proportional representation and deliberate introduction of complications in Western Europe has been the result of a desire to make numerous small interests get some form of political representation. Yet, this trend has been permitted, and very gradually, only within the limits of such an overall, highly simplified electoral process as does not permit the proliferation of political parties or the atomization of political communities. It will be of little use for India to adopt proportional representation, particularly when the actual results of an opposite system have produced the worst features of the proportional system. There is an unmistakable and urgent need for the introduction of an overall simplification of the electoral system to reduce the number of parties.

It is not possible to recapture here in a few paragraphs the dynamics of the stable and successful German democratic system, which has also become an economic giant, in relation to the new electoral system. But, by way of contrast with the pre-war German situation, the most salient features of post-war Germany can be traced.

As stated earlier, German politics and parliament have come to be dominated by two political parties despite proportional representation. The electoral law has made it impossible for the parties of the extreme Right and extreme Left, which had vitiated the politics of the country ever since the First World War, to make any serious headway. It is true that some parties of the extreme like the communists and neo-Nazis have been legally banned, but even before the ban was imposed their respective political strength was insignificant. Besides, the banned parties, as was expected, reappeared under different names, but their strength did not improve. The communists are functioning within the German Peace Party, and this party was able to secure only 1.9 per cent of the votes in the 1961 elections. The Right-wing extreme parties like the German Party and the All-German Block were equally unsuccessful in influencing the voters.

As a consequence, the role of ideology, which was paramount in the days of the Weimer Republic and divided the nation against itself, has been reduced to only legitimate proportions. The growing affluence of the people has further strengthened resistance against violent and paranoiac ideologies. The main contending parties and the mass of their supporters, conscious of the ugly past and their newly won freedom and economic prosperity, feel a tremendous stake in political stability and moderation. Voting has become a conscious act of political faith and a matter of active participation in the resurgence of new Germany.

The elimination of smaller parties and Independent candidates, which presumably represented small interests, has brought the two main parties in direct contact and close link with various group, class, and small community interests. This levelling tendency has forced the CDU and the SPD to project to the public not a sectarian but a national and social image by political absorption of these interests. Consequently, the old rigid alignments have disappeared. For example, whereas 76 per cent of the Catholic votes were polled for CDU in 1953, it dropped to 61 per cent in 1961. On the other hand, the working class vote for the SPD has declined from 75 per cent to 65 per cent during the same period.

A vast and efficient party machine has emerged for each party and it is in this fact that the organizational and institutional strength of German democracy lies. Germany is not a unitary but a federal State and its units have vast powers. Yet, the balance of power has not been upset and the federal structure not weakened because of the growing strength and power of the main parties. By contrast, the Indian Union has vast powers and yet this Union has been gradually weakened for lack of party balance.

In India, we need similar reforms to rationalize and streamline the party system. The Election Commissioner recognizes parties at the national and State levels if they get a certain number of votes but this recognition is neither constitutional nor effective, for there is no restriction on unrecognized parties; the number of parties is in fact increasing with every new election. It is a meaningless extra-constitutional authority enjoyed by the Election Commission. For example, recognizing two splinter communist parties, as was recently done, does not help anybody, least of all the communists.

The reforms needed in India will have to go a little further than those in Germany, Austria, etc. In the first instance, the electoral law should provide straightaway that every candidate must be a party candidate and the party must be registered at least one year before the general elections. There should be no such entity as Independent candidates officially recognized or otherwise. Secondly, if a party does not get certain minimum percentage of votes polled—say 3 per cent in parliament and 5 per cent in the State legislatures—it would lose the right of being represented at all. These two provisions would materially stimulate smaller parties to merge with bigger parties of similar or nearly similar political opinions, and further proliferation of the parties will be stopped. Parties will compete with each other on more distinct programmes and policies. Parties will have to build their machines, cadre, and organization to remain as a live political force. Above all, with the elimination of small parties, political parties will not be regarded as a nuisance and source of corruption. The essentiality of political parties will be recognized and understood after a period of transition.

Once a balanced party position is crystallized, a platform will be created for the youth and the intellectuals—who are nowhere near politics today—to participate. The party in power will also be forced to have clearer policies, a greater sense of responsibility, and a stimulus for greater efficiency. The Congress Party may remain in power if it becomes a more coherent and acceptable party, or may be replaced if it does not satisfy these conditions. There is a small but illusory loss of freedom to Independent candidates and small parties. They can always remain, and more usefully, as constituents of a party if they so desire.

In the final analysis, no change in the electoral system alone can bring about a political millenium. It is a matter of how far the spirit of democracy has gone deep into the minds of the people. Voting is a mental and not merely a physical act. But a proper and suitable electoral system is of supreme importance so long as the democratic institutions function and their prestige and respect needs to be maintained.

April 1966

15

QUALITATIVE CONTENT OF POLITICAL LIFE IN INDIA

THE SUBJECT OF quality of political life anywhere, more so in India, is difficult to deal with. There are two reasons for this. First, the criteria for judgment about quality are highly biased towards value-orientation and cannot be strictly objective. Anybody claiming open-mindedness or strict objectivity about quality is only concealing his or her personal prejudices. Second, whatever I have to say is highly impressionistic and may or may not stand this or that rigorous test of even a value-judgment. However, it would be futile to assume that, in the absence of objective criteria, the discussion has no objective meaning. What needs to be recognized is that the very criteria for objectivity are inevitably qualitative.

One other relevant question is whether any quantitative or institutional test can be applied in judging the quality of political life. For example, four factors which are often mentioned, stamping the democratic character of Indian polity as a superior entity, fall in this category: (1) India is quantitatively the biggest democracy in the world. Adult franchise and fair and orderly conduct of three general elections in which millions upon millions cast their free votes without fear of rigging or violence are cited as an evidence for the democratic character or quality of political life in India. (2) The establishment and continued functioning of a host of democratic institutions at all levels through which at least a politically conscious segment of the society freely conducts political activity. That the formal political structure in India, unlike in many other countries, has not crumbled under the pressure of repeated crises and foul winds points towards the sound foundations of a healthy society. (3) Growing mobility, horizontal and vertical, in economic, social, and political life reveals the dynamic character of political forces. (4) Tremendous development of educational facilities and expansion of mass communicating media are signs of actual or potential political awareness and the gradual strengthening of the infrastructure for informed public opinion. All these are very valuable and pertinent criteria, particularly for those who believe in the behaviourist, institutional, or legalistic approach to politics as the only valid, scientific, and relevant approach. But a formal institutional mechanism divorced from its social and political dynamism is nothing but deadwood. At best it is boundary-spanning and does not permit any direct qualitative evaluation of the aforementioned factors, because the matrix of forces in which politics is assumed to operate does not require a quality coefficient. Therefore, it is imperative that we look for some indirect index of political development (to judge the formal structure) associated with other variables of the system to measure the level and quality of political practice.

For example, as against the above-mentioned quantitative factors I would like to set a few questions for each factor, though a number of other questions still remain to be answered: (1) Do there exist before the voters clear choices of policy or programme-oriented parties or candidates? Do voters exercise their votes intelligently and rationally? (2) Is the formal political structure yielding at least some minimum results and showing signs of dynamic improvement? Is there a growing respect or contempt for it among the citizens? (3) Does mobility and participation mean a progressively better behaviour and more well-informed acts of participation? (4) Has the quality of education improved with the expansion of educational facilities? Are the educated people increasingly participating in political life or are they being alienated from politics? Answers to these and other similar questions can tell us something about the social and functional dynamism or stagnation of the system and not merely its formal structure.

There are two other dangers in adopting either institutional or behaviourist criteria. First, in doing so not only do we assume political equilibrium but also put a premium on the *status quo* and deny the validity of any political theory other than behaviourist functionalism. Second, the end process of such an approach is a moral and ethical nihilism in the sense of secularization and elevation of political activity as an end in itself. However, there is one good aspect of this criteria: they provide us the mechanism to tell us what is politically crucial or insignificant, and block any drift toward metaphysical or air-fairy theorizing.

While talking about the quality of life we must not fall prey to the danger of going to the other extreme of approaching the problem from some utopian criteria, sanctimonious and sterile moralizing, or a romantic image of good life and model citizenry for political practice. The model of man in the contemporary social and political life cannot be wholly of a fraud or of a saint. One often comes across the tendency to absolutize the model of a political crook as the chief political activist or the strong temptation or disposition to measure political activity by the image of Mahatma Gandhi. These tendencies must be squarely met for they cannot be dismissed; they make the age-old conflict, of every era and every nation, between normative political activity and its counterpart, an escape into a value-free "scientific" theory.

We are living in an era of nation-States. The model one seeks for a healthy and rational political practice belongs to strong unified nations and not to weak and loosely knit political entities. A nation-State not only provides its members a certain identification, pride, and stake in the nation as an entity but also permits experiments with new political systems, ideas and practices, the passion and devotion which are relevant and consistent only with a certain developed degree of nationalism. Of course, nationalism can develop perverted forms. The question, however, that needs answering is whether Indian nationalism which claimed to have resilience and receptivity as well as the capacity to reflect the complex and composite character of Indian culture is still a vital force. Except for a sudden very short-lived and emotionally focussed uspsurge that came in the wake of Chinese and Pakistani aggressions, there is ample evidence for a general decline of the collective conscience having taken place in India over the last decade or so. And I am not sure whether to recompense that decline; individual consciousness in the sense of greater personal freedom and expansion of choices has increased in the same period. The argument often put forward for this decline, namely, that we borrowed ideas and institutions from abroad for a wrong milieu, is only a half-truth because the real question is whether the consciously accepted institutions and the technology of political action, borrowed or indigenous, have become functional and India-focussed. The answer is in the negative. Growing contempt for borrowed as well as indigenous institutions is a common factor. With the single exception of our armed forces, all other unifying factors, like the power of the Centre, Planning Commission, common language, and national political parties, have weakened considerably.

In modern political analysis, three types of incentives are recognized as motives for political activity: material, solidary, and purposive. The last two have gradually been eliminated in India dragging with them the strong legacy of nationalism. Apart from history and tradition, the strongest and the most positive force for nationalism is the existence of a minimum consensus both as a system of values and a code of political conduct. Nehru's contribution during the first decade was the creation of this consensus, which unfortunately he totally undid in the second decade by a policy of turning his face from conflict-resolution to total appeasement. Consensus without conflict-resolution is untenable. Consensus has been replaced by ideological conflicts which are carried to such absurd limits as to have become inimical to the very existence of the State. I do not consider it a healthy political sign of Indian democracy if pro-Chinese or pro-Pakistani or for that matter pro-US and pro-USSR elements should conduct themselves as open agents of foreign powers with immunity from law and more so from public opinion. Several studies have shown how this decline in the collective conscience can be traced to the formal political structure itself. It is not possible to examine the causes here, but it must be mentioned that the shift of the power from the Centre to the States, dependence on caste and communal groups rather than on national parties for personal political identification, precedence of ideology over national interests, and refusal to forge links for a unified culture lie at the root of the weakening national consciousness and can be traced to such institutions as federalism, the so-called democratic decentralization, constitutional provisions on language, and empty idealistic assumptions underlying the Constitution of India.

Political activity, like other activities, has its own goals and objectives. In developed societies, democracy has travelled a long way and has made political activity also a rational end in itself. However, if objectives become blurred and mutually irreconcilable, lack minimum consensus, and impart intellectual cynicism and escapism, the autonomous political activity degenerates into pseudo-politics. This phenomenon is quite common in underdeveloped and unstable societies. It is one of the most serious challenges India faces today.

Pseudo-politics is "analytically distinguished from rational political activity by the type of motivation or purpose, the alleviation of neurosis and morbid passion for the promotion of private good against an improved satisfaction of human needs according to universalistic values." One other feature of pseudo-politics is that it considers the existing politico-economic system as the best and resists change. While politics is fast becoming an end in itself, there is also taking place a general deterioration in ordinary political norms and a disregard of the determinants and consequences of this type of political activity. Most of our political leaders talk all the time in terms of total normative dimensions. It is a sign of the same pseudo-politics that political activity in India is massively encumbered by flashes of mutually hating, pseudo-ideological positions. It is amazing how the ideology of equality and socialism has degenerated into non-discrimination against stupidity and incompetence, and the ideology of liberalism has become a tool for the maintenance of the illiberal *status quo* and the exploitation of the weakest sections of the society. Paradoxically, the same attitude is reflected in the emphasis on a high pressure pseudo-moral bias rather than on a technical bias. Worst of all, the sharpening ideological saliency has been accompanied by a decline in political involvement as well as by a general depoliticization of the educated and thinking people. Besides, while the political intensity of caste, communal, or factional groups has increased, there has simultaneously taken place a wide-spread political passivity among the citizens. One aspect of this passivity is the small size of the differential which the electorate thinks is likely to result from the choice of one or the other alternative open to him.

In developing democracies, politics can be an end in itself only if it is a manifestation of the underlying tensions or struggle for the stratification and the transformation of the society. Explicitly, some of the generalized attitudes that are related to these underlying conditions of political behaviour are: political alienation or participation, presence or absence of a sense of civic duty, personal commitment or non-commitment to certain values, acceptance or rejection of intellectual and rational premises, etc. These attitudes largely determine the quality of life and it would be a rash man who would claim that India has improved in these matters.

There is one thing common between all competing political models, democratic or otherwise, namely, the unique role of the rational-activist elite which imparts continuity, comparability, and direction to mass political activity and mass party organizations. Democracy is unthinkable without some guidance from quality elite. It is the quality elite which tackles the problems of political socialization of the people, recruitment of lower rank leaders, interest articulation and aggregation, and political communication. We unmistakably know now that Nehru, unlike Gandhi, totally neglected the problem of finding and training new political leaders; in fact, he was responsible for the frustration, elimination, or corruption of some of the second-rank leaders of the Gandhi era. Nehru believed more in the creation of personal vassals than in the creation of disciplined, conscious, and honest lieutenants, so much so that it has become very difficult today to speak of the integrated structure of national leadership. Whereas the old elite at the top was the product of mass politics with a single purpose in view, the new elite at the top is the product of a mass alienation of voters or their hostility to or disenchantment with politics. The ministers or legislators are not looked upon by voters as ministers or legislators but those who intercede with the administration on behalf of this or that group. In fact, the elite is not understood for its true functions at all. At the States' level, political relations between the elite and the mass of party men or voters are highly personalized and are based more on caste, communal, or dynastic loyalties than on straight political affinities. The result is an unreliable and floating elite, and one sure evidence of this is the low ratio of party members to voters in almost all the parties, including the Communist Party. The parochialism of this type of group politics has impaired the personnel and tactical continuity of party leadership and its authority. It is a great irony that democratic decentralization which was introduced to create local leadership and participation has declined both in authority and function precisely because of the non-emergence of really able people interested in local bodies. There is in fact very little involvement of competent and well-informed men at the bottom, although the existence of such men is not in doubt.

It is the almost complete alienation of the intellectual elite from mass politics which is the most dangerous aspect of the fast deteriorating leadership. A large number of highly educated and politically conscious persons have been absorbed in the administration and one would have hoped that, at least in administration, the positive role of the elite would find its manifestation. Unfortunately, the quality of administration has deteriorated faster than anything else over the last decade. Non-administrative intellectuals have withdrawn into their world of academics and its power, out of sheer disgust with the low quality of politics of the late Nehru era which stoods in sharp contrast with the Gandhi era. A very peculiar and perverted association between social status and political participation has come to stay and this model is totally anti-intellectual. Even the so-called Leftist intellectuals abhor rubbing shoulders with rural or urban low-class elite. The conservative intellectuals on their part have failed in explaining satisfactorily the quality of relationship between economic development and political structure in India or the relevance of freedom and democracy to the contemporary political structure, and therefore stand completely isolated from the mainstream of politics. Worst of all, no dialogue of any substance takes place between intellectuals of different political persuasions. The more the material gains are acquired by them, the more insecure they feel and the more frightened they appear as political animals. The only way in which these people can be brought back to the mainstream of politics and can earn the respect of the masses is to set and practise a minimum code of conduct in politics. In India the "change will not come by means of administrative and sociological devices, but by the example the nation's elite set of service to the community, of simple living, and refusal to tolerate exclusiveness." These are the words not of Gandhi or Bhave but of a modern political analyst, H. Tinker.

An indirect measure of the quality of political life is the presence or absence of the will, knowledge, and capacity for change whenever change is desirable. A healthy democracy is characterized by the actual alternations in Government or the existence of a potential alternative to an unsatisfactory Government. After eighteen years of the Congress rule no one can overlook the all-pervasive rot that has spread into the society and yet there is neither any alternative to the Congress Government in sight nor is there any chance of the Congress becoming a more coherent and responsive body. Despite the establishment of a comprehensive institutional mechanism and the ushering in of concomitant processes, the forces of social and political dynamism are weak, bribed, and suppressed, resulting in a growing digsust for the democratic institutions. One cannot imagine a more frustrating spectacle of hysterical and irresponsible legislatures as well as the cruelty and incompetence of the administrative juggernaut. The general political atmosphere is one of an acutely felt need for drastic political change and the utter impossibility of having one, a contradiction which leads to political pessimism and alienation on the one hand, and ruthlessness and cynical disregard of most political values with which the Indian experiment in democracy was launched, on the other. A widespread political fragmentation lies at the root of all this.

The chief features of political fragmentation are: (*i*) A party structure of innumerable parties which does not correspond to the electoral realities so much so that the party in power is perpetually in power with minority votes; (*ii*) lack of party indentification in terms of programmes and policies; (*iii*) intervention of thousands of independent candidates of whom only less than

5 per cent ever win, most of them entering the field with the clear intention of losing the elections or being bribed; (*iv*) increase of factionalism has gone to the extent of becoming completely inconsistent with political efficiency. For example, the efficiency of the Congress Party has been seriously undermined by a peculiar kind of factionalism, the party does not find opposition or support to itself as a party or to its policies but to its various factions each of which can be paired with one or the other opposition party. Political quality is a function of the political structure; and the political structure in India has become more and more diffused and less and less functional in the sense that its most active political manipulation yields very poor results.

In the absence of (1) streamlined political parties and lack of identification, (2) sufficiently developed and articulate interest groups, the politics of protest, which is an inevitable feature of demorcracy, has become by and large ugly, violent, and somewhat purposeless. Two trends are worth noting. First, the Congress Party has absorbed, in itself protest movements by the reward of office, money, or even empty promises. It is this particular phase of absorption of protest movements which marks the most corrupt and unprincipled growth of the Congress Party and its corrosive factionalism. Second, a vastly expanded Government activity and administration, instead of transferring the politics of protest to rationality and responsibility, has led to the sanctification of distortions and injustices, which are sustained bossism, and complacency and insensitivity on the part of the administration. Consequently, whereas the basic reasons for political protest have multiplied, the channels for conflict resolution have been increasingly blocked, resulting in violence, bloodshed, and even complete diversion from the very purpose of the protests. Politics itself has become the victim of political violence. For example, politicians are universally blamed for protest movements by students, workers, and others taking violent turn. D.H. Bayley has pointedly drawn attention to this fact and has also very convincingly shown how politics and its quality have deteriorated as a result of the degeneration of protest movements in India. Other effects are: (*i*) stopping of functional response; (*ii*) weakening of consensus between the ruler and the ruled; (*iii*) creation of tactical advantages for non-democratic political opposition; (*iv*) increasing alienation of the people from political activity; (*v*) intensification of elite isolation; (*vi*) confirmation of authoritarian tendencies, and (*vii*) corruption of administration.

If the preceding analysis is correct, it would follow that political modernization must have also been slowed down or distorted if not stopped under the pressure of elite alienation, concentration on parochial rather than national issues, and lack of political dynamism for change. Political modernization is also an independent factor and its absence or distortion must have, in turn, contributed to the emergence and strengthening of other corrosive factors. It is not difficult to see that the movement towards modernization and scientific attitude has been slow in general; there is ample evidence for that. Our basic approach to political action, in contrast to formal political structure, has been one of political philosophy, so heavily dogged by traditionalism, rather than of political theory, leading to the neglect of making a distinction between problems of fact and value, and between concepts and their operation. Some of the anti-rational, anti-scientific, and even anti-intellctual approaches were part and parcel of the national movement of the Gandhi era. To some, Gandhi was responsible for halting the incipient renaissance movement which started earlier under the modernizing influences of the British rule. Gandhi certainly did not have a systematic political theory, and whatever his philosophy, it was highly moralistic, ethical, and religious rather than political in orientation. Values can be divided into categories that can be labelled as goals and instruments, but he refused to make a distinction between ethical evaluation and empirical explanation. In fact, as somebody has remarked, Gandhi's philosophy began where political doctrine ended. But he was also a political tactician and knew his country thoroughly well. He could not wait for social transformation to take place before independence was granted; the superimposition of traditionalism on politics was meant to hasten political deliverance.

However, it was his successor Nehru, a modernist, who failed to stem the tide of traditionalism as well as to salvage the functional part of it. His attitude remained without change one of futile ambivalence. He talked big about science, physical laboratories, atomic age, socialism and planning, but in practice appeased every irrational and unscientific movement from cow protection to politicization of castes and communal forces inside the Congress, so much so that he ended his rule with complete normative neutrality of the political system in theory and its utter corruption in practice. In a sense, both Gandhi and Nehru were outside the political processes, and yet one with avowed traditionalism produced a better quality of political life than the other, a sworn scientist. It is said that traditional politics believes in withdrawal and transcendence while modern politics in participation, and yet Nehru was more aloof than Gandhi from Indian politics. Today we find a very ugly combination of withdrawal and participation; those who would like to be in politics are just not there and those who should not be there are sitting pat on it. Nehru's ambivalence and procrastination in introducing social and economic reforms really killed the political technology of modernization. Instead we got pseudo-politics of the *status quo* by substituting conformism for critical enquiry and rushing to accept the regressive theory of "villageism" and support to technologically most backward small-scale industries and a whole set of other backward-slopping and traditional ways of life. The same attitude has also affected social research by our putting sole emphasis on microsociology of political behaviour rather than bringing out an overall model of political change in which modernization would be an inevitable motivation. On the other hand, under the impact of the same ambivalence, the so-called modernization had also degenerated into imitating only the superficial and formal aspects of the Western society. Traditionalism is totally denounced as illiberal, undemocratic, and unfunctional, thereby lavishing scorn on every tradition, good or bad. This attitude has resulted in ignorance of and revulsion against the entire Indian culture and history. Our leaders fail to realize that it is not a matter of simple conflict between tradition and modernity but their dynamic and complex relationships and relativism in a society which ensures change. Sometimes traditional values result in superior performance, but for lack of political understanding and competence we resort to total condemnation. Political competence grows with higher education and occupational status and yet this has not happened. It is so because our education is not attuned to the growing needs of a changing society. Paradoxically, the most modern education has led either to political withdrawal and transcendence or to superficiality and futile imitation. We all recognize the primacy of politics in developing societies and yet political leadership is far away from giving a lead in modernizing the society. Historically, political modernity derived its capacity from two polar patterns of coercion on the one extreme and consensus, induced change and civic political culture on the other. We adopted the latter and did not succeed, for we are back at where we began, because we failed to develop techniques which make rapid social transformation possible while retaining the pattern of an open society. Shall we be obliged to adopt coercion?

This brief sketch of the main features of the deteriorating quality of political life in modern India should go some way to explain the howling cynicism, pessimism, and disgust that have encompassed the minds of thinking men in India. To some extent these moods are phoney because they are borrowed from contemporary Western societies. But Western societies have attained such levels of social, economic, and political maturity that their intellectual pessimism and scepticism are no more than signs of restlessness about the future. If a comparison is necessary, it is between the overwhelming concepts and ideas of progress in the West during their period of the political take-off, and the ideas of decadence and sentiments of political and cultural decline so widely prevalent in India today. It is important to note that during the rise of capitalism in the West it was the conservative classes that propagated the concept of decadence; in India today it is the so-called radicals and progressives who have fallen victims to it. Unfortunately, a general withdrawal from politics by the conservatives and the radicals has taken place. And this withdrawal implies simultaneous identification with no values and principles and unattainable values and principles. That is why our politics alternates between inactivity and hysteria or violence. These contradictions must be traced back to their original sins: we operate through most modern political institutions which have been superimposed on a socially rotten mileu. The answer is not to abolish the institutions but to have such social and economic reforms as would remove the social debris collected over centuries. This is the function of the political elite. I strongly feel that unless there is a wave of revolt by educated Indians against their normal condition of political alienation, there is little prospect of desirable political change through peaceful methods. Besides, apart from improving institutions and will to progress, there must be some political mechanism to improve individual qualities (and their reward), technical bias, sense of responsibility, discipline, and urge for public interest. It is a part of the larger problem of integration of values, facts, policies, and performance as well as of fixing some minimum political norms, the violation of which should bring forth the nation's wrath.

February 1966

GLOSSARY OF EVENTS

9 October 1963	K. Kamaraj is elected President of the Congress Party
27 May 1964	Nehru passes away
2 June 1964	Lal Bahadur Shastri is elected Prime Minister of India
5-20 September 1965	War with Pakistan
10 January 1966	Shastri passes away
24 January 1966	Indira Gandhi is sworn in as Prime Minister of India
7 December 1967	S. Nijalingappa is elected Congress President
7 December 1967	Indira Gandhi is re-elected Prime Minister of India
3 May 1969	Zakir Husain, President of the Indian Republic, passes away
12 July 1969	Congress Parliamentary Board nominates Sanjiva Reddy as Congress candidate for the Presidential election
16 July 1969	Morarji Desai is relieved of Finance Portfolio
19 July 1969	Fourteen major banks are nationalized
19 July 1969	Morarji's resignation accepted
20 August 1969	V. V. Giri is elected President of the Indian Republic
25 August 1969	Congress Working Committee endorses Unity Resolution